A NATION
IN CRISIS

A NATION IN CRISIS

How the Prophecy of Jeremiah
Speaks to Our Culture

RAY C. STEDMAN

with James D. Denney

Our Daily Bread
Publishing™

A Nation in Crisis: How the Prophecy of Jeremiah Speaks to Our Culture

© 2018 by Elaine Stedman
All rights reserved.

Requests for permission to quote from this book should be directed to: Permissions Department, Our Daily Bread Publishing, PO Box 3566, Grand Rapids, MI 49501, or contact us by email at permissionsdept@odb.org.

Scripture quotations, unless otherwise indicated, are taken from the Holy Bible, New International Version®, NIV®. Copyright © 1973, 1978, 1984, 2011 by Biblica, Inc.™ Used by permission of Zondervan. All rights reserved worldwide. www.zondervan.com.

Scripture quotations marked NKJV are from the New King James Version®. Copyright © 1982 by Thomas Nelson. Used by permission. All rights reserved.

Library of Congress Cataloging-in-Publication Data

Names: Stedman, Ray C., author. | Denney, Jim, 1953- author.
Title: A nation in crisis : how the prophecy of Jeremiah speaks to our
   culture / Ray C. Stedman with James D. Denney.
Other titles: Death of a nation
Description: Grand Rapids, Michigan : Discovery House, [2018] | " A Nation in
   Crisis is a revised and updated edition of Stedman's book Death of a
   nation, which was published in 1976"--ECIP. | Includes bibliographical
   references.
Identifiers: LCCN 2018027189 | ISBN 9781627078924 (pbk.)
Subjects: LCSH: Bible. Jeremiah--Criticism, interpretation, etc.
Classification: LCC BS1525.52 .S74 2018 | DDC 224/.206--dc23
LC record available at https://lccn.loc.gov/2018027189

Printed in the United States of America
21 22 23 24 25 26 27 28 / 9 8 7 6 5 4 3 2

CONTENTS

PUBLISHER'S PREFACE

From 1950 to 1990, Ray Stedman (1917–1992) served as pastor of the Peninsula Bible Church in Palo Alto, California. He was known and loved as a man of outstanding Bible knowledge, Christian integrity, warmth, and humility. Born in Temvik, North Dakota, Stedman grew up on the rugged landscape of Montana. When he was a small child, his mother became ill and his father, a railroad man, abandoned the family. Ray grew up on his aunt's Montana farm from the time he was six. He came to know the Lord at a Methodist revival meeting at age ten.

As a young man he moved around and tried different jobs, working in Chicago, Denver, Hawaii, and elsewhere. During World War II, he enlisted in the Navy, where he often led Bible studies for civilians and Navy personnel, and he even preached on local radio in Hawaii. At the close of the war, Stedman was married in Honolulu (he and his wife, Elaine, had first met in Great Falls, Montana). They returned to the mainland in 1946, and he graduated from Dallas Theological Seminary in 1950. After two summers interning under Dr. J. Vernon McGee, Stedman traveled for several months with Dr. H. A. Ironside, pastor of Moody Church in Chicago.

In 1950, Stedman was called by the two-year-old Peninsula Bible Fellowship to serve as its first pastor. Peninsula Bible Fellowship became Peninsula Bible Church, and Pastor Stedman served a forty-year tenure, retiring on April 30, 1990. During those years, he authored a number of life-changing Christian books, including the classic work on the meaning and mission of the church, *Body Life*. He went into the presence of his Lord on October 7, 1992.

A Nation in Crisis is a revised and updated edition of Stedman's book *Death of a Nation*, which was published in 1976. The revisions were done by James D. Denney, who has been involved in re-crafting Stedman's books for many years. In this book Stedman works his way through the life and the prophecy of Jeremiah—a man who stood up against criticism and persecution for his entire forty-year tenure as a prophet of God. Over and over he warned the southern kingdom of Judah that they needed to repent and return to God or face dire consequences. But his warnings fell on deaf ears. The nation was destroyed, and the people were taken into captivity.

As Stedman points out in this book, we can learn much from God's clear warnings for His people in the late sixth and early fifth century BC in Israel. We are reminded that there is always a way back to God for those who have either forgotten Him or who have never established a relationship with Him. We are reminded that God loves His people in ways we sometimes don't understand, helping us to see that trusting Him is always right because His wisdom is greater than ours and His love is eternal. And we are reminded that even when we face challenges that seem unprecedented—in our society or in our individual lives—the strength and wisdom of God are adequate to any challenge.

The book of Jeremiah is long, and sometimes it may seem like an arduous journey to traverse its fifty-two chapters. But if you keep *A Nation in Crisis* with you as you make your way through this important Old Testament book, you will be rewarded with renewed faith in God and His story and with inspiring new courage to face whatever modern society tosses your way. Allow this book to open up for you a new understanding of how God's Word addresses today's culture.

—Our Daily Bread Publishing

THE HEROIC PROPHET

Introduction

Suppose your pastor stood before your church on Sunday morning and said, "God is on the side of the terrorists. God is against America and He is for America's enemies. God is raising up the terrorists to punish the United States of America. God hates our religious worship. It is an offense to Him. And that is why God is going to use the terrorists to bring about the destruction of this nation."

What would you think of your pastor?

And suppose your pastor were arrested and charged with treason. Suppose he was publicly assaulted and all his writings were burned because of his condemnation of America's religious practices. And suppose your pastor not only refused to disavow his offensive words, but he repeated them even more forcefully.

That sounds a lot like the situation recorded in the book of Jeremiah. These were the kinds of messages Jeremiah was called by God to deliver to the kingdom of Judah.

God told Jeremiah to tell the nation of Judah that He hated the idolatrous religious practices of the nation. Because of Judah's disobedience, God was raising up the Babylonian Empire to punish and destroy the nation. Judah's only hope of survival lay in complete surrender to the Babylonians. It was a message that sounded treasonous to the people of Judah.

So the people rejected Jeremiah. They refused to listen to him. They isolated him and persecuted him day after day.

Imagine what it was like to be Jeremiah—hated and completely friendless. Imagine if all your old friends turned away from you and abandoned you. How would you feel if you didn't even have the comfort of a spouse because God had commanded you to remain single during the difficult days ahead?

That was the intolerable situation Jeremiah found himself in. Yet, in obedience to God, he endured the unendurable, day after day, year after year.

What if you wanted to give up the lonely life of a prophet? What if you wanted to quit? Suppose you prayed, "God, take this calling away from me! It's too hard. It's too lonely. And it's futile; the people won't listen to me. I'm just wasting my life trying to deliver this message to the nation." How would you feel?

Jeremiah wanted to walk away from his calling as a prophet and a preacher, but he couldn't. Why? Because the word of God burned within him. It kindled in the marrow of his bones; it blazed in his brain. Despite the harshness of his message, Jeremiah loved his people and his nation; and that's why he preached a message of judgment and terror against them. He wanted to bring them to their senses before it was too late—before God allowed the enemies of the nation to swarm over the borders and take the people into captivity in a foreign land.

I view Jeremiah as the most heroic of all the prophets. Each of the Old Testament prophets had a distinct calling and a distinct message from God. Ezekiel preached about the glory and majesty of God. Isaiah prophesied about the salvation of God and the coming of the Messiah. Amos thundered against the rich and powerful who oppressed the poor. But Jeremiah stands out from among all the prophets for his dauntless courage and perseverance in the face of persecution. He preached for forty years, and he never saw a glimmer of success in his ministry. The other prophets were able to see their message have at least some impact on the nation, but not Jeremiah.

God called Jeremiah to a ministry of failure. But God also called Jeremiah to a ministry of faithfulness. He was not focused on results. Whether or not the people responded to his message was up to the people—and to God. Jeremiah knew that his only responsibility was to faithfully deliver God's warning to a nation under judgment.

Jeremiah lived in the last days of a decaying nation. He was the last prophet to Judah, the southern kingdom. Judah was all that remained of the nation of Israel after the northern kingdom of Israel was conquered by Assyria. The ten tribes of the northern kingdom were led away into captivity by the brutal Assyrian conquerors. Those tribes never returned to the promised land but were absorbed and assimilated by their pagan captors. Today, they are known as the "Ten Lost Tribes of Israel." Jeremiah's mission was to preach to the remnant in the southern kingdom.

The prophet Jeremiah began his prophetic ministry during the reign of Josiah, the last good king of Judah. Josiah had become king at age eight after his father was assassinated. It was Josiah who led the last revival the nation experienced before the Babylonian conquest and captivity. Unfortunately, the revival under King Josiah was largely superficial, and it did not reflect a deep change of heart among the people. The prophet Hilkiah told the king that although the people went along with him in reforming the nation and returning to God, they did so *not* because they loved God but because they loved King Josiah.

Jeremiah preached to the nation of Judah during the reigns of five kings: Josiah, the last good king; Jehoahaz, who was on the throne only three months; Jehoiakim, one of the most evil kings of Judah; Jehoiachin, who was captured by King Nebuchadnezzar of Babylon after only three months on the throne; and Zedekiah, a puppet ruler installed by Nebuchadnezzar. During Babylon's final siege of Jerusalem, the Babylonians captured Zedekiah, killed his sons in front of him, then put out his eyes and led him into captivity in Babylon. The city was destroyed and the temple of Solomon was razed.

Although most of the people of Judah were taken captive, Jeremiah was one of the few who was allowed to remain in the land. For decades, he had warned the nation that destruction was coming if the people didn't turn their hearts back to God. Finally, he witnessed the tragic fulfillment of those warnings.

The book of Jeremiah still speaks to us today. Are we listening?

The tragedy of Judah in Jeremiah's day is not merely a story of events from long ago. It is an urgent warning to us today. The same patterns of wickedness and idolatrous religion that stained the national character of Judah is rampant in the world today.

The book of Jeremiah is set in a time of national crisis and steep moral decline. The same kind of spiritual cancer that was slowly consuming the life of Judah is metastasizing in the nations of the world today. Across the globe, we see racial hatred and social injustice, rampant crime, and political corruption. When sin is widespread in a land, the natural consequences of that godlessness will result in the failure of the country to thrive.

So, no matter where we live, as we study the prophecy of Jeremiah, we need to ask ourselves: What can we learn from the history of Judah? How can we prevent history from repeating itself in our time? What is God saying to us from the pages of Jeremiah?

Though Judah failed to heed Jeremiah's warnings and was ultimately conquered and taken captive, that doesn't have to be our fate. Jeremiah taught the people of Judah what they must do when the world was falling apart around them. The answers are here in this book, and from Jeremiah's prophecy for that land, we can learn how to live as people of light in a culture of darkness. We can learn how God plants the seeds of new life amid destruction and judgment. The Lord says to us, as He said to the people of Judah, "If you repent, I will restore you" (Jeremiah 15:19). That reality works for any people in any time period.

In this book, we won't examine the book of Jeremiah verse by verse. Rather, we will capture the theme and message of this great prophecy, often applying the principles we find to our lives and our world today. Jeremiah speaks to us across the ages, and we desperately need both its warnings and its message of hope. As I have studied the book of Jeremiah, I have come to love it, and I think you will too.

1

CALLED FOR A CRISIS

Jeremiah 1

We live in an era of moral and spiritual crisis.

We live in a world that has turned its back on God.

Take the United States, for example. In its founding charter the nation's founders recognized that human beings are endowed by God with certain "unalienable rights."

If that document were being written today, however, any mention of God would likely be crossed out. Leaders in American government, the courts, the media, and universities are offended or embarrassed by America's God-based roots. Many want to remove "one nation under God" from the Pledge of Allegiance and "In God We Trust" from our coins. Some are even rewriting history, removing any references to faith in the Founding Fathers.

There are even many leaders in the church who no longer talk about the God of the Bible, or His Son, Jesus Christ. They no longer teach about heaven and hell, or that Jesus is the way, the truth, and the life. Instead, they teach that there are many paths to the same destination and that it doesn't really matter what you believe, as long as you're sincere. Some churches, embarrassed by the biblical story of Christ's atonement for our sin on the cross, have removed the cross from their buildings and their Sunday morning services.

We live in a time of moral and spiritual crisis every bit as dire and dangerous as Jeremiah's day. Like the ancient nation of Judah, it seems at times that our culture is rushing headlong toward its own destruction. And like ancient Judah, we have a choice: blessing or destruction, freedom or captivity, a new golden age—or a descent into darkness and death.

A WITNESS TO NATIONAL TRAGEDY

The book of Jeremiah opens with a full-length portrait of the prophet and the times in which he lived. The first three verses set the prophecy in its historical background:

> The words of Jeremiah son of Hilkiah, one of the priests at Anathoth in the territory of Benjamin. The word of the LORD came to him in the thirteenth year of the reign of Josiah son of Amon king of Judah, and through the reign of Jehoiakim son of Josiah king of Judah, down to the fifth month of the eleventh year of Zedekiah son of Josiah king of Judah, when the people of Jerusalem went into exile. (1:1–3)

This bare-bones description of the life and times of Jeremiah gives the facts without sensationalizing or embellishing it. But as we will see, these were troubled times in Judah, the southern kingdom. The northern kingdom, Israel, had already been carried into captivity by Assyria more than a century earlier. Judah, the southern kingdom, was rushing blindly along the same course the northern kingdom had taken toward judgment and captivity.

The book of Jeremiah is a collection of the prophet's messages, interspersed with historical narratives that portray the moral decline of the nation. The narrative begins in the days of Josiah, Judah's last good king, and it continues through the days of Zedekiah, Judah's last king. It is a time of moral decay and spiritual defection. The story portrays a nation in crisis, and it concludes with the death of that nation, which is the natural, predictable consequence of turning away from God. Jeremiah is the son of a priest, a "preachers kid." He grew up in the town of Anathoth, where only priests lived. His father's name was Hilkiah. Although that was a common name in those days, some Bible scholars think that Jeremiah's father may have been the high priest Hilkiah, who served in the temple in the days of King Josiah.

The high priest Hilkiah is notable for having rediscovered the law of Moses, which had been lost for years. We find the story in 2 Kings 22 and 2 Chronicles 34. Hilkiah was rummaging around in the rooms of the temple one day, looking over some old records and money boxes that had been stored there. Underneath some dusty ledgers he found a scroll. He dusted it off and began to read. To his amazement, he realized it was a copy of the law of Moses.

The spiritual life of the nation had declined so far that the Law, which had once been the central pillar of the Jewish nation, was now hidden away, lost, and forgotten. Hilkiah was stunned by what he read. He ordered a scribe to take the scroll to King Josiah. When the scribe read the scroll to King Josiah, the king rose to his feet and tore his robes in anguish.

King Josiah understood what the loss of the Law meant to the life of the nation, and he feared that the wrath of God would be poured out on Judah for failing to keep the Law. He made a covenant before the Lord to keep His commandments, and he set in motion the last national reform this nation would experience before the Babylonian exile.

We don't know whether this same Hilkiah, the high priest, was indeed Jeremiah's father. But we do know that Jeremiah began his ministry when Josiah was working to bring spiritual reform and revival to the kingdom of Judah. Josiah moved swiftly and brought his full authority to bear on the reform effort. He restored the worship of Jehovah and tore down the idols and pagan altars. We see in 2 Kings 23:10 that idol worship had so corrupted the Jewish nation that parents sacrificed their own precious children on the fiery altars of Molek (or Molech). Such acts are beyond our comprehension. Is it any wonder that a loving God would punish idolatry among His people?

When Josiah instituted his reforms, the law of Moses once again became the law of the land of Judah. It seemed for a while that the people had turned their hearts back to God. Tragically, however, the revival in Judah was temporary.

Soon after the king began his reforms, the king of Egypt, Pharaoh Necho, led his army up the Euphrates River to the east of Israel, and King Josiah met him in battle at Megiddo in northern Israel's Jezreel Valley. Necho killed King Josiah in battle, and when Josiah died, the spiritual life of the nation collapsed. The people of Judah anointed Jehoahaz, Josiah's son, as king. The new king, who was twenty-three years old, disregarded Josiah's reforms and did evil in God's sight.

After Jehoahaz had reigned for just three months, Pharaoh Necho came to Jerusalem and took Jehoahaz into custody. Apparently, the nation of Judah was in such a fallen state that the Egyptian king could simply stride into the king's fortress, arrest him, and march him away in chains. Jehoahaz spent the rest of his life in exile in Egypt. Necho installed Jehoahaz's brother Jehoiakim as a puppet king, and the Scriptures tell us that he also did evil in God's sight.

Jeremiah was a witness to many history-making events. He saw the mighty northern nation of Assyria crushed by the great empire to the east, Babylon. Then he saw Egypt, the great superpower to the south, humbled by Babylon at the Battle of Carchemish in 605 BC—one of the most pivotal, history-making battles of all time. During his lifetime, Jeremiah saw the Babylonian Empire under King Nebuchadnezzar rise to a position of world domination.

Finally, Jeremiah watched in horror as his own beloved land, the kingdom of Judah, was invaded by the armies of Babylon. The Babylonians surrounded Jerusalem and laid siege to the city for about two years. It was a time of terror, starvation, and unimaginable misery for the people trapped within the besieged city.

When Nebuchadnezzar carried off the Jewish people into Babylonian captivity, Jeremiah was left in a desolate land. The city lay in ruins, the temple was completely destroyed, and the entire countryside was ravaged by war. Later, Jeremiah was taken against his will to Egypt and there, tradition tells us, he was stoned to death by Jews who were angered by his preaching against their idolatry and disobedience to God. He died unmourned, and his body was consigned to an unmarked grave.

Here was a man who never outwardly experienced success in his prophetic calling. He lived to see his dire warnings of judgment and destruction fulfilled, but he never got to see the promises of future healing and restoration come to fruition. Yet, as he endured failure after failure and suffered persecution after persecution, he remained faithful to his calling. His heroism and perseverance are a source of encouragement to my heart.

A PROMISE OF PREPARATION

Next, Jeremiah writes of the calling he received from God, and how God prepared and commissioned him into the prophetic ministry when he was a young man. God does the calling, the preparing, and the empowering. It is all of God. All Jeremiah had to do was obey.

Notice, first, God's *preparation* of Jeremiah:

> The word of the LORD came to me, saying,
> "Before I formed you in the womb I knew you,
>   before you were born I set you apart;
>   I appointed you as a prophet to the nations." (1:4–5)

Perhaps you are familiar with the ministry of Cru (formerly Campus Crusade for Christ), founded by Bill and Vonette Bright at UCLA in 1951. The organization uses a simple gospel presentation called *The Four Spiritual Laws*, and the first of those four laws is this: "God loves you and has a wonderful plan for your life." That is similar to what the Lord is saying to Jeremiah in these verses.

God knew Jeremiah and set him apart even before he was conceived. Before Jeremiah existed, God appointed him to be His prophet to the nations. God had a wonderful plan for Jeremiah's life. He was preparing Jeremiah for a prophetic ministry not merely to *one* nation, Judah, but to *the nations*, plural. I believe that means that Jeremiah's prophecy speaks not just to Jeremiah's time, but to all times, and all nations.

In His commissioning message to Jeremiah, God told Jeremiah that He was preparing him for the ministry, and He was getting the world ready for him. God was working through Jeremiah's father and mother, his grandfathers and grandmothers, his great-grandfathers and great-grandmothers. He was arranging circumstances, influencing hearts and minds, generation by generation, with His eternal plan for history in mind.

This is a profound revelation of God's will as it operates in our lives. It's amazing to realize that God chooses us before we are born and that He has appointed us to become engaged in the spiritual and moral crises of our times. Jeremiah would need this powerful affirmation from God to carry him through the times of opposition and disappointment that lay ahead.

When human beings face a crisis, they turn to a leader or a government program or a powerful corporation for a solution. But when God confronts a crisis, he sometimes starts with a baby. Why a baby? A baby seems so helpless and (frankly) useless. What can a baby do? A baby cannot feed himself, change himself, or even crawl.

But a baby has unimaginable *potential*. God, who is outside of time and sees the past, present, and future at once, can see a crisis in society before it takes form. Knowing the crisis that is coming, He can choose a baby, even before it is conceived, and can prepare that baby to be His chosen solution to that crisis. Although there is nothing impressive about a baby, that helpless little baby is God's chosen method of changing the world.

- God made sure that a Hebrew baby born in Egypt was kept safe in a basket at the edge of the River Nile so that, at the right moment in history, Moses the Deliverer would stand before Pharaoh and demand, "Let my people go."

- God made sure that even though Abraham and Sarah were old and long past childbearing years, a baby named Isaac would be born to them at just the right moment in history, fulfilling the promise God had made to Abraham.

- And God made sure that a long-prophesied baby would be born in a stable in Bethlehem at just the right moment to become the Savior of the world.

Hidden in the heart of a baby are the most amazing possibilities. That is God's assurance to Jeremiah. Generations before Jeremiah was born, God was weaving together the circumstances to bring forth this baby at just the right moment in history so that Jeremiah might deliver His prophecy to a nation in crisis.

History tells us that the mother of Sir Walter Scott (author of *Ivanhoe*) was a sensitive woman who loved poetry and art, so it's not surprising that her son became a novelist and poet. The mother of British poet Lord Byron (1788–1824) was hot-tempered, proud, and violent; and Byron himself took on those same qualities. The mother of French leader Napoleon Bonaparte (1769–1821) was ambitious for herself and her children, so it's not surprising that Napoleon became a military leader of unbridled ambition. The mother of eighteenth-century British evangelists John and Charles Wesley was a godly and devout woman who prepared her sons to impact the world for Christ.

For good or ill, our earliest childhood experiences help shape the kind of adults we become. God knows us and begins shaping our character and our lives before we are born. This is true not just for prophets like Jeremiah. God prepares *every* child this way. He prepared me, and he prepared you.

People often say of some notable individual, "When God made him, when God made her, He broke the mold." In other words, that individual is special, unique, and there'll never be another person like him or her. What we fail to understand is that this is true of every person ever born. When God made me, He broke the mold. And when God made you, He broke the mold. God doesn't make people on an assembly line with cookie cutters. Every human being is unique, a one-of-a-kind individual. Of all the billions of people who have lived on this earth, or who ever will, no two are ever alike. God has individually, uniquely prepared each of us to play our part in His eternal plan.

That is why this passage (Jeremiah 1:4–5) is used, and rightly so, as part of a biblical rationale for Christian opposition to abortion. Human disobedience may result in an unwanted pregnancy, but the resulting child is not a mistake and is not unwanted by God. That child is loved, and God has a plan for that child's life. Human beings should never abort God's plan for that precious little life. God says to that unborn child, "Before I formed you in the womb I knew you; before you were born I set you apart." The abortionist who takes that life is playing God.

I once heard the story of a young pastor named David who was dying of cancer. His father and uncle, both of whom are pastors, came to visit him shortly before his death. David spoke with them for a while, then he said to the uncle, "Would you mind if I talked to my dad alone?"

The uncle left the room, and David and his father talked alone for a while. Sometime later, the father came out of David's room, and he was in an emotional state. He said to the uncle, "Let's go get some coffee."

Later, over coffee, the father said, "I want to tell you what David did while we were alone. He called me over to his bed and said, 'Dad, would you put your arms around me?' So I embraced him, and he said, 'Dad, I want you to know that the greatest gift God ever gave me, outside of salvation itself, was the gift of a father and mother who love God and taught me to love Him too.'"

That's what God is saying, in effect, to Jeremiah: "What a gift you have! I have prepared you for this moment through the generations that passed before you were born. I was preparing the way so that you might speak for me during this time of crisis for Judah and all nations."

GOD'S PROVISION

In addition to God's preparation, we see God's *provision* for us to be His people, carrying out His eternal plan:

"Alas, Sovereign LORD," I said, "I do not know how to speak; I am too young."

But the LORD said to me, "Do not say, 'I am too young.' You must go to everyone I send you to and say whatever I command you. Do not be afraid of them, for I am with you and will rescue you," declares the LORD. (1:6–8)

When God called Jeremiah, the young man's initial response was to shrink from the call. Many heroes of the Bible have had the same response—Moses, Gideon, Isaiah, and others. When God first called them to a challenge, they said, in effect, "I'm not adequate for this task. I'm not eloquent enough or wise enough or strong enough or mature enough. Lord, you should choose someone else." If you ever feel inadequate when God calls you, remember that you're in good company. God's servants often start with a sense of inadequacy.

Jeremiah was probably about thirty years old when God called him. That's when young prophets usually began their ministry in Israel and Judah. Jesus was thirty years old when He began His ministry.

Jeremiah was acutely aware of his inadequacy and inexperience, and I believe this awareness on his part indicates the sensitivity of this young man. Throughout this prophecy, you find Jeremiah being sensitive to the events going on around him. He is called to stand before kings, to thunder denunciations and judgments, to feel the lash of their recriminations, to endure their anger and defy their power, and to suffer with his people as he sees them rushing headlong to their own destruction. Jeremiah's other book, Lamentations, contains the cries of his heart as he witnesses the sufferings the people have inflicted on themselves through disobedience.

When Jeremiah protested that he was inadequate, God answered just as He had answered Moses and every other Bible hero who suffered from self-doubt and inferiority feelings. God said, "You must go to everyone I send you to and say whatever I command you. Do not be afraid of them, for I am with you and will rescue you" (1:7–8).

Do you worry that you lack eloquence and a strong speaking voice? Do you worry that you are too young and inexperienced for the challenge? Do you worry that you lack the courage and wisdom needed for the challenge? Stop worrying. God will be your voice. God will be your encourager. God will supply His wisdom. Whatever you need, He will give it to you.

Are you afraid you might appear foolish, that you might embarrass yourself? Well, that's possible. There have been many times, especially in my early days in ministry, when I prayed for God's wisdom, courage, and power, and I proceeded to do and say things that embarrassed me. Yet God worked through my weakness and foolishness, and He touched hearts with my awkward, tongue-tied speech.

When God calls you to a challenge, He doesn't call you to glorify yourself. He calls you to give glory to Him. He often receives the greatest glory through the weakest and most foolish of His servants. Don't worry about making a fool of yourself. Be available and obedient for His purpose, and that will be enough.

The Lord's message to Jeremiah in these verses is essentially the new covenant that Jesus has made with us in the New Testament. It's the promise He made before ascending into heaven: "And surely I am with you always, to the very end of the age" (Matthew 28:20). The old covenant—the law of Moses—is an external demand that God made upon His people: If you will do this, then I will do that. If you keep My commandments, then I will bless you. The people could not keep the old covenant, because it is impossible for fallen human beings to meet all the demands of the Law.

But the new covenant is different. It is a covenant that God places within us. It is God's own presence with us. It is God's promise to be with us always, to the very end of the age. It is the promise God made to Jeremiah: "Do not be afraid of them, for I am with you and will rescue you" (1:8). The same promise of God that encouraged Jeremiah has also been delivered to us. As a result, when God calls us to a challenge, we should never say, "Lord, choose someone else. I'm inadequate to this challenge." Instead, we should say, "Yes, Lord. I know I can't do this in my strength, but trusting in your promise to always be with me, I will obey you."

GOD'S PROMISE OF POWER

Next, we come to the third division of Jeremiah's calling from God—an amazing section I call the promise of *power* from God:

Then the LORD reached out his hand and touched my mouth and said to me, "I have put my words in your mouth. See, today I appoint you over nations and kingdoms to uproot and tear down, to destroy and overthrow, to build and to plant." (1:9–10)

This is a significant scene. It is reminiscent of the scene in Isaiah 6, where God commissions the prophet Isaiah to be His spokesman. Isaiah experiences a vision of God in all His glory and majesty, surrounded by angels of heaven. And Isaiah responds, "Woe to me! I am ruined! For I am a man of unclean lips, and I live among a people of unclean lips, and my eyes have seen the King, the LORD Almighty" (v. 5).

Then an angel flies to him with a hot coal in his hand and touches the burning coal to Isaiah's mouth, saying, "See, this has touched your lips; your guilt is taken away and your sin atoned for" (v. 7).

Similarly, the Lord himself reaches out and touches Jeremiah's mouth and says, "I have put my words in your mouth" (Jeremiah 1:9). The Lord's own words are the key to Jeremiah's power. He now has on his lips the burning, mighty power of the word of God.

By giving Jeremiah this power, God gave the prophet authority over nations and kingdoms. Please understand; this is not mere poetry. The message of the book of Jeremiah is addressed to all the great nations of Jeremiah's day—to Egypt, Assyria, Babylon, and many others, as well as the kingdom of Judah. And while the message was not addressed to us today, the principles and teachings can be applied to America, Great Britain, France, Russia, China, and all other nations, great and small, around the globe.

Imagine all the nations of the world, with their power and pomp, their rattling sabers, thinking themselves so powerful and behaving so arrogantly. But God has chosen an obscure young man, about thirty years of age, from a village no one has ever heard of, to confront the nations. God tells him, "Today I appoint you over nations and kingdoms to uproot and tear down, to destroy and overthrow, to build and to plant" (1:10).

This is also our heritage as believers in Jesus Christ. The apostle James wrote that the prayer of a righteous person releases great power. When you and I pray about the affairs of life, we can affect the fate of nations. It doesn't matter that we are obscure and that no one knows who we are. As Paul wrote to the church in Corinth, "But God chose the foolish things of the world to shame the wise; God chose the weak things of the world to shame the strong" (1 Corinthians 1:27).

God strategically placed Jeremiah amid the death and destruction that was coming upon Judah. He gave Jeremiah authority, through His message of judgment, "to uproot and tear down, to destroy and overthrow" (Jeremiah 1:10). In a sinful nation, there are many things that must be torn down. It may well be that the destruction and partitioning of Germany after World War II was an uprooting, a tearing down, due to the awful national sin of the Holocaust. And it may well be that the American Civil War was an uprooting, a tearing down, due to the shameful national sin of human slavery. There are other examples we could point to.

Judgment, destruction, and being overthrown are always the work of God, whether it is a nation that must be torn down or an individual human heart. When there is disobedience, when there is defection from God, when there is heart of rebellion against God's moral law, there are things that need to be uprooted.

I once had a conversation with a young man who said, "I don't understand what's wrong with my marriage. I'm trying to do everything right, but our relationship gets worse and worse. I can't put my finger on what's wrong."

I replied, "There's something wrong, and I believe God will show it to you. There are things you're doing in your marriage that you're not aware of, things you need to see. At this moment, you're blind to them. You think you're doing everything right, and you don't see what you're doing wrong. It baffles you, and it means there are things in your life that God needs to tear down. Maybe it's pride. Maybe it's a habit of discourtesy. Maybe it's a superior attitude your wife picks up on. Ask God to reveal it to you. It will hurt, because when God begins to point out and uproot your flaws, there's always pain involved. But one day you'll look back on the uprooting process, and you'll be grateful to God for this painful blessing in your life."

God never destroys simply to be destructive. He never tears down merely to be mean or cruel. He destroys only to build up again. He uproots only to plant again. He allows hurt only to heal again. This was God's word to Jeremiah.

THE ENTIRE NATION VERSUS JEREMIAH

Jeremiah closes chapter 1 with a depiction of his prophetic ministry in the land of Judah. This passage falls into three major divisions, beginning with verse 11. In the first division, the Lord gives Jeremiah a symbolic vision of what He will accomplish through Jeremiah's ministry:

> The word of the LORD came to me: "What do you see, Jeremiah?"
> "I see the branch of an almond tree," I replied.
> The LORD said to me, "You have seen correctly, for I am watching to see that my word is fulfilled." (1:11–12)

In the original Hebrew, there is a play on words here. The Jews called the almond tree "the watcher" (*shaqad*) because it was the first tree to blossom in the spring. They saw it as watching for the return of the sun and the warming of the earth, and therefore it was the first to herald the coming of springtime.

God said to Jeremiah, "You have seen correctly, for I am watching (*shaqad*) to see that my word is fulfilled" (v. 12). This is a picture of health and healing. Throughout this prophecy there are comforting passages that deal with God's plan to heal the land.

Later we will look in detail at an incident in which God sent Jeremiah to buy a piece of property while the city was being conquered by the Babylonians. Amid the death and terror of a city under siege, Jeremiah was to buy this property, get the title deed, and have it sealed and witnessed. Why? It was because God was testifying, through Jeremiah's actions, that He intended to restore the land. The property that Jeremiah purchased would still have value at some time in the future. This is God's message of hope in a time of death and despair. God always shows us a glimmer of hope in our darkest trials.

The next symbol God gives to Jeremiah is a vision of a boiling pot:

The word of the LORD came to me again: "What do you see?"

"I see a pot that is boiling," I answered. "It is tilting toward us from the north."

The LORD said to me, "From the north disaster will be poured out on all who live in the land. I am about to summon all the peoples of the northern kingdoms," declares the LORD.

"Their kings will come and set up their thrones
    in the entrance of the gates of Jerusalem;
they will come against all her surrounding walls
    and against all the towns of Judah." (Jeremiah 1:13–15)

The prophet saw a pot boiling, with steam rising and streaming in the north wind toward the south. God was giving Jeremiah a symbolic glimpse of the future. He was saying that He would bring the confederation of nations down from the north against Jerusalem, and these nations would be like a flood of boiling water, bringing disaster, horror, and destruction upon the city. This is a picture of hot, boiling judgment against sin and godlessness.

At that time, Egypt was the greatest power on earth, but God didn't choose Egypt to judge Judah. Instead, He seized upon Babylon as His instrument of judgment.

As the crow flies, Babylon is east, not north, of Jerusalem. But the Babylonians would not have invaded Judah by crossing the arid upper Arabian Desert. Instead, they went northwest along the Euphrates River, then south through Syria. From Jerusalem, the enemy would appear to descend from due north.

Next, God announces to Jeremiah the reason for His judgment against the kingdom of Judah:

> "I will pronounce my judgments on my people
> because of their wickedness in forsaking me,
> in burning incense to other gods
> and in worshiping what their hands have made." (1:16)

The nation that forsakes God ultimately dies. In the kingdom of Judah, the impending death of the nation is evidenced by two idolatrous religious practices:

First, the people burned incense to other gods. Any nation that worships anyone other than the one true God has a lot to answer for.

Second, the people worshiped the work of their own hands. In other words, they exalted humanity and pointed to human beings as the solution to their own problems. This is never a good approach, and we can see today what happens to a society that leaves God out and exalts mankind to the highest position. Wherever human beings gather to exalt themselves, death is just around the corner.

In the closing verses of chapter 1, God issues a command and makes a promise to Jeremiah:

"Get yourself ready! Stand up and say to them whatever I command you. Do not be terrified by them, or I will terrify you before them. Today I have made you a fortified city, an iron pillar and a bronze wall to stand against the whole land—against the kings of Judah, its officials, its priests and the people of the land. They will fight against you but will not overcome you, for I am with you and will rescue you," declares the LORD. (1:17–19)

When I was sixteen years old, I was arrested and charged with hunting out of season. I knew I was innocent, and I was eventually able to prove my innocence. But I remember the dread I felt when I opened an envelope from the state and found a warrant for my arrest. At the top of the document were these words: "The People of the State of Montana versus Ray C. Stedman." I thought, *That's not fair! Everybody in the state of Montana is against me.*

Jeremiah faced a situation in which all the people of the kingdom of Judah were against him. He was hated and persecuted by the kings of Judah, the government officials, the priests, and all the people of the land. They fought him and smeared his reputation and even sought his life. But God told Jeremiah, "Do not be terrified by them . . . for I am with you and will rescue you" (1:17, 19). God promised to make him as strong as a fortified city, as immovable as an iron pillar, as unbreakable as a wall of bronze.

As we will later see, Jeremiah will endure persecution far beyond anything you and I are likely to face. Not only will he be ostracized, rejected, insulted, and slandered but he will also be thrown into a cistern, mired in mud and filth, and left to die a slow, agonizing death. But God had commissioned him to speak. No matter what his enemies did to him, Jeremiah always said exactly what God told him to say. He was a man of unquenchable faith and unstoppable courage.

Over his life, Jeremiah learned four key truths: First, he learned that God is sovereign over the affairs of nations. He has absolute authority to raise one nation up and cast another down. Second, Jeremiah learned that God keeps His promises to judge sin and that those who serve other gods will not escape His judgment. Third, Jeremiah learned that God keeps His promises to bless those who love Him and obey Him. Fourth, Jeremiah learned that God is tenderhearted toward those who suffer, and God hurts with those who are hurting.

We will see Jeremiah go through times of discouragement in his ministry. There is a point where he loses all hope and cries out, "Alas, my mother, that you gave me birth, a man with whom the whole land strives and contends!" (see Jeremiah 15:10). Jeremiah was not only lamenting his own hurt over the rejection he suffered but he also hurt for his persecutors. He wept over them, knowing the sufferings they were inflicting on themselves by rejecting God.

Ultimately, Jeremiah realized that his sufferings echoed the pain that pierced the heart of God himself. The people had rejected Jeremiah—but even more, the people had rejected God. Jeremiah hurt for his Jewish brothers, but how much *more* did God himself agonize over His wayward chosen people!

God is just and righteous, and He must punish sin. But God is also tenderhearted and merciful, and He does not want to see His children suffer, even when they bring judgment on themselves through sin and idolatry.

As we continue to explore the book of Jeremiah, we will discover the depths of the justice, righteousness, mercy, and love of God. Also, we will discover the deep wisdom of His plan for our lives—and for all the nations and peoples of our world.

2

THE WAY BACK

Jeremiah 2–6

Jim Vaus was a wiretapper for a Los Angeles crime syndicate in the 1940s and '50s. One night, out of curiosity, he went to a Billy Graham Crusade in downtown L.A., and Dr. Graham's message moved him to go forward and receive Christ as his Lord and Savior.

Vaus knew he could no longer continue his life of crime, and he wanted to make restitution to the people he had hurt, but there was no way to find them. So he did the next-best thing. He sold his home, his car, and other possessions, and he used the money to start a Christian discipleship organization called Youth Development, Inc. (now called YDI), which continues to disciple and mentor young people today.

After his conversion, Vaus wanted his old friends in organized crime to hear about Jesus. One of the first people he witnessed to was notorious crime boss Mickey Cohen. Vaus took a risk in talking to Cohen about his need for Jesus. Cohen was a violent man who had killed countless people, and he was living in an armed fortress in Brentwood. Yet when Vaus told Cohen how Jesus had changed his life, the crime boss wanted to know more.

Jim Vaus arranged a meeting for Cohen with Billy Graham and Christian actors Stuart Hamblen, Roy Rogers, and Dale Evans. Dr. Graham explained the gospel to Cohen, and the crime boss said he wanted to receive Christ.

For a while, it seemed he had sincerely given his life to Christ. But within days, it became clear that Cohen had not altered his lifestyle in the slightest. He was still living a life of crime. Jim Vaus arranged another meeting between Cohen and the Graham evangelistic team. Dr. Graham explained to Cohen that he could not follow Christ and continue his criminal career. He had to repent of his crimes.

Cohen was shocked. "Why do I have to give up my career? There are Christian movie stars, Christian athletes, Christian businessmen. So why not a Christian gangster? If that's Christianity, count me out."[1]

No matter who you are, no matter what you have done, no matter how many sins you have piled up over your lifetime, there is a way back to God. But you have to let God change your life. One gangster, Jim Vaus, was willing to change, and he found God. Another gangster, Mickey Cohen, was unwilling to let God change him.

Mickey Cohen thought he could receive Jesus as Savior without receiving Jesus as Lord. But God doesn't save people to leave them in their sin. He saves us *from* our sins and gives us *new life* in Christ. It doesn't matter how deep a pit of sin you have dug, you are never beyond the reach of God's mercy and grace.

Jesus was crucified between two criminals. Both were guilty of horrible crimes. One repented of his sin and begged Jesus for forgiveness; he found the way to God. The other was unrepentant and abusive to his final breath; he rejected the way to God.

King David found the way back to God after he sinned with Bathsheba and tried to cover up his sexual sin by arranging her husband's murder. King David's sins were horrifying, yet he confessed his sins, repented, and found his way back to God. The apostle Peter, on the night that Jesus was betrayed, denied his Lord three times. On the third time, he sealed his denial with an oath. Yet Peter later confessed his sin, repented, and he was reconciled to God.

No matter how awful our sins, there is a way back to God if we will repent and accept His forgiveness. There was a way back for the kingdom of Judah, and there is a way back for America—and every other nation today—as more and more people see their need to repent of their sins and turn to Jesus for salvation.

FIRST WORD: *REMEMBER*

Jeremiah's opening message to the nation of Judah spans several chapters of the book. I will highlight selected passages to show what God has to say to us when we have begun to drift away from Him. Have you ever fallen away from God, strayed from your love for Him, or turned your back on Him in anger and rebellion? I can testify that there have been times in my life when I have lost the joy, the peace, and the excitement of being close to God. Gradually, almost imperceptibly, I have drifted away, and my love for Him has grown cold.

This was the tragic state of the nation of Judah. Morally, the nation had wandered away from God. Spiritually, the nation had turned its back on God. Many blamed God for the problems they were having (you may have gone through times of blaming God as well). The people said it was God's fault that they no longer worshiped Him and loved Him as the law of Moses required. They claimed that God did not deliver them from their enemies. They charged God with failing to keep His promises.

But God has a message for the people of Judah—and for you and me. His message is centered around four keywords of Jeremiah: *remember*, *realize*, *return*, and *beware*. These four instructive words point the way back to God. Remember them and follow them when you sense you are drifting from your relationship with God. These four words will point the way home to Him.

The first of these four words, *remember*, is found in Jeremiah 2:

The word of the LORD came to me: "Go and proclaim in the hearing of Jerusalem:

"This is what the LORD says:

"'I *remember* the devotion of your youth,
how as a bride you loved me
and followed me through the wilderness,
through a land not sown.
Israel was holy to the LORD,
the firstfruits of his harvest;
all who devoured her were held guilty,
and disaster overtook them,'"
declares the LORD. (2:1–3)

God says, "Remember!" Look back. Recall what life was like when you first fell in love with God. He says, "I remember the devotion of your youth, how as a bride you loved me and followed me through the wilderness, through a land not sown."

I counseled many married couples over the years. Some have been married twenty, thirty, or forty years; yet they are still having struggles, they are tense and angry, and sometimes they will not even speak to each other. How do you begin the healing process with a husband and a wife who refuse to communicate with each other?

I learned early in my ministry as a pastor that the best way to begin is to say, "Before we begin our counseling session, I'd like to get acquainted with you both. Tell me something about yourselves. How did you meet? How did you fall in love in the first place?"

That's always an excellent place to begin. I always sense a change in the atmosphere. Angry, tense faces begin to relax. Sometimes eyes glisten. Hearts soften. They recall moments of excitement, tenderness, and the first flutterings of the heart. They remember what it felt like to be in love—before the anger set in. Tender memories are a starting point where couples can begin to find their way back to a love relationship with each other.

Do you remember the early days of your relationship with the Lord? Do you remember the wonder and joy of knowing you belong to Him? Speaking through the prophet Jeremiah, God is reminding the people of Judah of their first love for Him. They followed Him as a loving and devoted bride follows her husband: trustingly and faithfully, even through a wilderness where fields and orchards have not yet been planted. In effect, God says to the drifting heart, "Remember what it was like when you were secure in My affection for you? Remember what it was like when you were faithful to Me, and you served no idols or foreign gods?"

I once traveled with a young man from our church. He told me he had listened to a sermon on the letters to the seven churches in Revelation 2. When the speaker got to the part where the Lord says to the angel of the church in Ephesus, "I have this against you, that you have left your first love," (2:4 NKJV) this young man felt something grip his heart.

In a flash of insight, this young man realized that he had allowed his love for Bible study about Jesus to overtake his love for Jesus himself. He realized that he needed to return to his first love—his love for the Lord Jesus himself. Bible study, as exciting and engaging as it is, should not take the place of a deep love for God. This young man remembered his first love, and that remembrance showed him the way back to a vibrant and exciting relationship with the Lord.

That's what the Lord says, in effect, to the people of Judah through the prophet Jeremiah: "Remember, Judah, those days in the wilderness when you walked with Me as a bride walks devotedly with her husband? Remember the joy you felt when you were exclusively Mine?"

SECOND WORD: *REALIZE*

The second word God uses to point the people back to a close relationship with Him is *realize*:

> "Your wickedness will punish you;
> your backsliding will rebuke you.

Consider then and *realize*
how evil and bitter it is for you
when you forsake the LORD your God
and have no awe of me,"
declares the Lord, the LORD Almighty. (2:19)

God calls the people of Judah to *realize* the suffering they will inflict on themselves by forsaking God. Realize the moral and spiritual bankruptcy of your current state. Realize the harm you are doing to your children and grandchildren. Realize that you have no one to blame but yourself when judgment falls.

He is trying to arrest the attention of the nation and help the people see their need of Him. God, the Master Illustrator, goes on to provide two powerful visual aids to help the people realize the condition they were in. These two visual aids are instructive to us as well. Speaking through Jeremiah, God says:

"My people have committed two sins:
They have forsaken me,
the spring of living water,
and have dug their own cisterns,
broken cisterns that cannot hold water." (2:13)

Here, the Lord shows us two signs of moral and spiritual decay in a nation. God is describing the decay that had taken place in the kingdom of Judah, but He is also describing the state of moral and spiritual decline that can take place in any country if people reject God and His plan. Could it be that He is also describing the moral and spiritual state of your heart and mind?

Picture a valley with a stream running through it—a beautiful stream flowing with cold, crystal-clear water from the melting snow in the mountains. What could be more inviting? This is living water, tumbling over waterfalls, swirling and shimmering over stones, pleasant and refreshing to drink. This water is freely available to all who would dip their pail into the stream and draw it out.

But the people have forsaken the streams of living water. Up on the barren, rocky hillsides, they dug cisterns to catch the water as it runs down the slope. The water that collects in the cistern is often fouled with dirt and leaves and bugs and dead mice. The cisterns leak and need continual repair. Yet even though there is a stream of living water nearby, the people go to the effort of digging cisterns that yield inferior, polluted water.

What a vivid picture God presents, and how devastatingly accurate it is! We all know people who do that, don't we? In fact, we can probably remember times when we have done so ourselves. The living water of God has been available to us all along, providing freshness, vitality, joy, peace, security, love, and life. Yet we have sought our satisfaction in the dirty, polluted cisterns of pleasure-seeking, wealth-chasing, false philosophies, and other things that simply do not hold water. When a nation, a church, a family, or an individual turns away from the living water of God and toward the polluted cisterns of this world, death is sure to follow.

God begs the people of Judah to turn back to Him and drink deeply of the living water. He urges them to find the cleansing, healing, and refreshment of the Holy Spirit. Why do we insist on having our own way when our way is foolish and destructive? God alone can satisfy the heart. Why do we keep chasing after satisfaction in places where it can never be found?

We are tempted to pity or condemn the foolish people of Judah for forsaking God and neglecting His Word while worshiping idols made of metal or stone. But what are we chasing? What are we worshiping? What are the cisterns in our lives that have replaced the living water of a deep, satisfying relationship with God?

THIRD WORD: *RETURN*

God, speaking through Jeremiah, gives us another prophetic image that is even more graphic:

> "Long ago you broke off your yoke
> and tore off your bonds;
> you said, 'I will not serve you!'
> Indeed, on every high hill
> and under every spreading tree
> you lay down as a prostitute.
> I had planted you like a choice vine
> of sound and reliable stock.
> How then did you turn against me
> into a corrupt, wild vine?" (2:20–21)

When we forsake the living God, it doesn't take long for deterioration and degeneracy to set in. We open ourselves to being used and exploited by false ideas, false doctrines, false teachers, and false beliefs. We become, God says, like prostitutes—spiritual prostitutes. We defile ourselves by lusting after strange ideas and false gods. The Lord goes on to say:

> "How can you say, 'I am not defiled;
> I have not run after the Baals'?
> See how you behaved in the valley;
> consider what you have done.
> You are a swift she-camel
> running here and there,
> a wild donkey accustomed to the desert,
> sniffing the wind in her craving—
> in her heat who can restrain her?
> Any males that pursue her need not tire themselves;
> at mating time they will find her." (2:23–24)

If you have ever worked around horses, you know what this imagery speaks of. Here is a mare in heat, lusting to mate with a stallion. God speaks frankly in His Word to get our attention and awaken us to our spiritual condition. God intends for us to learn from the animal kingdom. He gave animals a different kind of sexual nature than He gave to us so we might observe them and learn from them.

The mare in heat is a picture of how human beings behave once they begin lusting after every new idea and philosophy that comes along. While human sexuality is meant to be expressed within the protective enclosure of faithfulness in marriage, animal sexuality is wild, uncontrolled, instinctive, and unfaithful. Animals are slaves to their primal urges, and we human beings become out-of-control and animal-like when we defile ourselves with false philosophies and false gods, and when we seek our satisfaction in anything other than God.

This visual image, spoken by God through the prophet Jeremiah, would have been immediately understood by the people of Judah. They lived closer to the animal kingdom then most of us do today. They understood what an animal in heat looks like, and how it is driven—mindlessly, instinctively—to seek sexual gratification.

God uses this imagery to help us see ourselves from His perspective. He is saying to us, "This is what you are like—living for the moment, living for pleasure, living for every new idea or form of entertainment that comes along—and you are being led around by your base urges instead of finding your satisfaction in Me." God is trying to shake His people out of their stupor and show them a way back to Him.

How do we become the kind of noble, spiritual, intelligent beings God created us to be? How do we stop being instinctual brutes, led about by our lusts and urges? We find the answer in the third keyword Jeremiah uses in his message to Judah. The first two keywords were *remember* and *realize*; the third is *return*. God, speaking through Jeremiah, repeats this word several times throughout this prophecy. For example:

> The LORD said to me, "Faithless Israel is more righteous than
> unfaithful Judah. Go, proclaim this message toward the
> north:
> "'*Return*, faithless Israel,' declares the LORD,
> 'I will frown on you no longer,

for I am faithful,' declares the LORD,
'I will not be angry forever.'" (3:11–12)

Later, in verse 22, God says, "*Return*, faithless people; I will cure you of backsliding." And in 4:1, He says, "If you, Israel, will *return*, then *return* to me." The logic of this counsel is inescapable. If you are driving down the road and discover you are on the wrong road, should you keep going, hoping that the wrong road will somehow bring you to the right destination? That would be the height of insanity. When you realize you're on the wrong road, the only logical thing to do is to turn around and go back to the point where you lost your way.

Yet many of us, in our lives and in our walk with God, behave in completely illogical ways. We realize we are moving in the wrong direction, yet we keep going, thinking that it will somehow turn out all right. We refuse to make that U-turn. We refuse to repent. Why? Perhaps we are too proud to admit we've been wrong. Perhaps we are too stubborn and self-willed to return to God. Perhaps we are so addicted to sin that we cannot see what is in our own best interests.

Therefore, we refuse to turn around. We refuse to return. We keep going our own way instead of going God's way. Yet God continues to plead with us, as the prophet Jeremiah records:

> "'*Return*, faithless Israel,' declares the LORD,
> 'I will frown on you no longer,
> for I am faithful,' declares the LORD,
> 'I will not be angry forever.
> Only acknowledge your guilt—
> you have rebelled against the LORD your God,
> you have scattered your favors to foreign gods
> under every spreading tree,
> and have not obeyed me,'"
> declares the LORD. (3:12–13)

What must we do to return and find our way back to God? "Only acknowledge your guilt" (v. 13). But that's not easy, is it? We don't like to take a searching look at ourselves and realize that, yes, we are guilty before God. He sees the heart, and we cannot fool Him. It's easy to fool the people around us and convince them that we are oh-so-spiritual. But we can't justify ourselves before God.

But He wants us to know that we don't have to justify or excuse ourselves. If we will confess our sin to Him, He will forgive us, heal us, refresh us, and restore us to a right relationship with Him.

I worry about an unfortunate trend I see in Christian circles today. Many Christians seem to treat God's beautiful promise of forgiveness as if it were automatic. They seem to assume that God is so ready to forgive that he will instantly excuse any sin we commit, whether we confess it or not. In his book *The Cost of Discipleship*, Dietrich Bonhoeffer called the belief in instantaneous blanket forgiveness "cheap grace." He wrote:

> Cheap grace is the grace we bestow on ourselves. Cheap grace is the preaching of forgiveness without requiring repentance, baptism without church discipline, Communion without confession. . . . Cheap grace is grace without discipleship, grace without the cross, grace without Jesus Christ, living and incarnate.[2]

Cheap grace takes a diminished view of the awfulness of sin and a diminished view of the holiness and justice of God. It seems to say, "Sin isn't that big a deal to fellowship with God. The blood of Jesus covers my sin so I don't ever have to think about it, much less acknowledge it. Being a Christian means never having to say I'm sorry." That sort of thinking is a lie from Satan himself.

The way to return is to acknowledge our guilt. As long as our sin remains unacknowledged and unconfessed, we cannot return to God. We need to take sin as seriously as He does.

Pastor and author Stuart Briscoe once told me of an incident that took place in his church. A teenage boy had come to Christ through the witness of some of the believers in the church. They had reached out to this young man when he was strung out on drugs and unable to get clean. After he received Christ as his Lord and Savior, God freed him from his addictions.

This young man was so grateful and excited about his newfound faith that he asked these believers how he could be baptized and become a member of the church. One Sunday morning a few weeks later, he was accepted into membership, and he asked Stuart if he could say a few words to the congregation. Stuart agreed.

The young man stood and said, "I want to tell you about my life before I knew Christ. I was messed up on drugs. I hated myself. I had no future. Then some people from this church found me and loved me as I've never been loved before. They told me how to receive Jesus as my Lord and Savior, and I asked Him to take over my life.

"I was eager to come to this church, and I wanted to find out what there was about this place that had people in it like that. But you know what? The first time I came here, I was disappointed. Some of you didn't like my long hair; I could see it in the way you looked at me. Some of you ignored me. Some of you seemed to be mad at me, and I didn't know why. And I have to admit it—it made me mad that some of you looked down on me. I almost didn't want to come back.

"But God dealt with my heart. He made me realize that it was wrong for me to be bitter toward you. If some of you here can't accept me, or you look down on me, well, that's between you and God. But I was wrong to be angry with you, and I had to settle that with God. I confessed to God that I had a sinful attitude, and He has forgiven me. But I also need to confess it to you, and I ask you to forgive me and receive me as a member here."

Stuart Briscoe told me that many in the church were convicted by those words. As a result of that young man's confession, a new attitude of openness swept through the church—a welcoming attitude toward people like this young man. It all began with this young man's acknowledgment of guilt. Once he confessed his own sin to God, he found his way back to God, and he found his way into the fellowship of that church.

God goes on to say through Jeremiah, "Then I will give you shepherds after my own heart, who will lead you with knowledge and understanding" (3:15). God is reaching out to His people. He says, *Return, come back, it's not too late. I will restore you. I will feed you. I will open your eyes.* We do not have to walk in ignorance and darkness anymore.

FOURTH WORD: *BEWARE*

We've looked at the first three words Jeremiah used to point the way back to God. But there is a fourth word that Jeremiah found it necessary to add. That fourth word is *beware*. God says:

> "Should I not punish them for this?"
>   declares the LORD.
> "Should I not avenge myself
>   on such a nation as this?
> "A horrible and shocking thing
>   has happened in the land:
> The prophets prophesy lies,
>   the priests rule by their own authority,
> and my people love it this way.
>   But what will you do in the end?" (5:29–31)

The word *beware* doesn't actually appear in this text, but that is the message—a message of warning, a message to be wary. God is reminding us that life is finite and all too short, and we need to think about how we will face the end of life.

God gives us life so we can prepare ourselves to die. If we have spent our lives chasing after wealth or status or pleasure or success instead of investing our lives in a relationship with God, that final day will come and we won't be ready to die. We won't be prepared. We won't look forward to meeting our Lord face-to-face.

Jesus said that life is like building a house. When you build a house, you can either build it on the firm foundation of the rock, or you can build it on sand. The rock is God—a close, loving, lifelong relationship with Him. And the sand? If you build your life on any system of thought, any philosophy, any set of values, any purpose other than Jesus himself, you are building your house on sand.

You can build a beautiful house on the rock, and you can also build a beautiful house on sand. People driving by will admire that beautiful house regardless of what foundation it rests on. You might be able to live in your house on the sand for quite a while without experiencing any problems.

But a time of testing eventually comes. The winds of adversity blow, and the waves of trials pound against the house. The testing you face may come from a troubling medical diagnosis, a devastating personal loss, a traffic accident that robs you of your health, a bankruptcy, the ruin of your reputation, or some other crisis. But I guarantee that sooner or later testing *will* come into your life. No matter how beautiful and comfortable your house may have been up until now, the time of testing will prove whether your house will endure. It all depends on your foundation.

At the end of your life, will you be eager to meet Him or will you be afraid? Will you have spent your entire life preparing for this moment or avoiding reality? Beware the trap of thinking your life will just go on and on. Beware the trap of putting off your decision to follow Christ—your decision to return to God.

Perhaps you've been going to church for years, but you've never given your life to Christ. Or perhaps you've been a Christian for many years, but your love for God has faded. God has made a way back for you. Acknowledge your guilt, repent, and turn away from your sins. Receive the free gift of God's mercy and salvation. He will heal you of your waywardness and faithlessness.

If you reject his offer of a way back to Him, if you choose not to think about what the end of life has in store for you, then you'll have to face death unprepared. Please consider this question God puts to you: *What will you do in the end? Will you be prepared to meet Me?*

Remember. Realize. Return. Beware.

God has made a way back for you. He loves you and wants to have a deep and abiding relationship with you. He wants to open the fountains of living water to refresh your spirit. Walk with Him day by day, and when the final day comes, you'll be ready to walk through the door of death, because you won't have to walk through it alone.

3

LOVE'S LAST RESORT

Jeremiah 7–10

The most baffling times in my Christian experience have been when God acted in ways that were contrary to my expectations. Again and again throughout my life I have found that there is a gap between the God of my expectations and the God of reality. I want a God who fits compactly into the box of my expectations and my understanding, but the God of reality, the God of the Bible, does not fit in that box. He comes to me on His own terms, not mine.

It's a dangerous thing to try to put God in a box. It's a dangerous thing to try to draw borders and boundaries around Him and say, "God, this is who you are. This is how you must operate, what you must do and not do, according to my theological notions of you."

Why is it dangerous? Because the discovery that God is not confined by our theological box can often lead to disillusionment. And disillusionment can lead to rejection and rebellion. When God fails to meet our expectations, we become disappointed and angry with God. We may even turn away from Him.

When Jesus came to Earth two thousand years ago, many were excited to discover that their Messiah had finally come. They followed Him from town to town, they were awestruck by His miracles, and they hung on every word of His sermons. On what we now call Palm Sunday, Jesus the Messiah entered Jerusalem exactly as the Old Testament prophets had foretold. The people lined the streets and shouted "Hosanna! Save us, Son of David! Blessed is He who comes in the name of the Lord!"

The people expected the Messiah to lead a revolt against Roman oppression. They expected Him to restore the nation of Israel to its former glory. Jesus was the God of their expectations. But when Jesus failed to meet their expectations, things changed. In less than a week, the people of Jerusalem had gone from shouting "Hosanna!" on Palm Sunday to shouting "Crucify Him!" on Good Friday.

We must be careful with expectations. We must make sure we worship the God of reality, not the God of our expectations. When God refuses to fit in our box, when He seems to change His character and act in ways that contradict our expectations, it's time to toughen up our faith. It's time to recalibrate our expectations.

It is not a sin to have expectations of God. We come by our expectations of God honestly. We have studied the Scriptures, which are God's revelation of himself. We read certain promises that God has given us, and we treasure them—as we should. God has bound himself to act in accordance with His promises, and we have every right to expect Him to keep His word.

The problem is not that God doesn't keep His promises but that we don't fully understand them. We don't know all of God's promises, how they all fit together, and what the total reality of God is. So we limit God according to our imperfect understanding of God and His Word. We pick out one part of God's promise and miss the rest.

Who of us is wise enough to understand the full intellect, wisdom, majesty, and might of God? That is the question Jeremiah faces as he prepares to deliver his second message to the nation of Judah. Here we will see God tell this young man to do two astonishing things.

The first astonishing thing God tells Jeremiah to do is found in chapter 7, verse 16. There God says to the prophet, "So do not pray for this people nor offer any plea or petition for them; do not plead with me, for I will not listen to you" (7:16). Imagine this: God commanded Jeremiah to *stop* praying for the people of Judah. He ordered the prophet to *stop* asking God to deliver the people. God told Jeremiah *not* to cry out to God on behalf of His people, nor fast for them, nor intercede for them in any way. Have you ever heard of a situation in which God said, "Don't pray"?

The Bible contains numerous exhortations about prayer. We are to pray continually (1 Thessalonians 5:17), pray for our loved ones (James 5:16), pray for our leaders (1 Timothy 2:1–2), and even pray for our enemies (Matthew 5:44). Surely, God would never command us to stop praying, yet here in Jeremiah 7, God gives the prophet this strange command. We all have our favorite Scripture verses, but I suspect that this verse, "Do not pray for this people," is not on anyone's list of favorite texts.

In 1 Samuel, there is a scene in which the prophet Samuel is sent by God to tell the people of Israel that they have turned away from God and have rejected Him as King. The people are demanding to have a king rule over them as all the surrounding nations have. Samuel tells the people that God will grant their request and give them a king, but they won't like the result. In spite of the disobedience of the people, Samuel says these words, which are treasured to this day by many believers: "As for me, far be it from me that I should sin against the LORD by failing to pray for you. And I will teach you the way that is good and right" (1 Samuel 12:23).

We love words like Samuel's promise of prayer and intercession. We rightly quote Samuel's words as biblical teaching on prayer. When we intercede in prayer, we express love and caring for another person. Prayer is an expression of faith in God's power and provision. Prayer is an appeal to God for His blessing. So, it's strange to hear God command Jeremiah *not* to pray for His people.

What do we do with this command from God to Jeremiah? As if this command wasn't bad enough, God goes on to tell Jeremiah, "When you tell them all this, they will not listen to you; when you call to them, they will not answer" (7:27). It seems out of character for God to issue such a command and make such a statement. It confounds our expectations of Him.

As we come to Jeremiah's second message to Judah, we see that His command not to pray is just the first of two actions by God that do not match our expectations of Him. Jeremiah's second message was delivered about five years after the first, during the eighteenth year of the reign of King Josiah. This second message is very different from the first, both in its content and in its impact on Jeremiah himself.

God told Jeremiah to stop praying but to continue preaching. I'm sure that was very hard for Jeremiah to do, especially since God told Jeremiah that the people would not listen to him. They were going to continue sacrificing to false gods and disobeying the Law. This was one of the most difficult assignments God has ever given one of His servants.

There have been many times during my ministry as a pastor when I knew that people were not listening to my preaching, were not interested in my counsel, and were not living the way God wanted them to live. It was a great privilege and comfort for me to go to my knees and pray: "Lord, please help them. Lord, please open their eyes to your truth. Lord, please soften their hearts and make them receptive to your wisdom."

Imagine that someone you loved is violating God's Law, practicing a false religion, destroying his own future. God says to you, "Don't pray. Talk to him, preach to him, witness to him. But he won't listen to you. Whatever you do, don't pray for him." How hard would that be?

Jeremiah loved his people. He yearned for them to repent, turn back to God, and escape the coming judgment. The Lord's command must have filled Jeremiah with anguish beyond our imagining.

Hypocritical religion

To understand why God would issue such a strange command to Jeremiah, let's look at the historical setting of this section of the book, beginning with the opening words of chapter 7:

> This is the word that came to Jeremiah from the LORD: "Stand at the gate of the LORD's house and there proclaim this message:
> "'Hear the word of the LORD, all you people of Judah who come through these gates to worship the LORD. This is what the LORD Almighty, the God of Israel, says: Reform your ways and your actions, and I will let you live in this place. Do not trust in deceptive words and say, "This is the temple of the LORD, the temple of the LORD, the temple of the LORD!" If you really change your ways and your actions and deal with each other justly, if you do not oppress the foreigner, the fatherless or the widow and do not shed innocent blood in this place, and if you do not follow other gods to your own harm, then I will let you live in this place, in the land I gave your ancestors for ever and ever.'" (7:1–7)

We find additional insight into this era in 2 Kings 22 and 2 Chronicles 34. As we previously noted, young King Josiah, in his attempt to turn the nation back to God, gave orders to clean the temple, which had become filled with clutter, like an old warehouse. During the clean-up operation, the high priest Hilkiah unearthed the old scroll of the law of Moses, probably a copy of the book of Deuteronomy.

The scroll revealed the regulations for the celebration of the Passover. The Law had fallen into such disuse that the nation had not celebrated the Passover since the time of Hezekiah, a hundred years earlier. The king ordered a great celebration of the Passover, like never before. Josiah went all-out, ordering sacrifices according to the Levitical commandments—with the priests well-prepared to conduct the ceremony.

The great day arrived when the sacrifices were to be offered in the temple. The choirs of singers and chanters were prepared, and the great procession, headed by King Josiah himself, was on its way to the temple to perform the Passover supper. We can imagine the priests swinging their incense pots to and fro, chanting as they went, along with the choir: "The temple of the LORD, the temple of the LORD, the temple of the LORD."

The people of the land of Judah heaved a sigh of relief, thinking, *God is now satisfied and He will save us. Now we'll be safe from our enemies because we have settled our religious accounts with God.* And as the choir chanted this chorus and the procession moved toward the temple, Jeremiah climbed to a prominent place on the temple steps. The astonished crowd fell silent and the young prophet called out:

> "Hear the word of the LORD, all you people of Judah who come through these gates to worship the LORD. This is what the LORD Almighty, the God of Israel, says: Reform your ways and your actions, and I will let you live in this place. Do not trust in deceptive words and say, 'This is the temple of the LORD, the temple of the LORD, the temple of the LORD!'" (7:2–4)

Jeremiah was saying, in effect, "Who do you think you're kidding? Do you really believe God only cares about religious rules and rituals? Do you really think you can put on a religious show and God will be fooled?" Jeremiah went on to describe the reality of their lives, which they were trying to cover up with a public show of religious rituals:

> "If you really change your ways and your actions and deal with each other justly, if you do not oppress the foreigner, the fatherless or the widow and do not shed innocent blood in this place, and if you do not follow other gods to your own harm, then I will let you live in this place, in the land I gave your ancestors for ever and ever. But look, you are trusting in deceptive words that are worthless.
>
> "Will you steal and murder, commit adultery and perjury, burn incense to Baal and follow other gods you have not known, and then come and stand before me in this house, which bears my Name, and say, 'We are safe'—safe to do all these detestable things? Has this

house, which bears my Name, become a den of robbers to you? But I have been watching! declares the LORD." (7:5–11)

Do these words sound familiar? Of course, they do. The injustices and hypocritical religion of Jeremiah's day foreshadowed the time, centuries later, when the Messiah himself would stand in the temple, brandishing a whip of cords He had fashioned with His own hands, and He would drive out the money changers, saying, "You have turned my Father's house into a den of robbers" (see Matthew 21:13).

Jeremiah has dramatically interrupted the proceedings, and he has delivered the message God gave him for the people. These people thought God looked on them with favor, and they counted on the fact that the temple was now clean and the Law was being restored. Then Jeremiah told these people that their outward rituals were worthless if they were inwardly full of corruption, lies, and idolatry. He said:

> "'How can you say, "We are wise,
>   for we have the law of the LORD,"
> when actually the lying pen of the scribes
>   has handled it falsely?
> The wise will be put to shame;
>   they will be dismayed and trapped.
> Since they have rejected the word of the LORD,
>   what kind of wisdom do they have?'" (8:8–9)

The people trusted in their performance of an outward ritual. They didn't understand that God judges the heart, not the performance. When people become so blind to their own hypocrisy that they imagine God can be fooled by religious fakery, there is no hope for them. The only thing that can open their eyes is God's judgment. God says to them through Jeremiah:

"Go now to the place in Shiloh where I first made a dwelling for my Name, and see what I did to it because of the wickedness of my people Israel. While you were doing all these things, declares the LORD, I spoke to you again and again, but you did not listen; I called you, but you did not answer. Therefore, what I did to Shiloh I will now do to the house that bears my Name, the temple you trust in, the place I gave to you and your ancestors. I will thrust you from my presence, just as I did all your fellow Israelites, the people of Ephraim." (7:12–15)

It was at this point that God told Jeremiah not to pray for the people any longer, because God had decided to impose His judgment upon them.

THE PROPHET'S HEARTSICK CRY

Let's not misunderstand what God is saying. He's not losing His temper and saying, "I've had it with these people! I'm through with them, and I'm going to destroy them!" God is not throwing a tantrum, nor is He being cruel and unloving. God still loves His people, but He is acknowledging that this generation will not respond to Jeremiah's message.

Jeremiah, however, cannot understand God's purpose. He is deeply grieved by God's decision to judge His people. So in Jeremiah 8 we see the prophet's emotional response:

> You who are my Comforter in sorrow,
>   my heart is faint within me.
> Listen to the cry of my people
>   from a land far away:
> "Is the LORD not in Zion?
>   Is her King no longer there?"
> "Why have they aroused my anger with their images,
>   with their worthless foreign idols?" (8:18–19)

Jeremiah knows the horrors that are coming up on the nation of Judah, and he is heartsick over the death, suffering, and destruction that is to come. He is particularly burdened over the suffering that will overtake the women and girls of the kingdom of Judah, as we are about to see. At this point, I need to depart from the New International Version, because I believe it mistranslates this next passage. The NIV reads:

> "The harvest is past,
>   the summer has ended,
>   and we are not saved."
> Since my people are crushed, I am crushed;
>   I mourn, and horror grips me.
> Is there no balm in Gilead?
>   Is there no physician there?
> Why then is there no healing
>   for the wound of my people? (8:20–22).

Other translations, such as the King James Version, the American Standard Version, and the New American Standard Bible refer not just to the wound "of my people" (v. 22) but to the wound or brokenness "of the *daughter* of my people." The Hebrew word *bath* in this passage is translated "daughter" throughout the NIV Old Testament, but (inexplicably) not here. Let's look at the NASB version of these verses:

> "Harvest is past, summer is ended,
> And we are not saved."
> For the brokenness of the daughter of my people I am broken;
> I mourn, dismay has taken hold of me.
> Is there no balm in Gilead?
> Is there no physician there?
> Why then has not the health of the daughter of my people
>   been restored?"
> (8:20–22 NASB)

I don't know why the NIV translators glossed over the word *bath* ("daughter") in Jeremiah's text, but I think Jeremiah, with the help of the Holy Spirit, chose those words carefully. He was grieved and brokenhearted over the terrors that would be suffered by the daughters (women and girls) of Judah when God's judgment would fall upon the nation.

Later, in Jeremiah 16, we will see that God tells Jeremiah that he must remain unmarried because of the coming judgment:

> Then the word of the LORD came to me: "You must not marry and have sons or daughters in this place." For this is what the LORD says about the sons and daughters born in this land and about the women who are their mothers and the men who are their fathers: "They will die of deadly diseases. They will not be mourned or buried but will be like dung lying on the ground. They will perish by sword and famine, and their dead bodies will become food for the birds and the wild animals." (16:1–4)

Jeremiah feels so intensely grief-stricken over the coming judgment that he cries out, in effect, "God, where are You? Where is the healer? Where is the One who can heal the wounds of the daughters of Judah? Where is the One who can restore the people? Where is the balm in Gilead, the medicine that can make a sick person well?"

Have you ever felt like that? Have you ever suffered over a loved one, crying out in anguished prayer, "God, where are You? Where is the Great Physician?" That is Jeremiah's heartsick cry. He cannot understand what God is doing.

JUDGMENT IS COMING

In chapter 7, God describes His response when an individual or an entire nation turns away from Him: "While you were doing all these things, declares the LORD, I spoke to you again and again, but you did not listen; I called you, but you did not answer" (v. 13). When we begin to drift away from God, He calls to us, He warns us, He pleads with us, He alerts us to the danger we are in. His message to us is the same word of warning Paul delivered to the church in Galatia: "Whoever sows to please their flesh, from the flesh will reap destruction;

whoever sows to please the Spirit, from the Spirit will reap eternal life" (Galatians 6:8).

God does not bring judgment upon us without warning. He always warns us that sin will leave its scars, even after the wound is healed. He warns us that sin has consequences. He calls to us and speaks to us. God loves us, and He longs to draw us to himself to comfort and heal us. But all too often when He calls, we do not answer. When He speaks, we do not listen. Why does He call to us? Why does He speak to us? The answer, in a word: *Love.* In our rebellion and self-will, we forget how much He loves us. When He calls to us, He is trying to awaken a response of love and gratitude within us. He is trying to call us back. He will not force us against our will, but He pleads with us to willingly return to Him.

God is like the father in the story of the prodigal son. In the story Jesus told, the father watched the horizon day after day, hoping to see his wandering son return. That is a portrait of the heart of God, who patiently looks for His children to return to Him and to the protective embrace of His loving arms. That is why he called, again and again, to the people of Judah.

What does God do when we do not respond to His love? He only has one recourse remaining: *judgment.* But it's important to understand that judgment is *not* God's way of saying, "I'm through with you." It is not a mark of the abandonment of God. It is God's last-ditch act of love, His last resort in an attempt to call us back to himself. C. S. Lewis put it beautifully when he wrote, "God whispers to us in our pleasures, speaks in our conscience, but shouts in our pains: it is His megaphone to rouse a deaf world."[3]

Jeremiah had to learn this principle. He didn't understand that the nation of Judah had reached such a state of willfulness and rebellion that the only way to heal the people was to judge them. They were sacrificing their own children to the demon gods of the pagan nations. How could a God of love permit such horrors to continue among His chosen people? They left Him no choice but judgment. And judgment meant the pain of invasion, the tragedy of exile, the leveling of the temple and the Holy City, and the loss of their sovereign nation.

People ask how a God of love could judge the nation so harshly. The real question is this: How could a God of love *not* judge the people when they were degrading themselves and murdering their own children? The judgment of God flowed directly from the love of God.

Now, perhaps, you can see why God commanded Jeremiah to cease praying for the people but to continue preaching to them. If you read through the Scriptures, you see that prayer delays judgment, but preaching hastens it. And what the nation of Judah needed for its healing was judgment. It would have been cruel to delay the judgment through prayer. It was merciful to hasten God's judgment by preaching and warning the people.

God was telling Jeremiah, in effect, "Don't delay My judgment through your prayers. Don't hold Me back. If you want to be merciful and kind to the people of Judah, then let Me perform radical surgery on the people as soon as possible. Keep preaching, but stop praying."

In Genesis 18, the prayers of Abraham held off judgment in the case of Sodom and Gomorrah. Abraham asked God if He would spare Sodom if there were fifty righteous people living there. God said He would spare the city for the sake of fifty righteous people. Then Abraham asked if He would spare the city for forty-five righteous people, then forty, then thirty, then twenty, then ten—and then he didn't dare lower the number any further. Abraham's prayer delayed God's judgment.

But preaching hastens judgment, because God's Word is true, and when the truth is proclaimed, people are forced to make a choice. God calls adultery, theft, murder, and perjury by their rightful names. As Jesus said of the Pharisees, "If I had not come and spoken to them, they would not be guilty of sin; but now they have no excuse for their sin" (John 15:22). Preaching hastens judgment.

As Jeremiah begins to understand God's program for the people, a plan of judgment compelled by love, he breaks down and weeps before

God. You cannot read these passages without feeling the anguish of Jeremiah and realizing that the prophet echoes the brokenhearted sobs of God. If Jeremiah loves the people of Judah, and he does, God loves them even more. If Jeremiah weeps for them, God weeps even more. Amid Jeremiah's despair over the coming judgment, God tenderly and beautifully speaks to the prophet, giving him a message of hope:

> This is what the LORD says:
> "Let not the wise boast of their wisdom
>   or the strong boast of their strength
>   or the rich boast of their riches,
> but let the one who boasts boast about this:
>   that they have the understanding to know me,
>   that I am the LORD, who exercises kindness,
>   justice and righteousness on earth,
>   for in these I delight,"
> declares the LORD. (9:23–24)

This is one of the great statements in Scripture on the character of God. Here we see the wisdom, might, and mercy of the God we serve. How small and insignificant is the power of a human being by comparison. Let not the wise boast of their wisdom, because the wisest human being who ever lived (excluding Jesus, of course) still sees reality through the wrong end of the telescope. Human understanding is finite and fragmentary. From God's perspective, even our wisest philosophers and greatest scientists have such a dim understanding of reality that they don't even know what questions to ask.

As human knowledge increases, human problems multiply. People are smart enough to split the atom, but they lack the wisdom not to build atomic bombs. People are smart enough to invent all kinds of industries and technologies, but they lack the wisdom not to pollute the planet. People are smart enough to create functioning governments and societies and universities, but they lack the wisdom to prevent war and terrorism.

Some philosophers believe that human beings can create a utopia on earth. We who believe the Bible know that this can never happen through mankind's actions. Human wisdom is woefully inadequate to the task of creating a heaven on earth. T. S. Eliot stated the problem well in his pageant play, *The Rock*.

> All our knowledge brings us nearer to our ignorance,
> All our ignorance brings us nearer to death,
> But nearness to death no nearer to GOD.[4]

We cannot trust human wisdom. The more we know, the better we understand how little we know. Our knowledge brings us an awareness of our ignorance, and our ignorance leads not to life, but to death.

Let not the strong boast of their strength. Why not? For one thing, the man with great power and authority tends to become a dictator, a tyrant, an oppressor. For another thing, our great strength often becomes a source of weakness.

At the end of World War II, America appeared to be an invincible force in the world. America had led the fight against Japanese imperialism in the Pacific theater and against Nazi fascism in the European theater. America had twice used the most frightening weapon ever made, the atomic bomb. Was any nation stronger than the United States?

Then came the Vietnam War, which lasted from 1955 to 1975. The United States lost more than 58,000 soldiers in that war; North Vietnam may have lost more than a million. In the end, the United States lost that war to a much smaller and more primitive country because the North Vietnamese were fighting a different kind of war than America was fighting. Atomic bombs were useless in that war.

Let not the wise boast of their wisdom or the strong boast of their strength. There is only one righteous boast, and that is boasting of our relationship with God, who has shown kindness and mercy to us, and in whom we delight.

As the prophet Jeremiah comes to the end of this discourse, he reflects on all that God has taught him: "LORD, I know that people's lives are not their own; it is not for them to direct their steps" (Jeremiah 10:23). What a profound lesson this is, and what a difficult lesson to learn! We do not belong to ourselves, but God has authority over our lives. It's not up to us to direct our own steps; we must let God direct the path we take.

I once visited Minneapolis during a blizzard. As I looked around at the city, I remembered how, more than three decades earlier, I had passed through Minneapolis for the first time—a young man twenty-one years of age riding a bus on my way to Chicago. I was fresh from the plains of Montana, and I had obtained a job through the mail. I was a country boy on my way to the big city, and I was scared to death. I didn't know where I should go or how I should react to people.

Now, returning to Minneapolis after so many years, all those old feelings and fears and insecurities came flooding back. Yet I also remembered that, through all the intervening years, the hand of God had guided me at critical moments in my life. He had opened doors, corrected me, taught me, rebuked me, and helped me to grow in character and in the Christian faith. I was glad to acknowledge that my life was not my own. If it had been up to me to direct my own steps, I would have made a much bigger mess of my life.

During my visit to Minneapolis, thinking back over my life, I bowed my head in my hotel room, and I gave thanks to God because He had directed my steps. And I remembered those wise words from the book of Proverbs: "Trust in the LORD with all your heart and lean not on your own understanding; in all your ways submit to him, and he will make your paths straight" (Proverbs 3:5–6).

The prophet Jeremiah suffered anguish over the fate of his people, who refused to repent and turn to God. But he learned the lesson God had for him, and he prayed:

> Discipline me, LORD, but only in due measure—
>   not in your anger,
>   or you will reduce me to nothing.
> Pour out your wrath on the nations

that do not acknowledge you,
    on the peoples who do not call on your name.
For they have devoured Jacob;
    they have devoured him completely
    and destroyed his homeland. (10:24–25)

Here, Jeremiah's second message to Judah concludes. He ends by saying, in effect, "Lord, I know you have the right to discipline me as I should be disciplined. And I know you have the right to judge the nations. But Lord, please judge the enemies of your chosen people. Judge the nations that devour your people and destroy their land."

God has opened the eyes of the prophet Jeremiah to catch a glimpse of His truth—truth that you and I need to grasp for our lives today. Our lives are not our own; we need to allow the Lord to direct our steps. We need to glory in our relationship with God, not in our own puny wisdom or strength. Jeremiah has learned these lessons, but there is so much more God wants to teach this young prophet.

And more God wants to teach you and me.

4

FAITH AT THE BREAKING POINT

Jeremiah 11–15

When a church puts out the call for a pastor, the advertisement ought to read something like this:

WANTED: A minister for a challenging position in a growing church. Applicant should have expertise and experience in the following fields: CEO, CFO, COO, board chairman, sales manager, politician, diplomat, social worker, vocational counselor, marriage counselor, psychologist, theologian, missionary, educator (adept at teaching all levels, from preschool to university), Boy Scout leader, writer, artist, funeral director, wedding consultant, master of ceremonies, and standup comedian. Must be skilled at solving problems connected with birth, death, and every significant life event in between. Must be flexible and willing to work endless hours of overtime without compensation. Must be willing to work weekends. Must be willing to accept unfair criticism and abusive behavior from church members, always with a cheerful attitude. Must be loving and forgiving at all times. Must be a captivating public speaker. Anyone applying for this position after reading this far must have their sanity questioned.

That, unfortunately, is what many churches demand of their pastors. Yet I'm happy to report that increasing numbers of churches are discovering the biblical truth that the ministry of the church was never intended to rest entirely on the shoulders of the so-called "minister" of the church.

Who, according to Scripture, is the *real* minister of the church? Everyone! All of God's people are ministers, and we are all in the ministry. God has given you a ministry, according to the spiritual gifts that He has apportioned to you. If you are not using your gifts and carrying out your ministry, then you are not fulfilling the purpose God has given you.

We should all be engaged in the ministry God has given us. God prepared Jeremiah to minister to the people of Judah in a time of national decline and decay. God called Jeremiah to a strange and difficult ministry, and He prepared and toughened Jeremiah for the assignments he was to carry out in the nation of Judah.

Jeremiah struggled with the commission God gave him. He wept over it. He pleaded with God on behalf of the people. He begged God to extend mercy to these idolatrous people. And the more Jeremiah wept and pleaded, the more adamant God seemed to become—and the more determined to judge.

As we come to the next section of the book of Jeremiah, thirteen years have passed since Jeremiah's previous message. King Josiah, the last godly king of Judah, has made a valiant effort to reform the nation and to eradicate idol worship from the land. Josiah has tried to establish the worship of Jehovah, the God of Abraham, Isaac, and Jacob. Outwardly, the people went along with him, but inwardly, there was still a deep-seated mood of rebellion and idolatry.

In 2 Chronicles 35, King Josiah meets his death. Although he has tried all his life to live for God, at the very end of his life, he disobeys the word of God. He goes out to do battle with Necho, the king of

Egypt, who is on his way to fight the Babylonians at the Battle of Carchemish. There on the plain of Megiddo, where the last battle of human history will be fought—the battle of Armageddon—King Josiah met his death. He was mourned in Israel, and Jeremiah eulogized him in the book of Lamentations.

The death of King Josiah plunged the nation of Judah into crisis. The young and inexperienced son of Josiah, Jehoahaz, was anointed as the new king. He was weak and incapable of governing, and Necho, the king of Egypt, deposed him and placed Jehoahaz's brother Jehoiakim on the throne. The prophet Jeremiah could only watch these events unfold, knowing that history was moving inexorably toward judgment.

The tiny kingdom of Judah was as helpless as a cork bobbing in the ocean. All around it were the great superpowers of the era, contending with one another for supremacy in the affairs of the world. Egypt and Assyria were kingdoms in decline, yet still powerful and as dangerous as cornered beasts. Babylon was on the ascendancy. In this time of unrest and war, tiny Judah was caught in the grip of a vice as the three great empires asserted their power and expanded their borders.

A PLOT AGAINST JEREMIAH

In Jeremiah 11, God sends the young prophet back to the nation with another word of warning. This latest message is similar to the previous messages Jeremiah has delivered. It combines a stern denunciation with an urgent appeal for the people to put away their idolatry and sin, and turn back to God for salvation and restoration. Jeremiah warned them that if they continued in unbelief and disobedience, God would have no recourse but to judge them. His justice would be sudden and terrible.

Here again, God tells Jeremiah not to pray for Judah: "Do not pray for this people or offer any plea or petition for them, because I will not listen when they call to me in the time of their distress" (11:14). Again, God is placing a gag order on Jeremiah that appears harsh and merciless at first glance but is actually an expression of God's mercy. He is telling Jeremiah, in effect, "Don't prolong their suffering by delaying My judgment."

Jeremiah is already distressed by God's unwillingness to hear his pleas. But there is worse to come. When the prophet returns to his hometown of Anathoth, he learns that his own neighbors and friends have plotted to take his life. Here is his account of the murder plot against him:

> Because the LORD revealed their plot to me, I knew it, for at that time he showed me what they were doing. I had been like a gentle lamb led to the slaughter; I did not realize that they had plotted against me, saying,
>
> > "Let us destroy the tree and its fruit;
> > let us cut him off from the land of the living,
> > that his name be remembered no more."
>
> But you, LORD Almighty, who judge righteously
> and test the heart and mind,
> let me see your vengeance on them,
> for to you I have committed my cause. (11:18–20)

Jeremiah realizes that he has been naïve and blind in trusting his neighbors and friends in his hometown. He didn't even suspect they would conspire against him. When he learns of their plot, he goes to the Lord and cries out to Him for vengeance. He didn't take vengeance into his own hands, but he trusted God to be his Vindicator. He said, "Let me see your vengeance on them, for to you I have committed my cause" (v. 20).

When someone tries to harm us, what is our instinctive response? For many people, it is revenge. Either they try to attack their enemy directly, or they try an indirect approach, spreading rumors to destroy the other person's reputation. But Jeremiah, when he was attacked, took his case straight to the Lord.

Was Jeremiah's approach completely righteous? Probably not. He didn't go to God and say, "Lord, these people have plotted against me. Please deal with it and vindicate me by whatever means you think is best." No, he went to God and told God exactly how He should deal with the problem. "Let me see your vengeance on them," he said. Jeremiah wanted God to strike them down or inflict a plague on them or some other terrible thing, and he wanted to be there to see it happen. Jeremiah records the Lord's response:

> Therefore this is what the LORD Almighty says: "I will punish them. Their young men will die by the sword, their sons and daughters by famine. Not even a remnant will be left to them, because I will bring disaster on the people of Anathoth in the year of their punishment." (11:22–23)

God says to His prophet, in effect, "You're right, Jeremiah. I will punish these evil men, but I will do it in My time. They will suffer their punishment in the judgment that is coming upon Judah. They will suffer in the coming invasion by the Babylonians, and in the famine that follows. But their doom will come when I say, to satisfy My justice, not your hunger for revenge."

I can identify with Jeremiah, and I'm sure you can too. We want God to act according to our timetable. But God has His own schedule. We say, "Lord, you should do this and this. Just follow my advice, Lord, and everything will work out." But God ignores our suggestions, and He replies, "I'll do what I choose to do, when I choose to do it." This was a lesson Jeremiah had to learn, just as you and I do.

THE BREAKING POINT

In Jeremiah 12, the prophet proceeds to present his complaint before the Lord:

> You are always righteous, LORD,
>   when I bring a case before you.
> Yet I would speak with you about your justice:

Why does the way of the wicked prosper?
Why do all the faithless live at ease?
You have planted them, and they have taken root;
    they grow and bear fruit.
You are always on their lips
    but far from their hearts.
Yet you know me, LORD;
    you see me and test my thoughts about you.
Drag them off like sheep to be butchered!
    Set them apart for the day of slaughter!
How long will the land lie parched
    and the grass in every field be withered?
Because those who live in it are wicked,
    the animals and birds have perished.
Moreover, the people are saying,
    "He will not see what happens to us." (12:1–4)

It's interesting that Jeremiah begins by telling God, "You are always righteous, LORD," but in the next breath, he suggests that God's judgment and His justice are a little out of whack. In essence, Jeremiah asks the questions that continue to trouble us today: Why do evil people seem to prosper? Why do wicked people seem to get away with their crimes?

I once taught a Bible class to a Young Life group in Fort Worth, Texas. I noticed that these young people seemed far more serious than most of the Young Life groups I had visited before. I paused during the study and asked, "Why are you all so somber?"

They told me that a popular Christian high school girl in that city had disappeared a few days earlier. For days, no one knew where she was. All her Christian high school friends had prayed for her, believing that God would protect her and bring her home safely.

But just an hour before our Bible study met, the news media reported that her body had been found. She had been sexually assaulted and murdered. These young people were stunned, and the same question was on the heart of everyone there: "Why? If God is all-loving and all-powerful, why did He let this happen?"

This is one of the great questions that is thrown at our faith, again and again: Why does God allow the innocent to suffer? Why does God seem to allow injustice to go unpunished? Why do evil people prosper? That's the line of questioning Jeremiah puts to God, and God's response is not the answer we might expect:

> "If you have raced with men on foot
>   and they have worn you out,
>   how can you compete with horses?
> If you stumble in safe country,
>   how will you manage in the thickets by the Jordan?" (12:5)

In other words, God tells Jeremiah, "What are you going to do when things get worse? The men of your town plotted to murder you. That's bad—but that's far from the worst thing that will happen. If you let an incident like this upset your faith, if you doubt Me because of what evil men do, what will happen to your faith when it is *really* tested? How will your faith withstand what is to come if it is already at the breaking point?"

God uses an analogy of running a race. He says that if you become tired while racing against men on foot, what will you do when you have to race against horses? And if you stumble while running over smooth, level ground, how will you stay on your feet when you are running through thorn bushes by the riverbank? God is warning Jeremiah that things are going to get worse—much worse—and he needs to mentally, emotionally, and spiritually prepare himself for the days ahead.

The Lord's question to Jeremiah, and to us, is this: If your faith can't withstand the mere *beginning* of sorrows, what are you going to do when the *real* devastation begins? How will you compete with horses, when you can't even stay in a race against men?

Jeremiah apparently expected God to make things right before they got worse. I think most of us are due for a shock in our Christian lives when we discover that God doesn't always work out our problems on easy terms. In contrast to what many preachers and televangelists are teaching these days, God has not promised us a lifetime of health and wealth if we follow Him. God has promised us persecution (2 Timothy 3:12) and tribulation (Romans 12:12).

That is where Jeremiah finds himself in chapter 12. He wanted God to say, "Don't worry, Jeremiah. I'll work out your problems. I'll take care of everything. You won't have any more stress or strain." Instead, God said, "Jeremiah, it's going to get worse—a lot worse. What are you going to do then? Will your faith stand the test of the terrible days ahead?"

CAN A GOD OF LOVE . . . HATE?

God then began to detail some of the frightening events to come. If Jeremiah was troubled by the fact that his friends plotted to kill him, he had an even greater disappointment in store. God told him:

> "Your relatives, members of your own family—
>   even they have betrayed you;
>   they have raised a loud cry against you.
> Do not trust them,
>   though they speak well of you." (12:6)

God was saying to the prophet, "Jeremiah, your own family is part of the plot." How do you think Jeremiah felt when God revealed this truth to him? How lonely and friendless he must have felt! Jeremiah thought he had heard the worst when he learned that his friends, his own townspeople, were plotting to kill him. But no, the truth was even worse than he thought. He never suspected that his own family would want him dead.

The Lord went on to tell Jeremiah there would be no mercy for the nation. Judgment was inevitable:

> "I will forsake my house,
>   abandon my inheritance;

> I will give the one I love
> > into the hands of her enemies.
> My inheritance has become to me
> > like a lion in the forest.
> She roars at me;
> > therefore I hate her." (12:7–8)

For most of us, it is hard for our theology to encompass these words. The Scriptures tell us, "God is love" (see 1 John 4:8). Yet here, God says of His own chosen people, "I hate her." Do you find this confusing?

I believe the way to understand this passage is in light of what theologians call the "anthropomorphisms" of Scripture. An *anthropomorphism* is "the attributing of human characteristics to animals, inanimate objects, or to God." Here, God is speaking as though He were a man. It is true that the inherent nature of God is love, and He can never be anything other than a God of love.

Yet, we all know that when love has been rejected, offended, and insulted, love often acts as though it hates. God is expressing His response to the rejection and insult of the people of Judah in terms that the prophet Jeremiah will understand.

God goes on to describe how he will deliver the nation of Judah to judgment and how He is going to devastate the land:

> "Has not my inheritance become to me
> > like a speckled bird of prey
> > > that other birds of prey surround and attack?
> Go and gather all the wild beasts;
> > bring them to devour.
> Many shepherds will ruin my vineyard
> > and trample down my field;
> they will turn my pleasant field
> > into a desolate wasteland.
> It will be made a wasteland,
> > parched and desolate before me;
> the whole land will be laid waste

> because there is no one who cares.
> Over all the barren heights in the desert
>   destroyers will swarm,
> for the sword of the LORD will devour
>   from one end of the land to the other;
>   no one will be safe.
> They will sow wheat but reap thorns;
>   they will wear themselves out but gain nothing.
> They will bear the shame of their harvest
>   because of the LORD's fierce anger." (12:9–13)

This is an image of absolute devastation and desolation. Yet in the closing verses of this chapter the Lord gives Jeremiah a gleam of light, a ray of hope:

> This is what the LORD says: "As for all my wicked neighbors who seize the inheritance I gave my people Israel, I will uproot them from their lands and I will uproot the people of Judah from among them. But after I uproot them, I will again have compassion and will bring each of them back to their own inheritance and their own country. And if they learn well the ways of my people and swear by my name, saying, 'As surely as the LORD lives'—even as they once taught my people to swear by Baal—then they will be established among my people. But if any nation does not listen, I will completely uproot and destroy it," declares the LORD. (12:14–17)

Here we see that the "hate" God felt for the people of Judah was not the bitter, stone-hearted, unforgiving hatred so common among human beings. Clearly, God is still a God of love, a God of mercy, a God of forgiveness. He promises compassion for the people of Judah. He promises to bring them back to their own inheritance and their own country. It is, of course, a conditional promise, and God will only bless the people if they listen and obey the God who loves them.

God is still a God of love, yet He is a God who sometimes acts in strange ways that we cannot understand at the time. This is one of the most challenging issues of the Christian faith. One of the greatest tests of our faith is when we discover we can no longer understand what God is doing, and His actions do not seem to be in line with His promises. Then we must say with the apostle Paul:

> Oh, the depth of the riches of the wisdom and knowledge of God!
> How unsearchable his judgments,
> and his paths beyond tracing out!
> "Who has known the mind of the Lord?
> Or who has been his counselor?" (Romans 11:33–34)

As we will soon see, God is not through with Jeremiah. He is still teaching profound lessons in faith to this great prophet—and to you and me.

A STRANGE VISUAL AID

In Jeremiah 13, God provides a strange visual aid to teach this young prophet an important truth. I call this visual aid "the sign of the unwashed shorts." Jeremiah writes: "This is what the LORD said to me: 'Go and buy a linen belt and put it around your waist, but do not let it touch water.' So I bought a belt, as the LORD directed, and put it around my waist" (13:1–2).

What the text calls a "linen belt" is essentially underwear—linen shorts. Jeremiah was to purchase a linen cloth that would wrap around his midsection like underwear. He was to wear them, but not wash them. What was God trying to teach Jeremiah, and us, through this surprising imagery?

Jeremiah did as God told him. He bought the linen cloth, wore it, took it to the place God directed him to, and hid it in the crevice of the rock. After many days, he retrieved it, and it was ruined. Standing there with that worthless, rotting, filthy piece of linen in his hand, he tells us:

Then the word of the LORD came to me: "This is what the LORD says: 'In the same way I will ruin the pride of Judah and the great pride of Jerusalem. These wicked people, who refuse to listen to my words, who follow the stubbornness of their hearts and go after other gods to serve and worship them, will be like this belt—completely useless! For as a belt is bound around the waist, so I bound all the people of Israel and all the people of Judah to me,' declares the LORD, 'to be my people for my renown and praise and honor. But they have not listened.'" (13:8–11)

This visual aid makes several points.

First, God uses the ruined condition of the linen cloth to illustrate the ruined pride of Judah when His judgment falls. The people have spurned God's word to them, and they have served false gods. They have rejected God's purpose for their lives and made themselves useless to Him.

Second, a human life or a human society, once it has turned away from God, begins to rot and become disgusting and unusable. Apart from God, we cannot be fully human. We were made in His likeness, and we were designed to be in intimate fellowship with Him. When we violate our design and purpose by rejecting God, we lose our power, our usefulness, our purpose, and our beauty. We become good for nothing.

Third, even though the people of Judah have made themselves like that linen cloth—ruined, filthy, and useless—God still binds them to himself. He has not thrown them away. He created them for His own praise and honor, and even though they have not listened to Him, God still wears His people as a man wears a pair of shorts.

The remaining verses of Jeremiah 13 show us how God's unusual visual aid impacted the heart and soul of the prophet Jeremiah. He immediately went before the people and pleaded with them:

> Hear and pay attention,
>   do not be arrogant,
>   for the LORD has spoken.

Give glory to the LORD your God
before he brings the darkness,
before your feet stumble
on the darkening hills.
You hope for light,
but he will turn it to utter darkness
and change it to deep gloom.
If you do not listen,
I will weep in secret
because of your pride;
my eyes will weep bitterly,
overflowing with tears,
because the LORD's flock will be taken captive. (13:15–17)

The prophet takes no pleasure in pronouncing doom upon the people of Judah. In fact, he pleads with them with tears of compassion. God's visual aid of the filthy and worthless linen cloth moves Jeremiah deeply. God has given the prophet a message of utter destruction, and it practically destroys his soul to deliver this message to the people:

"I will scatter you like chaff
driven by the desert wind.
This is your lot,
the portion I have decreed for you,"
declares the LORD,
"because you have forgotten me
and trusted in false gods.
I will pull up your skirts over your face
that your shame may be seen—
your adulteries and lustful neighings,
your shameless prostitution!
I have seen your detestable acts
on the hills and in the fields.
Woe to you, Jerusalem!
How long will you be unclean?" (13:24–27)

The first rumblings of the coming destruction are just around the corner. And still, the people refuse to listen and turn to God.

WHEN GOD DOES NOT BUDGE

In Jeremiah 14, God sends a severe drought upon the land. As Jeremiah describes the scene, the cisterns have no water, the ground is cracked, the farmers are filled with dread, the crops are withered and dried, and the animals pant and thirst. This is the first wave of God's hand of judgment. As the divine hand of discipline descends upon Judah, Jeremiah again questions God:

> Although our sins testify against us,
>   do something, LORD, for the sake of your name.
> For we have often rebelled;
>   we have sinned against you.
> You who are the hope of Israel,
>   its Savior in times of distress,
> why are you like a stranger in the land,
>   like a traveler who stays only a night?
> Why are you like a man taken by surprise,
>   like a warrior powerless to save?
> You are among us, LORD,
>   and we bear your name;
>   do not forsake us! (14:7–9)

Can you identify with these words? Have you ever felt the emotions Jeremiah describes? There have been many instances in Scripture when the prayers of a righteous man have turned aside the judging hand of God by pleading the glory of God himself. Moses prayed a prayer like this, and God chose not to punish the people. Samuel prayed a prayer like this, and again God chose not to punish the people. It's a prayer that says, "Lord, you know how sinful and rebellious your people are. You have every right to destroy us all. But for the sake of your name and your glory, so that your name will not be lost among the nations, please don't destroy your people. Be merciful to them for your name's sake."

That is Jeremiah's cry in these verses. He is reaching up to God on the highest level of prayer possible. He closes the chapter with an eloquent plea to God:

> Have you rejected Judah completely?
>   Do you despise Zion?
> Why have you afflicted us
>   so that we cannot be healed?
> We hoped for peace
>   but no good has come,
> for a time of healing
>   but there is only terror.
> We acknowledge our wickedness, LORD,
>   and the guilt of our ancestors;
>   we have indeed sinned against you.
> For the sake of your name do not despise us;
>   do not dishonor your glorious throne.
> Remember your covenant with us
>   and do not break it.
> Do any of the worthless idols of the nations bring rain?
>   Do the skies themselves send down showers?
> No, it is you, LORD our God.
>   Therefore our hope is in you,
>   for you are the one who does all this. (14:19–22)

Notice that Jeremiah does not ask God to spare "them," the people of Judah. He identifies with the people. He is one of them. Even though Jeremiah himself is innocent of any idolatry or rebellion, he prays as a representative of the people, saying, "We acknowledge *our* wickedness, Lord, and the guilt of our ancestors; *we* have indeed sinned against you."

Next, Jeremiah records God's reply:

Then the LORD said to me: "Even if Moses and Samuel were to stand before me, my heart would not go out to this people. Send them away from my presence! Let them go! And if they ask you, 'Where shall we go?' tell them, 'This is what the LORD says:

> "'Those destined for death, to death;
> those for the sword, to the sword;
> those for starvation, to starvation;
> those for captivity, to captivity.'" (15:1–2)

God does not budge an inch. What are you going to do with a God like this? When God shows His will to be immovable, it's a challenge to our faith. But God is not through with Jeremiah. Although He seems harsh and unyielding, and He goes on to repeat His judgment to the nation, He has something more to say.

GOD ANSWERS JEREMIAH'S DOUBTS

At the close of Jeremiah 15, the prophet, after being forbidden by God to pray for the people, cries out for himself:

> LORD, you understand;
> remember me and care for me.
> Avenge me on my persecutors.
> You are long-suffering—do not take me away;
> think of how I suffer reproach for your sake. (15:15)

Jeremiah thinks back to King Josiah's day, when the word of God was found in the temple. He writes:

> When your words came, I ate them;
> they were my joy and my heart's delight,
> for I bear your name,
> LORD God Almighty. (15:16)

But Jeremiah is wretched, hurt, and at the point of despair. He doesn't understand God's will, and he cries out:

> Why is my pain unending
>   and my wound grievous and incurable?
> You are to me like a deceptive brook,
>   like a spring that fails. (15:18)

In his suffering, Jeremiah wonders why God seems insensitive to his pain and unresponsive to his prayers. The prophet even wonders if God has been lying to him, and he prays to God in terms that are blunt and candid, to the point of being accusatory.

Have you ever felt that way about God? Those times when God seems silent, when He seems to be indifferent to our pain and unmindful of our prayers, and our times of testing. Our faith is tested to the nth degree—even to the breaking point. Do you know how Jeremiah feels? Then notice how tenderly and gently God deals with Jeremiah in his time of pain and doubt:

> Therefore this is what the LORD says:
> "If you repent, I will restore you
>   that you may serve me;
> if you utter worthy, not worthless, words,
>   you will be my spokesman.
> Let this people turn to you,
>   but you must not turn to them.
> I will make you a wall to this people,
>   a fortified wall of bronze;
> they will fight against you
>   but will not overcome you,
> for I am with you
>   to rescue and save you,"
> declares the LORD.
> "I will save you from the hands of the wicked
>   and deliver you from the grasp of the cruel." (15:19–21)

Notice how God answers his own questions. In Jeremiah 12, he had asked Jeremiah, "If you have raced with men on foot and they have worn you out, how can you compete with horses? If you stumble in safe country, how will you manage in the thickets by the Jordan?" (12:5). God's answer is this: Even when the whole world seems to be collapsing all around you, when there is no one you can depend on, no one you can turn to, you can rest in Him. The Lord will strengthen you and see you through anything—even the destruction of your civilization, the captivity of your people. The Lord is your only source of strength in a time of trouble. Any other source will fail you. As the old hymn reminds us:

> When through the deep waters I call you to go,
> The rivers of sorrow shall not overflow;
> For I will be with you, your troubles to bless
> And sanctify to you your deepest distress.[5]

"I am with you to rescue and save you," declares the Lord. This is God's promise to Jeremiah, and this is still His promise to us today. God pours on the pressure sometimes, as we see in the book of Jeremiah. His goal is not to destroy us but to prepare us for the challenges and crises ahead.

Surely, this is how God is dealing with Christians around the world today. We are facing challenges and threats and burdens that are unprecedented in our history. No individual, no people, no nation is adequate for the crises of today and tomorrow.

But the strength and wisdom of God are adequate to any challenge. His promise to us is sure: "I am with you to rescue and save you."

5

DEATH OF A NATION

Jeremiah 16–17

English historian Edward Gibbon published the first volume of *The History of the Decline and Fall of the Roman Empire* in 1776, the same year the United States of America declared its independence. Gibbon published the sixth and final volume of that work in 1789, the year the United States Constitution went into effect.

Somehow, it seems fitting that Gibbon's massive work, which chronicled the demise of one of history's greatest empires, should have been published during the span of time that the United States was being founded and established as a constitutional republic. In all sincerity, I don't think that timing was a coincidence. I believe God intended that Edward Gibbon's work should serve as a warning to the fledgling American nation *not* to follow the pattern of decline and fall that was set centuries earlier by the Roman Empire.

America was warned, but America seems to be ignoring that warning. Today, we see the US following a similar pattern of decline and fall that led to the collapse of Rome and the beginning of the Dark Ages.

What were the chief factors that led to the demise of Rome, one of the most powerful empires in history? Rome didn't fall because of climate change or a massive earthquake or an epidemic. Edward Gibbon found that the root causes of the collapse of Rome were largely moral and spiritual: The decline of individual morality and civic virtue. The breakdown of the family. The rise of unrestrained hedonism and living for sexual gratification. The declining influence of religion.

For the better part of three centuries, Christianity was a persecuted religion in the Roman Empire. Christians were imprisoned, tortured, and executed for their faith by the Roman government, yet the Christian faith continued to spread and thrive throughout the empire. Then, in AD 313, Constantine I declared that Christianity would be officially tolerated throughout the Roman Empire. Within decades, Christianity even became the official state religion of the Roman Empire. As the institutional Christian church triumphed, it quickly became rich, powerful, and corrupt. Moral decay set in, and by the fifth century, the church had largely ceased to be a force for morality and virtue in the empire.

A Roman Christian writer of that era, Salvian the Presbyter, wrote about how Roman Christian Spain had been conquered by Germanic barbarian tribes from the north. He believed it was God's judgment against the immorality of Christianized Roman culture. He wrote:

> The barbarians are now cleansing by chastity those lands which the Romans polluted by fornication.... God gave all [of Roman Spain] to the weakest enemies to show that it was not the strength of numbers but the cause that conquered.... We are right now being overcome solely by the impurity of our vices....
>
> I ask: What hope of pardon or of life can there be for us in the sight of God when we see chastity among the barbarians and are, ourselves, unchaste? I say: Let us be ashamed and confused....
>
> You, O Roman people, be ashamed; be ashamed of your lives.[6]

Once the Roman Empire began to crumble, the social order of Rome collapsed quickly. The Visigoths laid siege to the city of Rome, beginning in AD 408. At that time, the city of Rome had not been conquered in eight hundred years, and the Romans thought their city was completely immune from attack. But the Visigoth siege held the Romans in the grip of terror. The Christian church in Rome had become so feeble and apostate that Pope Innocent I permitted Christians to offer sacrifices to pagan idols in the hope that the false Roman gods might protect them from the invaders.[7] Imagine, the head of the Christian church officially sanctioning idolatry!

On August 24, 410, the Visigoths entered Rome through the Salarian Gate. For three days, they raped and slaughtered and took many Roman citizens as slaves. Rome had reached the pinnacle of power and culture, yet the empire was collapsing like a sand castle under an ocean wave.

The reasons for the sudden final collapse of the empire, Gibbon concluded, were a decline of morality, the breakdown of the family, and the crumbling influence of religion. One of the first people to own and read Gibbon's six-volume work on the fall of Rome was America's first president, George Washington. In his farewell address to the nation after serving two terms as America's first president, Washington said:

> Of all the dispositions and habits which lead to political prosperity, religion and morality are indispensable supports. In vain would that man claim the tribute of patriotism, who should labor to subvert these great pillars of human happiness, these firmest props of the duties of men and citizens. . . . And let us with caution indulge the supposition that morality can be maintained without religion. . . . Reason and experience both forbid us to expect that national morality can prevail in exclusion of religious principle.[8]

Edward Gibbon and George Washington were convinced that the foundation for a strong society is neither a dominant military force nor a strong economy, but rather a citizenry with strong moral fiber, strong religious faith, and strong God-centered families. As we come to Jeremiah 16 and 17, we find that the convictions of Gibbon and

Washington are affirmed by the prophet Jeremiah and by God himself. America, and every other nation, needs these convictions to prevent going the way of the Roman Empire—and of the kingdom of Judah.

A RAY OF HOPE IN THE DARKNESS

Jeremiah has been watching the death of a nation, the decline and fall of the kingdom of Judah. The people of Judah have been infected by the idolatry and evil that had spread across the land, starting with Judah's godless king and trickling down to the common people. This infectious moral disease has been leading the nation toward the inevitable climax of God's judgment—the conquest of Jerusalem and the exile of the Jews to Babylon.

The decline and fall of Judah has been gradual, almost imperceptible. Jeremiah's ministry of preaching against the sin and idolatry of Judah has lasted more than forty years, and God has patiently withheld judgment, giving Judah every opportunity for repentance. But the people of Judah have persisted in their rebellion against God, and it is only a matter of time before God's judgment falls and the kingdom is overthrown.

Throughout Jeremiah's ministry, God has been preparing him, strengthening him, toughening him up so that he will stand firm even as the nation is collapsing around him. The time is growing short. The people are growing increasingly more wicked. God's judgment is looming and appearing more and more certain, despite Jeremiah's faithful preaching.

He doesn't understand why he is having so little success in his calling as a prophet. In times past, prophets have preached the warnings of God with intensity and power, as Jeremiah has, and the people have turned back to the Lord in repentance. But the words of Jeremiah seem to fall on deaf ears. He is deeply hurt by this and has even tried to stop preaching for a while. But God won't let him stop.

In Jeremiah 16 and 17, we come to the centerpiece of the entire prophecy of the book of Jeremiah. These two chapters contain two messages—the first two of four messages Jeremiah delivers near the end of the reign of King Jehoiachin. King Jehoiachin was a wicked king who succeeded his brother Jehoahaz to the throne and reigned for eleven years.

This section opens with a dire warning addressed to Jeremiah himself:

> Then the word of the LORD came to me: "You must not marry and have sons or daughters in this place." For this is what the LORD says about the sons and daughters born in this land and about the women who are their mothers and the men who are their fathers: "They will die of deadly diseases. They will not be mourned or buried but will be like dung lying on the ground. They will perish by sword and famine, and their dead bodies will become food for the birds and the wild animals." (16:1–4)

Here, God reaffirms His determination to judge this wicked kingdom and its people. The Lord begins by setting a stringent limitation upon the prophet: He forbids Jeremiah to get married and start a family. Clearly, the life of a prophet is a harsh and difficult calling. It demands great personal sacrifice. Jeremiah already feels defeated and rejected, and now God tells him he is never to know the joys of a home, a wife, or children.

Was God trying to deal harshly with Jeremiah? No. In fact, as we are about to see, these limitations God places on Jeremiah are prompted by God's love for him. God wants to spare this prophet even greater sorrow, so He places these restrictions on him. God's command that Jeremiah not marry reminds us of the words of the apostle Paul:

> Because of the present crisis, I think that it is good for a man to remain as he is. Are you pledged to a woman? Do not seek to be released. Are you free from such a commitment? Do not look for a wife. But if you do marry, you have not sinned; and if a virgin marries, she has not sinned. But those who marry will face many troubles in this life, and I want to spare you this. (1 Corinthians 7:26–28)

God looks ahead to the day of Judah's judgment, and He foresees the grief that Jeremiah and his wife and children would experience on the coming day of death and destruction. God wanted to spare Jeremiah this additional grief, so He forbade him to be married as the nation hastened to its doom.

Next, God laid two more restrictions on Jeremiah:

> For this is what the LORD says: "Do not enter a house where there is a funeral meal; do not go to mourn or show sympathy, because I have withdrawn my blessing, my love and my pity from this people," declares the LORD. . . .
> "And do not enter a house where there is feasting and sit down to eat and drink. For this is what the LORD Almighty, the God of Israel, says: Before your eyes and in your days I will bring an end to the sounds of joy and gladness and to the voices of bride and bridegroom in this place. (16:5, 8–9)

God tells Jeremiah that there is no time left for the normal social amenities. There is no time left to mourn those who die. There is no time left to celebrate at weddings. The judgment of God is about to fall, and the civilization of Judah is coming to an end.

Then God gives Jeremiah another word of instruction:

> "When you tell these people all this and they ask you, 'Why has the LORD decreed such a great disaster against us? What wrong have we done? What sin have we committed against the LORD our God?' then say to them, 'It is because your ancestors forsook me,' declares the LORD, 'and followed other gods and served and worshiped them. They forsook me and did not keep my law. But you have behaved more wickedly than your ancestors. See how all of you are following the stubbornness of your evil hearts instead of obeying me. So I will throw you out of this land into a land neither you nor your ancestors have known, and there you will serve other gods day and night, for I will show you no favor.'" (16:10–13)

The people of Judah will be like a patient with a terminal disease who refuses to accept the diagnosis. When the judgment of God begins to fall on Judah, the people will act completely surprised. Jeremiah has been warning them for forty years, yet they will seem not to have heard a word he said. "What wrong have we done?" they will ask. And they will be appalled at Jeremiah's words.

One of the surest signs that the end of the nation is near is when its people have become so callous to sin, so steeped in idolatry, that they don't even realize how evil they have become. They think there's nothing wrong with worshiping false gods alongside the one true God. They think there's nothing wrong with mingling the obscene practices of the Canaanites and Philistines with the rituals and sacrifices prescribed in the Law of Moses. They are breaking most of the Ten Commandments, yet they don't understand why God is judging them.

The Lord tells Jeremiah to tell them that this judgment is coming upon them because their ancestors rejected God and followed false gods, and the people themselves have committed even worse idolatries than their apostate parents. That is why they will be thrown out of the land and sent into exile in a foreign land to serve false gods day and night.

But in the midst of this darkness, God gives Jeremiah a ray of hope: He promises to restore the people to the land after their exile. Meanwhile, the land of Judah will be overrun by enemies who will hunt the people down like animals and carry off the wealth and the treasures of the nation. In the meantime, although God will one day restore the people to their homeland, they will pay a heavy price for their disobedience.

Jeremiah 16 closes with an amazing dialogue between Jeremiah and the Lord. If God had told you that He was about to destroy your nation and allow all of your people to be either slaughtered or led into captivity, and if he placed all these restrictions on you, how would you respond? Would you be bitter toward God, or would you praise Him? After God tells Jeremiah about the coming terrors of judgment, Jeremiah responds:

> LORD, my strength and my fortress,
>   my refuge in time of distress,
> to you the nations will come
>   from the ends of the earth and say,

"Our ancestors possessed nothing but false gods,
    worthless idols that did them no good.
Do people make their own gods?
    Yes, but they are not gods!" (16:19–20)

Here, Jeremiah lifts his eyes to the future, looks down through the course of the ages and sees the end of history. Although his present circumstances are hard to bear, Jeremiah knows that God is his stronghold, his place of refuge. One day the nations will understand their folly, and they will realize that the so-called "gods" they have trusted in are not gods at all, but mere man-made statues of inert metal. People might as well pray to a table lamp or a hat rack, for all the good it will do them. One day, people will know. But for this generation, it's already too late!

THE SECRET OF LIFE

The next verse, Jeremiah 16:21, begins God's response to Jeremiah. After that verse, there is a chapter break and Jeremiah 17:1 begins, continuing God's response. It's important to realize that while the Word of God is inspired by God, the chapter and verse divisions were added centuries later and were not inspired. In fact, some chapter divisions, such as the division between Jeremiah 16 and 17, are unfortunately placed, because they interrupt the flow of the text. So I will treat verse 16:21 as it was originally intended—as the first few lines of the much longer response from God to Jeremiah. God says:

"Therefore I will teach them—
    this time I will teach them
    my power and might.
Then they will know
    that my name is the Lord." (16:21)

Through the time of judgment to come, God will teach the nations—both His own chosen people in the kingdom of Judah and the ungodly nations that surround Judah. What will He teach them? He will show them the emptiness of the false gods they have trusted. He will show them His true power and might. And He will teach them that He alone is the Lord. They will learn that other gods are false gods. How will God teach the people these lessons? By the only means they will understand. He will collapse everything they place their trust in. They have ignored all of Jeremiah's warnings. Now God will get their attention the only way He can, by bringing them to the end of themselves, by upending their society, by taking away everything, everything, *everything* they have depended on. Then their eyes will be opened, and they will know the God they have ignored, disobeyed, and disrespected.

God is patient, loving, and merciful. That's why He has delayed judgment for so many years. But the patience of God is not without limits. It's time for the people of Judah to learn about the God they have been ignoring. God goes on to say:

"Judah's sin is engraved with an iron tool,
    inscribed with a flint point,
on the tablets of their hearts
    and on the horns of their altars.
Even their children remember
    their altars and Asherah poles
beside the spreading trees
    and on the high hills.
My mountain in the land
    and your wealth and all your treasures
I will give away as plunder,
    together with your high places,
    because of sin throughout your country.
Through your own fault you will lose
    the inheritance I gave you.
I will enslave you to your enemies
    in a land you do not know,
for you have kindled my anger,
    and it will burn forever." (17:1–4)

Judah's sin is so deeply ingrained in the nation that nothing short of judgment can dislodge it. Could this be true of nations of the world today—even the United States? Evil and godlessness pervade many of our institutions. Vile ideas and images are piped into our homes through our electronic media and the internet.

Wickedness is engraved on the heart with a stylus of iron, so that it cannot be erased. Wickedness infects every generation, from the parents to the children to the grandchildren. God has appealed again and again to the people to repent and turn back to him, but their sin and rebellion only grows worse. So the hand of God must move in judgment.

The Lord continues His message to Jeremiah:

> This is what the LORD says:
> "Cursed is the one who trusts in man,
>   who draws strength from mere flesh
>   and whose heart turns away from the LORD.
> That person will be like a bush in the wastelands;
>   they will not see prosperity when it comes.
> They will dwell in the parched places of the desert,
>   in a salt land where no one lives.
> "But blessed is the one who trusts in the LORD,
>   whose confidence is in him.
> They will be like a tree planted by the water
>   that sends out its roots by the stream.
> It does not fear when heat comes;
>   its leaves are always green.
> It has no worries in a year of drought
>   and never fails to bear fruit." (17:5–8)

This section of Jeremiah 17, from verse 5 to the end of the chapter, is, in my view, the heart of the prophecy of Jeremiah. In these verses, God begins to open Jeremiah's eyes to what He is doing in human history. If you want to understand the strange, tumultuous events of Jeremiah's day—and if you want to understand the times in which we live—it's important to understand what God now teaches the prophet Jeremiah.

The Lord's first lesson to Jeremiah is that all human beings make a choice between one of two paths. There are only two paths; no more, no less. If you choose one, you reject the other. If you choose the other, you reject the one. You cannot travel both paths at the same time.

God sets forth the first path in verses 5 and 6—the path of trusting in man, drawing strength from mere human flesh, and living for self. This is the natural path of the flesh, the sin nature we inherited from Adam. This is the path of all those who rely on their own intellect, their own skill, their own cunning as the ultimate solution to their problems. This is the path of those who think they can save themselves.

The Lord tells Jeremiah, "Cursed is the one who trusts in man" (v. 5). In other words, everything they do ultimately comes to nothing. Those who follow this path "dwell in the parched places of the desert, in a salt land where no one lives" (v. 6). It's the path of death.

Next, God sets forth the second path—a path of blessing for those who place their trust solely in the Lord. "They will be like a tree planted by the water," God says, "that sends out its roots by the stream." A tree planted by a stream of water never has to worry about heat or droughts. Its leaves are always green, and it never fails to be fruitful.

When I was growing up in Montana, we often had long periods of drought in the summer months. No rain would fall on the land, and the ground would bake and become cracked and dry. Any trees, shrubs, or grass that grew on that parched land would turn brown and sere during the summer droughts.

But on the ranch where I lived, there was one tree that never turned brown. It was always green, no matter how dry the country around it became. It was planted near a hidden underground spring, which kept it watered, green, and fresh even during the drought. I always think of that tree when I read these verses in Jeremiah.

I want to be like that tree in my soul and spirit. I want to have my roots planted deep in the earth that is watered by a spring of living water. I want to be continually strengthened by a hidden reservoir of refreshment from God. That is the secret of life God reveals in Jeremiah 17.

GOD'S DIAGNOSIS OF OUR HEART TROUBLE

Next, God reveals the heart of the problem—and the problem is the heart: "The heart is deceitful above all things and beyond cure. Who can understand it?" (17:9).

In those few words, God has distilled an explanation of all the misery, wickedness, and injustice of life. When the Bible speaks of the "heart," of course, it doesn't mean the literal muscular organ that pumps the blood throughout our bodies. It speaks of our innermost being, the part of us that is bent by sin and makes bad choices—the aspect of our humanity that the Scriptures also refers to as "the flesh." The heart has two things wrong with it:

First, the heart is "deceitful above all things." It is desperately corrupt, dishonest, and full of lies. It can never function as God originally designed the human heart to function. It can never fulfill all our expectations. It can never achieve our best intentions and lofty ideals.

Second, the heart is infected with a fatal and incurable virus called sin. It cannot be healed. It cannot be fixed. It cannot be cured. There is only one way to solve the problem of the incurably sinful human heart: It must be put to death.

That's exactly what the Lord Jesus did when He was nailed to a cross 2,000 years ago. He took our fatal, incurable nature—our sin nature, our unfixable human heart—and He put it to death. That's all the human heart—our inmost being—is good for.

Now, many people have a problem with this notion. In fact, this statement: "The heart is deceitful above all things and beyond cure" divides humanity into two categories. It all comes down to those who believe this verse and live their lives on these terms *versus* those who deny this verse and say, "That's not true! Human beings are basically good! They can be fixed with the right social conditions, the right upbringing, the right education, the right caring."

If you belong to the second group, if you believe human beings are basically good, your argument is not with me. Your argument is with

God. He is the one who says that our hearts are overwhelmingly and incurably deceitful and sinful.

The secular worldview sees this statement as harsh and negative. But if you understand the biblical view of human nature, you understand that God created human beings in a state of moral innocence and purity, and He created us in His own perfect image. But in the garden of Eden, when Adam and Eve were tempted and sinned, God's perfect image in us was forever marred by sin. We have had a sin nature—a natural bent toward sin—ever since.

So the biblical view of human nature is not harsh, not negative—but realistic. It explains why there is so much good in us, why we want to do good, why we are often loving and generous and kind—that's the vestige of God's image that still resides in us. Yet the biblical view also explains why we sin even when we want to do good, why we sometimes hurt the people we love, why we lie or steal or lust or hate or over-eat or get drunk even when we try not to. Only the biblical view of human nature accounts for *both* the good we do *and* the evil we do.

"People are basically good" says the naïve and unrealistic secular worldview. "People are basically sinners" says the realistic, biblical worldview. There is no middle ground between these two ways of looking at the human heart. You must be on one side or the other. The side you choose will determine how you think about politics, education, legislation, and every other major issue in your life. Let me give you some examples:

Secularists, who believe that people are basically good, have a diametrically opposed view of education from biblical Christians who believe that people are basically sinners. If you believe people are basically good, that they are born good, you will blame the evil that people do not on people themselves, but on outside forces, on "society." The secularist thinks, "If we could just control all the external, social forces that cause people to do bad things, we could eliminate evil. We could educate people to be good."

The secularists try to control the thinking of children through education and indoctrination. Believing that people are basically good, they teach that there is no right or wrong, only safe and unsafe, tolerant and judgmental. So the secularists, for instance, want to teach our children how to use a condom and how not to be "homophobic."

As biblical Christians who believe that people are basically sinners, we have a very different view of education. We teach our children that their most basic struggle is not against outside forces but against the urges of their own sin nature. Instead of teaching children how to use a condom, we teach our children to rely on the Holy Spirit for the strength and wisdom to overcome lustful urges. Instead of teaching our children that all forms of sexual expression are equal and good, we teach that sex outside of God's plan for marriage is sin.

At the same time, we treat all people, including those who engage in sinful behavior, with courtesy, respect, and caring. We teach that it is godly to hate the sin but love the sinner.

Secularists, who believe people are basically good, blame society and social ills and even religion for the evil that people do. The evildoer, some would go as far as to say, should not be held accountable for his evil. People who do bad things don't need to be punished—they need to be taught that their actions are unhelpful. We need to understand the social, psychological, and environmental reasons the criminal commits crimes, the terrorist commits mass murder, the rapist commits sex crimes, and so forth. We need to help these people to see themselves as good people.

By contrast, biblical Christians believe people are basically sinners. While we seek to eliminate injustice and social ills because of our Christian compassion, we hold the sinner responsible for his or her sins.

Another major difference between those who see people as basically good and those who see people as basically sinners is how each side views God and religion. Those who see people as basically good believe that religion is (at best) without value. If people are basically good, why do they need religion? In fact, they say, religion actually does harm because it teaches people to be judgmental and intolerant of others, and it makes people feel guilty by telling them they are "sinners." Instead of making people feel bad about themselves, instead of telling people they need to be saved by the crucifixion of a Jewish teacher 2,000 years ago, people just need to hear that they are good people, and they will try to live up to that.

"The heart is deceitful above all things," God says, "and beyond cure." Do you agree with God about human nature—or do you disagree? Your response to God's diagnosis of the human heart in Jeremiah 17:9 will determine how you raise and educate your children, how you vote, how you view such issues as crime and terrorism and social justice and economics, and on and on. People increasingly fall for the "people are basically good" deception because we live in a post-Christian culture. The post-Christian mindset is radically reshaping society—and not for the better.

The Founding Fathers of the United States understood the deceitfulness of the human heart. Many of them were grounded in the truth of God's Word and understood that human beings are, by nature, desperately corrupt. When the Founding Fathers wrote the Constitution, they put safeguards into the document to ensure that they didn't entrust too much power in a single individual. They set up checks and balances so that each branch of government would keep the other two co-equal branches from becoming corrupted by too much power. The framers of the Constitution didn't trust the "goodness" of human nature—and I'm glad they didn't.

Winston Churchill, the prime minister of Great Britain during World War II, was an astute observer of life. He wrote, "While men are gathering knowledge and power with ever-increasing and measureless speed, their virtues and their wisdom have not shown any notable improvement as the centuries have rolled. . . . Under sufficient stress—starvation, terror, warlike passion, or even cold intellectual frenzy—the modern man we know so well will do the most terrible deeds, and his modern woman will back him up."[9]

Churchill's analysis echoed God's diagnosis of the human heart. Although human beings are made in the image of God, that image is warped and corrupted by sin, and no system of philosophy or psychology or politics or education can ever hope to eliminate the essential deceitfulness and wickedness that we are heir to as fallen human beings.

WHO CAN UNDERSTAND IT?

There is another aspect of the deceitful human heart that God describes, and we dare not ignore it: The heart is not merely corrupt and sinful but it is also deceitful above all things. The heart disguises its own evil. It is corrupt, but it doesn't look corrupt. It is sinful, but it wears many masks to give itself a saintly appearance. A heart full of hate cloaks itself in a disguise of insincere flattery. A heart full of greed puts on a mask of false generosity. A heart full of lust puts on a pious disguise. And a heart full of lies ingratiates itself, saying, "Trust me."

The deceitful human heart is like a well that pumps poisoned water up out of the ground. The water looks good to drink, but it will sicken you or kill you. Many of the theories advanced by secular psychologists and sociologists and educators and politicians—theories meant to purify the poisonous water of the human heart, are meaningless gestures. They are the equivalent of trying to purify a poisoned well by painting the pump.

The human heart not only tries to deceive others but it is also amazingly self-deceptive. How many times have you told yourself, "I'm really not a bad person. In fact, I'm just a few steps short of perfection. If I could just overcome this minor bad habit or that personality flaw, I would achieve perfection!" Do those thoughts sound familiar? If so, then you have experienced the deceitfulness of the human heart. You know firsthand what God was saying to Jeremiah.

The human heart is cunning, hypocritical, and deceitful above all else. This is the truth that divides the world. This is the truth that men and women must know if they are to understand life as it is. You won't learn this insight from humanism or secular psychology.

You won't learn it from Buddhism or Hinduism or Zoroastrianism. You won't hear about the deceitfulness of the human heart on CNN or on daytime TV talk shows. For a trustworthy, reality-based diagnosis of the human heart, you must go to God's Word. No wonder Jeremiah responds to this truth with the exclamation, "Who can understand it?" (v. 9).

If our hearts are so deceitful, so desperately wicked, beyond our capacity to understand, how can we function in this world? How can we live our lives? How can we solve our problems? How can we even recognize our problems and realize that they need solving? Our hearts, our emotions, our hidden and subconscious motives constantly deceive us and drive us to do things we don't even want to do. How can we penetrate the deception of our deceitful hearts?

Answer: We can't, but God can. He goes on to tell the prophet Jeremiah:

> "I the LORD search the heart
>   and examine the mind,
> to reward each person according to their conduct,
>   according to what their deeds deserve." (17:10)

Do you want to know the true inner workings of your heart? Do you want to peer behind the deception and disguises of your heart? God searches the heart and examines the mind, and He rewards us according to the actions that proceed from the inner workings of our hearts. If you want to know the depths of your heart, look at what comes out of your life. Even if our heart is deceptive, our actions reveal the truth. What God says to Jeremiah in this passage is mirrored by Paul's words to the believers in Galatia:

> Do not be deceived: God cannot be mocked. A man reaps what he sows. Whoever sows to please their flesh, from the flesh will reap destruction; whoever sows to please the Spirit, from the Spirit will reap eternal life. (Galatians 6:7–8)

Paul pictures our lives as a field in which we sow seed, hoping to reap a harvest. If we sow the kind of seed that only pleases our sinful, deceptive flesh, what kind of harvest can we expect to reap? Destruction. It is vitally important that we understand the workings of our hearts, so we can sow the kind of seed that pleases God and leads to eternal life.

Jeremiah responds to the Lord's teaching with a simile from nature:

> Like a partridge that hatches eggs it did not lay
>   are those who gain riches by unjust means.
> When their lives are half gone, their riches will desert them,
>   and in the end they will prove to be fools. (17:11)

How tragic it would be to discover midway through your life that you have wasted all those years and have nothing to show for it! How tragic to build your life on worldly wealth and riches, only to have those worldly goods abandon you and leave you desolate. You would find you had lived your entire life in a state of self-deception.

And in the end, you realize you've been a fool.

THE SANCTUARY OF GOD'S THRONE

Jeremiah goes on to say:

> A glorious throne, exalted from the beginning,
>   is the place of our sanctuary.
> LORD, you are the hope of Israel;
>   all who forsake you will be put to shame.
> Those who turn away from you will be written in the dust
>   because they have forsaken the LORD,
>   the spring of living water. (17:12–13)

Where do we find the answer to the riddle of life? Where do we find the solution to our deepest problems, the understanding of our own nature? Where do we find a place of sanctuary and protection when all the forces of the world are arrayed against us? There is only one place we can go: the throne of God.

One reason many people refuse to accept the fact that they are born with an evil nature is that if they admit they are basically evil, but reject faith in God, they have no place to go. They have no sanctuary. To accept that they are sinners rather than the good people they claim to be would be a kind of moral suicide. They would have to put their self-image ("I am a good person") to death.

To say, "People are basically sinful," we must first be willing to admit, "*I* am basically sinful." Many people simply can't bring themselves to make that admission. But until we face the truth, stated in God's Word, that we are sinners in need of a Savior, we cannot accept the good news of the gospel.

The good news of the gospel begins with the bad news that we are lost in our sins and incapable of saving ourselves. To receive the good news, you have to accept the bad news. You have to give yourself up and die to the notion that you are a good person with no need of a Savior.

The good news is that God has made it possible for us to die without dying. We can crucify the old, false notion that we are good people, we can accept the fact that we are sinners and we are lost—and then we can accept the sacrifice of Jesus on our behalf. We can allow *His* righteousness to become *our* righteousness.

We no longer have to pretend to be good people. We can admit that we are sinners saved by God's grace. We have no righteousness of our own, but all of our sins have been washed away by the blood of Jesus. We have been clothed in His righteousness. We can go to His glorious throne and find a sanctuary from judgment and condemnation.

Some people think that the Old Testament is about the Law and condemnation, while the New Testament is about grace and forgiveness. That's a false dichotomy. The entire Bible, from Genesis to Revelation, is about grace and forgiveness. Here we see Jeremiah pray, and his prayer is a beautiful testament to the grace of God: "Heal me,

LORD, and I will be healed; save me and I will be saved, for you are the one I praise" (17:14).

No one else can heal. No one else can save. Only the One who sits on the glorious throne of heaven can heal us. Jeremiah comes to the Lord saying, in effect, "Here I am with the heart I have inherited as a fallen son of Adam. My heart is desperately corrupt and deceitful above all things. I am helpless to save myself, so I come to you, Lord, and I say, 'Heal me, Lord, and I will be healed. Save me, and I will be saved.'"

Whenever the deceitful human heart rises up within us and says, "I'll take control," we need to run to the sanctuary of God's throne. We need to ask God to heal us and save us from the deceitfulness of the heart. That is a prayer God will honor. He will heal you, and He will save you.

GOD SPEAKS THROUGH THE SABBATH

At this point, God gives Jeremiah new instructions and sends him back to the nation of Judah. Also, He gives Jeremiah a message for the nation. This message closes Jeremiah 17. Jeremiah records God's word to him:

This is what the LORD said to me: "Go and stand at the Gate of the People, through which the kings of Judah go in and out; stand also at all the other gates of Jerusalem. Say to them, 'Hear the word of the LORD, you kings of Judah and all people of Judah and everyone living in Jerusalem who come through these gates. This is what the LORD says: Be careful not to carry a load on the Sabbath day or bring it through the gates of Jerusalem. . . . But if you are careful to obey me, declares the LORD, and bring no load through the gates of this city on the Sabbath, but keep the Sabbath day holy by not doing any work on it, then kings who sit on David's throne will come through the gates of this city with their officials. They and their officials will come riding in chariots and on horses, accompanied by the men of Judah and those living in Jerusalem, and this city will be inhabited forever. People will come from the towns of Judah and the villages around Jerusalem, from the territory of Benjamin and the western foothills, from the hill country and the Negev, bringing burnt offerings and sacrifices, grain offerings and incense, and bringing thank offerings to the house of the LORD. But if you do not obey me to keep the Sabbath day holy by not carrying any load as you come through the gates of Jerusalem on the Sabbath day, then I will kindle an unquenchable fire in the gates of Jerusalem that will consume her fortresses.'" (17:19–21, 24–27)

Why is God so concerned about the Sabbath during the final days of Judah? The nation is in crisis, yet God is telling the people not to carry a load through the city gates on the Sabbath day.

God set aside the Sabbath day as a day of rest, commemorating the day God ceased from the work of creation and rested on the seventh day. He tells us through the Scriptures that the Sabbath is a picture of the life of faith. We are to cease trying to save ourselves through our own effort, and we are to place our trust entirely in God and rest in Him. That is what it means to keep the Sabbath.

All the ceremonies and rituals human beings have created and added to the law of Moses were attempts by human beings to make up their own religion and reach God by their own efforts. God is saying through the Sabbath, "All the man-made ceremonies and rituals you have added to the faith I gave you through Moses are a false religion, a works-based religion, and they violate the Sabbath rest." As we read in the New Testament book of Hebrews, "for he who has entered His rest has himself also ceased from his works, as God did from His" (Hebrews 4:10 NKJV).

God does all the work of salvation, and we rest in Him. That is the Sabbath. We are at rest because Jesus did the work of salvation on the cross so we don't have to (we couldn't anyway). When we rest in the work God has done for us, we are like the tree planted by the river (see Psalm 1:3), a tree that remains green and fresh even in times of drought and disaster.

Because God has done all the work of salvation, we can enjoy the Sabbath rest, and we can say with Jeremiah, "Heal me, LORD, and I will be healed; save me and I will be saved, for you are the one I praise" (Jeremiah 17:14).

6

THE POTTER
AND THE CLAY

Jeremiah 18–19

During a trip to Israel, I visited the tomb of Abraham in the village of Hebron. I noticed a pottery house across the street from the tomb. I went inside, and that pottery shop was like a trip back in time. The potter sat at his wheel, making a clay pot in the ancient way. He operated the potter's wheel with his feet—no electrical motor. He shaped the clay with the skilled touch of his hands as it spun around and around on the potter's wheel.

I watched the potter turn a lump of clay into a useful utensil—and a work of art. The technique he employed had not changed since Jeremiah's day. There are only three ingredients to the process: the potter, the clay, and the wheel.

As we come to Jeremiah 18, the Lord sends Jeremiah to the potter's house, where he will see these same three ingredients at work. And Jeremiah will leave the potter's house having learned a lesson that he declares to the nation. The prophet writes:

This is the word that came to Jeremiah from the LORD: "Go down to the potter's house, and there I will give you my message." So I went down to the potter's house, and I saw him working at the wheel. But the pot he was shaping from the clay was marred in his hands; so the potter formed it into another pot, shaping it as seemed best to him. (18:1–4)

What did Jeremiah see at the potter's house? First, he saw clay. Jeremiah knew, as he watched the potter turning and shaping the clay on the wheel, that he was looking at a picture of himself, a picture of all human beings, and in fact a picture of every nation. God is the Potter; we are the clay, both individually and collectively. The prophet Isaiah uses the same imagery in describing our relationship to God our Creator:

"Woe to those who quarrel with their Maker, those who are nothing but potsherds among the potsherds on the ground. Does the clay say to the potter, 'What are you making?' Does your work say, 'The potter has no hands'?" (Isaiah 45:9)

Yet you, LORD, are our Father.
We are the clay, you are the potter;
we are all the work of your hand. (Isaiah 64:8)

The apostle Paul offers a similar insight in the New Testament:

But who are you, a human being, to talk back to God? "Shall what is formed say to the one who formed it, 'Why did you make me like this?'" Does not the potter have the right to make out of the same lump of clay some pottery for special purposes and some for common use? (Romans 9:20–21).

Here in Jeremiah 18, the prophet watches the potter shape and mold a clay pot on the potter's wheel. The wheel turns continuously under the control of the potter, and it is the turning of the wheel under the potter's hand that gives the pot its symmetrical beauty. The potter applies gentle pressure to the clay as it spins around and around, forming and molding the clay according to his plan for that piece.

As Jeremiah watches, an imperfection in the clay spoils the piece of pottery so that it becomes unsightly and unusable. The potter then kneads and reshapes the clay, fashioning it into a new shape, a new utensil that the potter finds pleasing and useful. The lesson God wants Jeremiah to learn from the potter is not hard to understand. Jeremiah writes:

> Then the word of the LORD came to me. He said, "Can I not do with you, Israel, as this potter does?" declares the LORD. "Like clay in the hand of the potter, so are you in my hand, Israel. If at any time I announce that a nation or kingdom is to be uprooted, torn down and destroyed, and if that nation I warned repents of its evil, then I will relent and not inflict on it the disaster I had planned. And if at another time I announce that a nation or kingdom is to be built up and planted, and if it does evil in my sight and does not obey me, then I will reconsider the good I had intended to do for it." (18:5–10)

Jeremiah understood that God is the Great Potter, and He has a sovereign right to do with the clay as He sees fit. The clay pot is shaped according to the image in the mind of the Potter, and He has a sovereign right to do as He pleases with the works of His hands. That clay might be a single individual—or a mighty nation. God has a sovereign right to shape that lump of clay and to tear down that lump of clay and to reshape it into something else.

Through the analogy of the potter and the clay, God sent a message to the nation, warning Judah that if it refused to repent of its sin, it would be like a lump of clay resisting the potter's gentle pressure. It would become ugly, misshapen, and no longer useful. It would be fit only to be torn down, kneaded back into a formless lump, and refashioned into something new and beautiful. Through this image, God was saying that the nation of Judah was about to be destroyed, crushed, and turned back into a formless lump of clay.

But that was not the end of the story. Through the imagery of the potter and the clay, God was also telling Jeremiah that the clay would be returned to the wheel, and the Potter would rework it and reshape it and restore that clay to usefulness and beauty. The Jewish people would be refashioned and made to conform to God's design.

God often deals the very same way with us as individuals. He is our Potter just as He is the Potter of the people of Israel. He puts us through pressures and trials that cause us to be reshaped. The pottery wheel of life spins us like a centrifuge, and God touches us, forms us, shapes us, bringing beauty and usefulness out of formlessness. If we resist His creative touch, He may be forced to radically remake us. When He takes us off the wheel and kneads us into a formless mass, it may seem at first as if He is destroying us—but no, the reshaping is merely an additional and necessary step in His creative process.

When we resist God's attempt to conform us to His image, that resistance comes from what the Bible calls "the flesh." It's the equivalent of the flaw in the clay that spoils the pot, forcing the Potter to rework the clay and start over again. Taking the clay off the wheel and turning it into a formless lump again is the equivalent of putting to death the flesh. God has to work out our imperfections and flaws, then He puts us back on the wheel and reshapes us into His likeness.

DOES GOD CONTRADICT HIMSELF?

This passage contains a fascinating description of the working of God's mind. Jeremiah writes that if a nation repents of its evil, God will "relent" and not impose judgment and destruction on the nation. And if a nation God blesses turns around and does evil in His sight, then He will "reconsider" and bring destruction on that nation. In some translations, the word *repent* is used instead of *relent* and *reconsider*. Can God repent? Can God change His mind, make a U-turn, and go in a different direction than He originally intended?

When we human beings repent, we change our minds and change the direction of our lives. But the Bible tells us that God never changes His mind; in fact, God never changes, period. James 1:17 tells us that God "does not change like shifting shadows." And the book of

Numbers says: "God is not human, that he should lie, not a human being, that he should change his mind. Does he speak and then not act? Does he promise and not fulfill?" (23:19).

Yet Jeremiah speaks here of God repenting. And there are other instances in Scripture where God is said to repent or change His mind. For example, we read in Genesis 6:6, when evil reigned in the days before the flood of Noah, that God "regretted that he had made human beings on the earth, and his heart was deeply troubled." And after Jonah preached to the people of Nineveh and they repented of their sin, we read that God "relented and did not bring on them the destruction he had threatened" (see Jonah 3:10).

Is this a case of Scripture contradicting itself? No. God never needs to change His mind, because God is never taken by surprise. He knows the end from the beginning. He has known everything about you and me since before the foundation of the world. God was not blindsided by the fall; He knew that Adam and Eve would eat the forbidden fruit. This doesn't mean Adam and Eve were programmed robots and had no free will. They had complete freedom of choice, but God knew in advance what their choice would be. And God knew before the foundation of the world that the crisis of sin would be solved by the death of His Son on the cross.

God is outside of time, and He sees our future as clearly as He sees our past. Past and future are all one to Him. But we human beings are limited by time. We experience time as the remembered past, the present moment, and the mysterious and unknowable future.

The Bible often presents God's actions to us in anthropomorphic (human-like) terms to make His actions understandable to us. Exodus 7:5 describes God as stretching out His hand; Psalm 33:6 speaks of God creating by the breath of His mouth; Psalm 34:15 refers to the eyes and ears of the Lord; and Psalm 89:10 speaks of God destroying Israel's enemies with His strong arm.

Similarly, when the Bible speaks of God repenting or changing His mind, it is using a metaphor, it is using anthropomorphic language to interpret God's actions in a way that makes sense to our limited, time-locked understanding. The Bible is not saying that God altered His plans because He suddenly discovered new information He never knew before.

God's nature is unchanging, and one aspect of His nature is His mercy. God responds to human repentance by showing mercy and forgiveness instead of judgment. But He knows in advance whether we will repent or not. We have free will, and we make choices in the present that will have consequences in the future. However, God, who is not limited by time, has always known what choice we will make, and He has always known whether His response to our choice would be forgiveness or judgment.

The nation of Judah had a choice to make. Jeremiah pleaded with the Jewish people to make the right choice. But God already knew what choice the people of Judah would make. Long before the day of judgment was set to fall upon the nation of Judah, God was preparing the godless, idol-worshiping Babylonians, increasing the ferocity and military strength of the nation for the day of Judah's destruction.

The people of the kingdom of Judah had every opportunity to repent and receive God's mercy and forgiveness. They said no to every opportunity Jeremiah presented to them, and when the Babylonians finally came and laid siege to the city of Jerusalem, the people of Judah were without excuse.

God is the Potter and all human beings, both as individuals and as entire nations, are the clay to be molded as He chooses. He says to us, "Can I not do with you, Israel, as this potter does? Like clay in the hand of the potter, so are you in my hand, Israel. If at any time I announce that a nation or kingdom is to be uprooted, torn down and destroyed, and if that nation I warned repents of its evil, then I will relent and not inflict on it the disaster I had planned" (Jeremiah 18:6–8).

Although God has always known what choice we will make, we are still free to make our own choice of our own free will. But we must accept the consequences of our choices.

A SIGH OF RELIEF

The Hebrew word that is translated *relent* or *reconsider* (or *repent* in other translations, including the King James Version) is *nacham*, a word that literally means "to groan or sigh with deep emotion, either a groan of grief, or a deep sigh of relief." So when God is said to *relent* or *reconsider* or *repent*, these English words are very weak words compared with the depth of emotion conveyed by the original Hebrew word.

In the original language, this passage of Scripture suggests that God responds to our repentance with a deep sigh of relief. God is relieved and happy that He no longer has to inflict His judgment and discipline on us. He is profoundly relieved that He can show us mercy and forgiveness instead. In effect, God is saying to the nation of Judah, and to all of us as His children, "If I am about to deal harshly with you because of your sin and rebellion, and then you turn back to me in repentance, I will heave a sigh of relief."

In 1961, the American government became aware that the Soviet Union was installing missiles in Cuba, and those missiles were aimed at the hearts of American cities. President John F. Kennedy reacted immediately. He ordered the US Navy to blockade the island of Cuba and stop and search any Soviet ships that were headed for Cuba. A naval blockade is an outright act of war. Both the United States and the Soviet Union were walking a tightrope. It was a time of global risk and uncertainty, and the entire world trembled at the horrifying prospect of nuclear war.

I will never forget how tense those days were, and I vividly recall the collective sigh of relief from the American people, and all the people of the world, when the Soviet Union backed down and removed its missiles from Cuba.

That sigh of relief the world experienced at the end of the Cuban Missile Crisis is similar to God's sigh of relief when His people repent of their sin. God, the Potter, has one goal in mind: to make us into beautiful, functional clay vessels according to His design. Nothing can stop Him from accomplishing His goal—not even our own stubborn will. But it pleases Him deeply when we freely choose obedience instead of rebellion. It pleases Him not to punish us.

God takes no pleasure in judging the human race or in disciplining individual people. He does not enjoy dealing harshly with us, though we often leave Him no choice. In the book of Lamentations, Jeremiah writes:

> For no one is cast off
>   by the Lord forever.
> Though he brings grief, he will show compassion,
>   so great is his unfailing love.
> For he does not willingly bring affliction
>   or grief to anyone. (Lamentations 3:31–33)

And the prophet Isaiah tells us that God's judgment is not the work He takes pleasure in. Instead, judgment is God's "strange work," His "alien task" (Isaiah 28:21). The act of inflicting pain or pressure on human beings conflicts with the desire of God's loving and merciful heart. That's why He is so patient with us, giving us many opportunities for repentance before He must bring pressure upon us. If we yield obediently to His touch, so that He does not have to inflict pressure on us, He breathes a sigh of relief.

But God sometimes breathes a sigh of sorrow, as we are about to see.

A SIGH OF SORROW

In the next two verses, we see the fingers of the Great Potter at work, preparing to radically reshape the clay that has deformed itself upon His wheel:

"Now therefore say to the people of Judah and those living in Jerusalem, 'This is what the LORD says: Look! I am preparing a disaster for you and devising a plan against you. So turn from your evil ways, each one of you, and reform your ways and your actions.' But they will reply, 'It's no use. We will continue with our own plans; we will all follow the stubbornness of our evil hearts.'" (Jeremiah 18:11–12)

God gives the people of Judah and Jerusalem every opportunity to repent, every chance to receive mercy and avert their own disaster. But the people stubbornly refuse to accept the will of God. They tell him, in effect, "Forget it, God! It's no use trying to reason with us, trying to warn us, trying to save us from our own stubbornness and sin. It's no use trying to be merciful to us. We reject your warnings and your mercy. We choose the consequences of disobedience."

So God heaves a sigh of sorrow and grief, and this is His response:

Therefore this is what the LORD says:

> "Inquire among the nations:
>   Who has ever heard anything like this?
> A most horrible thing has been done
>   by Virgin Israel.
> Does the snow of Lebanon
>   ever vanish from its rocky slopes?
> Do its cool waters from distant sources
>   ever stop flowing?
> Yet my people have forgotten me;
>   they burn incense to worthless idols,
> which made them stumble in their ways,
>   in the ancient paths.
> They made them walk in byways,
>   on roads not built up.
> Their land will be an object of horror
>   and of lasting scorn;
> all who pass by will be appalled
>   and will shake their heads.
> Like a wind from the east,
>   I will scatter them before their enemies;
> I will show them my back and not my face
>   in the day of their disaster." (18:13–17)

Here, the Lord expresses wounded amazement that the people of Judah would insist on rebelling against Him even though it means their own destruction. Why would people willingly choose sorrow instead of joy, suffering instead of healing?

God speaks of the snow on the Mount Lebanon range of mountains that extend along the Mediterranean coast. The highest peak of the Lebanon range is more than 10,000 feet in height, and there is snow on its slopes much of the year, sometimes even in the summertime. The runoff from melting snows feeds cold, refreshing streams in the lowlands of Lebanon and Israel.

These snowy mountains, and the continual blessing of the cold, refreshing streams that flow from those snows, represent the goodness of God. People who turn away from the goodness and refreshing provision of God are as foolish as people who would grow thirsty walking across the land, then cross a cool refreshing stream without taking a drink. Why would anyone do that? It makes no sense, yet that is what the people of Judah have chosen to do.

So the Potter heaves a deep and sorrowful sigh, then He takes the lump of clay, pushes it down, works His fingers into it, erasing every trace of its former shape so He can reshape it into something new and beautiful again.

To translate from metaphorical language to historical reality, God used the Babylonians to topple the walls of Jerusalem, tear the temple to the ground, remove all traces of the great culture and civilization of Judah, and carry the people off into exile in a foreign land. He smashed down the southern kingdom of Judah (he had already obliterated the northern kingdom of Israel, using the Assyrians as the instrument of His judgment, decades earlier), and He turned the nation into a formless lump. His plan was to bring Israel back into the land seventy years later and completely reshape the nation.

Although God took no pleasure in the destruction of Judah, he was prepared to carry out his "strange work" of judgment against His stubbornly disobedient people.

Jeremiah responds in the flesh

Following this statement by God, Jeremiah interjects a personal note. The king and other officials of the government of Judah are enraged over Jeremiah's warning of coming destruction. So they decide to take action against Jeremiah. The prophet writes:

> They said, "Come, let's make plans against Jeremiah; for the teaching of the law by the priest will not cease, nor will counsel from the wise, nor the word from the prophets. So come, let's attack him with our tongues and pay no attention to anything he says." (18:18)

Jeremiah's enemies have decided to squelch his prophetic message by ruining his reputation. They will defame him, smear him, and undermine his prophetic authority so no one will listen to him. Perhaps they had dug up some information on him (what politicians today call "opposition research") to twist into accusations against him. Or perhaps they simply made up a pack of lies about him.

This new attack on Jeremiah's reputation drove him back to the Lord in prayer. He ran to God, which is always the right place to go when you are under attack. This is the prayer Jeremiah prayed:

> Listen to me, LORD;
>   hear what my accusers are saying!
> Should good be repaid with evil?
>   Yet they have dug a pit for me.
> Remember that I stood before you
>   and spoke in their behalf
>   to turn your wrath away from them.
> So give their children over to famine;
>   hand them over to the power of the sword.
> Let their wives be made childless and widows;
>   let their men be put to death,
>   their young men slain by the sword in battle.
> Let a cry be heard from their houses

> when you suddenly bring invaders against them,
> for they have dug a pit to capture me
> and have hidden snares for my feet.
> But you, LORD, know
> all their plots to kill me.
> Do not forgive their crimes
> or blot out their sins from your sight.
> Let them be overthrown before you;
> deal with them in the time of your anger. (18:19–23)

Jeremiah has been interceding for the people of Judah—the people he loves. He is trying to save them from their own foolishness. He sees the destruction coming upon them, and he is shouting a warning to them to change course. He prays for the nation, he preaches to the nation, and he pleads with the nation to turn back to God and avoid the coming wrath.

And how do the leaders of the nation repay Jeremiah's efforts to save them? They seek to destroy his reputation. And that is just a first step. As we will later see, Jeremiah's enemies will eventually seek to take his life.

How does Jeremiah respond to the plot against his reputation? When his enemies slap him on one cheek, does he turn the other to be slapped as well? Does he pray for his enemies? Does he react the way the Lord would later prescribe in His Sermon on the Mount?

No. Jeremiah responds in a perfectly natural human way. He responds in the flesh. He doesn't pray *for* his enemies; he prays *against* them. He says in effect, "Get 'em, Lord! Kill their children in a famine! Kill the men with a sword, and make childless widows of their wives!" He is like so many people today who say, "I love humanity. It's *people* I can't stand."

Now, Jeremiah's reaction shouldn't surprise us. He is probably reacting no differently from the way you or I would in the same situation. His vindictive prayer against his enemies is simply a confirmation of what Jeremiah learned about himself in chapter 17, verse 9: "The heart is deceitful above all things and beyond cure. Who can understand it?"

Even the heart of a godly prophet can give way to the passions and temptations of the flesh. Even God's chosen spokesman can, under the pressure of opposition and attack, pray, "Wipe them out, Lord!" Think about how far this is from the response of the One who would pray from the cross, "Father, forgive them, for do not know what they are doing" (Luke 23:34).

One of the most instructive lessons of the book of Jeremiah is that this mighty prophet, who fulfilled a faithful ministry to the nation of Judah, had times of weakness and times of responding in the flesh.

THE SERMON AT THE GARBAGE HEAP

God responds to Jeremiah's prayer by giving him these instructions:

> This is what the LORD says: "Go and buy a clay jar from a potter. Take along some of the elders of the people and of the priests and go out to the Valley of Ben Hinnom, near the entrance of the Potsherd Gate. There proclaim the words I tell you, and say, 'Hear the word of the LORD, you kings of Judah and people of Jerusalem. This is what the LORD Almighty, the God of Israel, says: Listen! I am going to bring a disaster on this place that will make the ears of everyone who hears of it tingle. For they have forsaken me and made this a place of foreign gods; they have burned incense in it to gods that neither they nor their ancestors nor the kings of Judah ever knew, and they have filled this place with the blood of the innocent. They have built the high places of Baal to burn their children in the fire as offerings to Baal—something I did not command or mention, nor did it enter my mind. So beware, the days are coming, declares the LORD, when people will no longer call this place Topheth or the Valley of Ben Hinnom, but the Valley of Slaughter.'" (19:1–6)

God was sending Jeremiah back to the potter's house to buy a clay jar, a flask that had already been fired in the kiln. He was to take the jar outside the city gates at the southern part of Jerusalem, to the valley of Hinnom, which people in the New Testament days would know as the valley of Gehenna. It was a garbage dump, a place where trash and the bodies of dead animals were left to rot. It was a place where the bodies of criminals were dumped after execution. It was a vile and stinking place. Jeremiah was to go there and speak to the elders of the people and the senior priests. He was to tell them that God was going to bring disaster upon them for abandoning Him and turning to alien gods and sacrificing their own children to the fires of demonic idols.

This is a statement of God's sovereignty, the sovereignty of the Potter over the clay. Men make plans, but human plans always shatter when they come up against the plans of God.

The statement God told Jeremiah to make at the garbage heap at the valley of Hinnom continues:

> "'In this place I will ruin the plans of Judah and Jerusalem. I will make them fall by the sword before their enemies, at the hands of those who want to kill them, and I will give their carcasses as food to the birds and the wild animals. I will devastate this city and make it an object of horror and scorn; all who pass by will be appalled and will scoff because of all its wounds. I will make them eat the flesh of their sons and daughters, and they will eat one another's flesh because their enemies will press the siege so hard against them to destroy them.'" (19:7–9)

This prophecy was fulfilled, literally and precisely, a few years later when the armies of Nebuchadnezzar surrounded the city of Jerusalem and laid siege to it. The famine that resulted from the siege was so severe and horrifying that the people resorted to cannibalism and ate their own children. Then the Babylonian armies broke down the gates of the city and knocked the walls to the ground. Jerusalem became a scene of such destruction that anyone who passed by was amazed and horrified by its desolation.

CREATIONS OF THE POTTER'S HANDS

God also gave Jeremiah instructions about the clay jar he had purchased at the potter's house:

"Then break the jar while those who go with you are watching, and say to them, 'This is what the LORD Almighty says: I will smash this nation and this city just as this potter's jar is smashed and cannot be repaired. They will bury the dead in Topheth until there is no more room. This is what I will do to this place and to those who live here, declares the LORD. I will make this city like Topheth. The houses in Jerusalem and those of the kings of Judah will be defiled like this place, Topheth—all the houses where they burned incense on the roofs to all the starry hosts and poured out drink offerings to other gods.'" (19:10–13)

God is the Great Psychologist as well as the Great Potter. He knows that to convey a message powerfully and with impact you need to make that message visual, emotional, and memorable. So God told Jeremiah to employ a striking visual aid to make sure there was no mistaking His meaning. Jeremiah was to take the jar and violently smash it, to show the people what God was about to do to the nation of Judah.

I believe God is doing a similar work on an even larger scale as the world slides closer to the Great Tribulation. According to the prophetic Scriptures, the world is going to be wracked by suffering and catastrophes beyond our imagining, so that men's hearts will fail them out of fear. People will cry out against God for being harsh and unfair, even though they have only brought God's judgment upon themselves with their sin and idolatry.

The image of the Potter and the clay is an amazingly apt picture of our relationship to God. This image is not merely about judgment. It is also about God's law. The Potter does not hate His creations. He loves them. He doesn't smash the failed pot down into a shapeless mass of clay in a fit of rage. His goal is to reshape the clay into something new and beautiful and functional for His glory. That is the great lesson Jeremiah learned at the potter's house. It's a lesson we need to learn as well.

Jeremiah's prophecy about the Potter and the clay reminds me of Paul's second letter to Timothy, where he writes:

In a large house there are articles not only of gold and silver, but also of wood and clay; some are for special purposes and some for common use. Those who cleanse themselves from the latter will be instruments for special purposes, made holy, useful to the Master and prepared to do any good work. (2 Timothy 2:20–21)

We must never forget that we are the creations of the Potter's hands, and He has a sovereign right to use us in any way He chooses. We will feel the pressure of His fingers as He molds us and conforms us to His image. If we allow Him to do His perfect work through us, we will never have to suffer the pain of His "strange work." We can relax and trust Him, knowing that this Potter, through His Son Jesus, has suffered with us and knows how we feel.

Out of His great love for us, He is determined to form us into vessels that are beautiful and fit for the Master's use. The Potter sees all of time at once, and He has a purpose in mind for us. He has the skill and ability to fulfill that purpose, and He will perform His purpose through us, whether we respond in grateful obedience or we force Him, through our stubborn disobedience, to reshape us and make us over.

God has the sovereign right to make of us whatever He chooses, yet we have free will and the ability to choose to make it easier on ourselves by obeying Him. The people of Judah chose the hard way of disobedience.

May you and I have the wisdom to lovingly, gratefully, obediently cooperate with the wise and skilled hands of the Great Potter.

7

A BURNING
IN THE BONES

Jeremiah 20

Paul Robert Schneider was an evangelical pastor in Germany. After Adolf Hitler became chancellor of Germany in 1933, Schneider realized that Hitler was stoking hatred and anti-Semitism in Germany, and he became an early and outspoken critic of the Nazi leader. He became the Jeremiah of his day, calling for Hitler and the German people to repent, while warning that the nation faced judgment and destruction if it did not repent.

In early 1934, Schneider became the pastor of two congregations, one in Dickenschied, the other in Womrath. He joined the Confessing Church, an organization that sought to unify Protestant opposition to Hitler. Week after week, he boldly preached against Nazi hate and violence.

In June 1934, Pastor Schneider agreed to conduct a funeral for a member of the Hitler Youth organization, Karl Moog, who had died at age seventeen. In his eulogy, Schneider gave a powerful presentation of the gospel of Jesus Christ. After he spoke, a local Nazi party organizer, Heinrich Nadig, got up and spoke at length about the glory of belonging to the Hitler Youth, adding, "Comrade Karl Moog, you have now been enlisted in Horst Wessel's battalion in heaven." (Horst Wessel was a Nazi stormtrooper leader who had been murdered in 1930.)

Pastor Schneider stood up and refuted Nadig, saying that God would welcome young Karl Moog into heaven, but there was no stormtrooper battalion in heaven. Nadig argued back, and Pastor Schneider retorted sharply that he would not allow the Christian gospel to be contaminated during a Christian burial ceremony. Pastor Schneider was arrested the following morning and jailed for a week.

Schneider was also arrested without warrant in March 1935 for criticizing the Nazi government from his pulpit. During 1935 and 1936, he was interrogated a dozen times and told to stop speaking out against the Nazis. He told his interrogators that he would continue to follow his conscience. His friends and parishioners pleaded with him to stop speaking out, but he replied that God had called him to prepare the church for eternal life, not to ensure his own physical well-being or that of the church. He continued to preach that Hitler, the Nazi government, and the German people must repent of their sins and turn to Christ for salvation.

In 1937, the Nazis arrested him and sent him to Koblenz prison. After two months, Nazi officials released him, told him not to return to his church and to stop preaching, or else. He did stay away from his church for two months.

Then, on the morning of October 3, 1937, the Sunday of Harvest Thanksgiving, he returned and preached to his congregation at Dickenschied. Pastor Schneider told his parishioners, "Confessing Jesus will carry a price. For His sake we will come into much distress and danger, much shame and persecution. Happy the man who does not turn aside from these consequences." He ended by quoting the prophet Jeremiah: "O land, land, land, hear the word of the LORD!" (Jeremiah 22:29).

News of Pastor Schneider's sermon spread like wildfire. That evening, he was on his way to preach in the neighboring town of Womrath when he found the road blocked by police. They arrested him and took him to the concentration camp at Buchenwald. To prevent him from preaching the gospel to fellow prisoners, prison officials placed him in solitary confinement. They soon found that this meddlesome preacher just wouldn't shut up. He preached the good news of Jesus Christ to his fellow prisoners from the tiny window of his prison cell.

During his time at Buchenwald, Pastor Schneider was often beaten and tortured, but the prison guards could not break his spirit. On Easter Sunday, as the prisoners were assembled in the yard, Pastor Schneider climbed to the window of his cell and shouted, "Comrades, people are tortured and murdered here, so the Lord says, 'I am the resurrection and the life!'" Moments later, guards entered his cell and gave him another beating.

In July 1939, Pastor Schneider became ill and was taken to the camp infirmary. There, a guard injected him with a massive overdose of a heart stimulant, strophanthin. He died, the first Protestant martyr of the Nazi regime. He died as a twentieth-century Jeremiah—a fearless Christian witness who refused to be intimidated into silence.

Violently unrepentant

In the closing verses of Jeremiah 19 and on into Jeremiah 20, we encounter the first act of violence against Jeremiah. The last two verses of chapter 19 belong to the narrative of chapter 20. After delivering his dramatic speech to the leading officials of Jerusalem at the garbage heap at Hinnom, Jeremiah continues to issue a call for national repentance. His message encounters mounting opposition:

Jeremiah then returned from Topheth, where the LORD had sent him to prophesy, and stood in the court of the LORD's temple and said to all the people, "This is what the LORD Almighty, the God of Israel, says: 'Listen! I am going to bring on this city and all the villages

121

around it every disaster I pronounced against them, because they were stiff-necked and would not listen to my words.'"

When the priest Pashhur son of Immer, the official in charge of the temple of the LORD, heard Jeremiah prophesying these things, he had Jeremiah the prophet beaten and put in the stocks at the Upper Gate of Benjamin at the LORD's temple. (19:14–15; 20:1–2)

Jeremiah's enemies have crossed a line. They have gone from trashing his reputation to physical violence. They've beaten him bloody, then fastened him in stocks that bind his arms and legs, putting the bruised and battered prophet on public display. Anyone passing through the gate near the temple of Solomon would see him, suffering and humiliated. It was the kind of treatment normally reserved for Jerusalem's worst criminals.

The prophet's first encounter with violent persecution took place in the fourth year of the reign of King Jehoiakim. At this point, the armies of Nebuchadnezzar of Babylon were already marching toward Jerusalem. King Jehoiakim had heard of the approach of the Babylonians, and fear gripped the hearts of the people and the king himself. (This attack by Nebuchadnezzar in 597 BC would result in the death of Jehoiakim and the deportation of many high-ranking Jews; the siege and destruction of Jerusalem and the death of Zedekiah, Judah's last king, would take place around 586 BC.)

Jeremiah was sent by God to warn King Jehoiakim and the people of Jerusalem. This brutal beating and imprisonment in the stocks was Jerusalem's answer.

The book of Jeremiah is a testament to the patience of God. At this point in the narrative, Jeremiah has been pleading with the nation and warning the people *for twenty-two years,* and still God has stayed His hand of judgment. But the kingdom of Judah remains stubbornly and violently unrepentant.

There is a saying that "no good deed goes unpunished." That has certainly proven true in the life of the prophet Jeremiah. Many spiritually immature Christians have the notion that if you obey God and do what is right, you will never have any problems in life. In reality, our obedience to God is often the very thing that gets us into trouble. As Paul told his spiritual son Timothy, "everyone who wants to live a godly life in Christ Jesus will be persecuted" (2 Timothy 3:12).

Here is Jeremiah, locked in stocks, bleeding and bruised, the pain from his beating compounded by being forced into an unnatural and uncomfortable position, while being jeered and mocked and spat on by everyone who passed by. He would sit in those stocks through the heat of the day and the cold of the night. For what? For obeying God. For speaking God's truth. For trying to warn and save the very people who had beaten and imprisoned him in the stocks. He had no court to appeal to, no constitutional rights, no defense attorney, no journalists who would interview him and publish his side of the story. He was alone, one prophet versus the chief temple officer, the king, the leaders of the city, and the people of the kingdom of Judah.

And the opposition against him was getting more stubborn and more violent with each encounter.

DECEIVED BY GOD?

At this point, Jeremiah has reached the depths of discouragement. This prophet was no spiritual Superman, always rejoicing no matter how grim his circumstances, no matter how deep his pain. No, throughout the book of Jeremiah, he is candid with us about his spiritual low points—and this was definitely one of them. Cut him, and he bleeds. Beat him, and he experiences hurt and despair, just as you and I would.

The next time you find yourself in deep trouble, experiencing anxiety, fear, doubt, or despair, turn to Jeremiah 20 and realize that you are in good company. You will identify with Jeremiah as he seesaws between doubt and faith, between despair and hope, between questioning and confidence in God. One of the first emotions Jeremiah experiences in this situation is distrust and suspicion toward God:

> You deceived me, Lord, and I was deceived;
>   you overpowered me and prevailed.
> I am ridiculed all day long;
>   everyone mocks me. (20:7)

These are shocking words. Jeremiah charges God with lying to him, overpowering him, and placing him in a position where he is mocked and ridiculed. Have you ever felt that way toward God? Have you ever felt that God has deceived you, let you down, and tossed you aside? Jeremiah is probably thinking back to his youth, when God first called him to be a prophet. At that time, Jeremiah had told God he didn't feel qualified to be a prophet of the Lord. But God had responded with a counterargument:

> But the Lord said to me, "Do not say, 'I am too young.' You must go to everyone I send you to and say whatever I command you. Do not be afraid of them, for I am with you and will rescue you," declares the Lord.
>   Then the Lord reached out his hand and touched my mouth and said to me, "I have put my words in your mouth. See, today I appoint you over nations and kingdoms to uproot and tear down, to destroy and overthrow, to build and to plant." (1:7–10)

Jeremiah remembers God's promise to appoint him over nations and kingdoms, and now he is treated like a common criminal. In effect, he is saying to God, "What happened, Lord? What happened to your promise? You said you would be with me to rescue me. You said I would have authority to uproot and tear down! You said I would have the ability to build and plant! And here I am, bruised and bleeding, unable to move, threatened with death. Where is that rescue you promised? Lord, you deceived me. You let me down."

A wounded heart can easily feel this way toward God. You may have experienced such thoughts yourself in times of suffering and fear. But God has never lied to you, and God never lied to Jeremiah. God made promises to Jeremiah, and He will keep those promises. Like so many of us, Jeremiah interpreted God's promises to him in a superficial way. He made some faulty assumptions about those promises.

Jeremiah probably thought that when God promised to "rescue" him, it meant that God would shield him from any harm or hurt. But God never said that. In fact, the word *rescue* implies that there will be danger and harm that he would need to be rescued from. If we are never in danger, we'll never need to be rescued.

It may be that Jeremiah had some youthful misconceptions about himself. He saw himself as a prophet who would go before the people, declare God's word to them, and God would give His angels charge over him, keeping him safe from the anger of the crowd. Where were those angels? Why didn't they keep him out of the stocks? Why didn't they prevent him from being beaten? So Jeremiah, in the depths of his discouragement and disillusionment, charged God with lying to him.

Lying, of course, is the one thing God cannot do (see Numbers 23:19; 1 Samuel 15:29; Titus 1:2; Hebrews 6:18). He always keeps His promises. Yet Jeremiah feels, as you have probably felt at one time or another, that God has failed His promise. I cannot count the number of people who have come to me and said, "Pastor, I know what the Bible says, I know what God promised, but I've done that, and it doesn't work. God's promise isn't true." That was Jeremiah's predicament.

TERROR ON EVERY SIDE

The second complaint Jeremiah makes is fascinating. Nowhere in verse 7 does Jeremiah complain about being beaten and bloodied, nowhere does he complain of his pain and the discomfort of the stocks. What does he complain about? Being mocked. Being made a laughingstock.

Parents teach their children a little rhyme to give them a perspective on being mocked and taunted: "Sticks and stones will break my bones, but names will never hurt me." Yet Jeremiah seems more wounded by the mockery, jeering, and name-calling than the physical beating he has suffered.

Perhaps you can identify with Jeremiah. You might feel that a physical pummeling is easier to take then mockery—especially when that mockery comes from people you are trying to warn, people you are trying to save, people who won't listen. There are some who could mock you, and you'd scarcely even hear it. There are others who could speak to you with the faintest hint of sarcasm, and it would wither your soul. The mockery of the people of Jerusalem got under Jeremiah's skin and depleted his spirit. It caused him to doubt God's caring for him.

Jeremiah's message of judgment was unwelcome in Judah. He delivered God's warning to the people with devastating logic, and the people had no answer to his message. So they answered him the only way they could—with ridicule and ad hominem attacks. This is always the refuge of petty minds. When people cannot argue their point rationally, they attack their opponent personally and try to destroy him.

So as Jeremiah languished in the stocks, groaning in his pain, they laughed at him, they ridiculed him, even as the fierce Babylonian enemy was marching toward them, as Jeremiah had predicted. Ridicule is hard to bear. Mockery is as corrosive as battery acid. It had taken its toll on Jeremiah and his faith.

Jeremiah continues his complaint:

> Whenever I speak, I cry out
> proclaiming violence and destruction.
> So the word of the LORD has brought me
> insult and reproach all day long.
> But if I say, "I will not mention his word
> or speak anymore in his name,"
> his word is in my heart like a fire,
> a fire shut up in my bones.
> I am weary of holding it in;
> indeed, I cannot. (20:8–9)

Jeremiah finds he has an inner conflict, an unbearable tension within himself. He has always loved God, wanted to serve God, and wanted to speak God's word. Just a few chapters back, he gloried in God's message and declared:

> When your words came, I ate them;
>> they were my joy and my heart's delight,
> for I bear your name,
>> LORD God Almighty. (15:16)

Now, however, he finds that the prophetic message of God has only brought him insult and reproach. Yet, if he were to stop preaching, God's message would be like a fire in his bones, burning in his heart, desperate to be spoken. He can't keep from speaking God's word, yet whenever he speaks, he suffers unbearable consequences.

What can he do? How can he resolve this seemingly insoluble tension?

Have you ever experienced what Jeremiah calls "a fire shut up in my bones" (20:9)? Maybe you haven't been called to preach. But perhaps you have seen some injustice in your family, your church, your community—some scandalous conduct, some act of abuse, and even though you feared to speak out, you couldn't keep quiet about it. You knew that if you spoke up, no one would thank you. In fact, you would expose yourself to attacks and ridicule. If you've ever felt that way, then you know something of the feelings Jeremiah struggled with.

Jeremiah goes on to say that he has been living in a state of fear and insecurity:

> I hear many whispering,
>> "Terror on every side!
>> Denounce him! Let's denounce him!"
> All my friends
>> are waiting for me to slip, saying,
> "Perhaps he will be deceived;
>> then we will prevail over him
>> and take our revenge on him." (20:10)

There is no one Jeremiah can trust—no friend, no family member, no counselor, no ally of any kind. Even people he used to consider friends now whisper against him. His fears have reached a paranoiac level; there is terror on every side. Everyone is out to get him. He even feels that God has deceived him.

This is a vivid description of how fear can seize the mind and distort reality to such a degree that we actually come to believe that God, our truest, most faithful Friend, has turned on us. This is also a fitting description of satanic attack. For clearly, Satan is mentally and emotionally assaulting God's prophet, trying to silence him and prevent him from speaking God's message.

If you have ever gone through a feeling that everyone has turned against you and that even God has abandoned you, then you know you can't talk yourself out of those feelings with intellectual arguments. The problem confronting you is not intellectual in nature—it is spiritual.

Now, to some degree, Jeremiah's outlook is accurate. His friends really have abandoned him. His nation really has turned against him. He has been beaten and mocked. Where his perception of reality has become distorted is in his relationship with God.

Jeremiah has begun to think that God would lie to him. His painful circumstances have twisted his perception of God. And there is only one solution to this problem, only one way to correct the distortions in his thinking about God: Jeremiah must return to his original faith in God. And that is what Jeremiah does next:

> But the LORD is with me like a mighty warrior;
>   so my persecutors will stumble and not prevail.
> They will fail and be thoroughly disgraced;
>   their dishonor will never be forgotten.
> LORD Almighty, you who examine the righteous
>   and probe the heart and mind,
> let me see your vengeance on them,
>   for to you I have committed my cause. (20:11–12)

Jeremiah's faith comes to rescue him and strengthen him. Faith provides a counterattack to the assault of Satan against his mind and emotions. Jeremiah fights back against Satan's assault of lies by lobbing a bombardment of God's truth at the enemy. Jeremiah reminds himself that God is with him like a mighty warrior. Even though Jeremiah is being mocked now, his persecutors will be disgraced. The Lord examines the righteous, and He is their Defender.

THE DARK NIGHT OF THE SOUL

Whenever your mind is being assaulted by Satan or by frightening circumstances, it's time to return to the basic truths of your faith. Begin with God. He is unchangeable, He is loving, He is the One who sees reality as it is. Ask Him to help you see reality clearly and accurately. Ask Him to lead you into an understanding of the truth.

That's what Jeremiah does here. He starts with God. He affirms that the Lord is with him, a mighty warrior who knows how to repel the assaults of Satan and wicked men. Therefore, Jeremiah can be assured that his enemies will fail. Once Jeremiah is able to see reality clearly, he is able to lift his heart in praise to God:

> Sing to the LORD!
> Give praise to the LORD!
> He rescues the life of the needy
> from the hands of the wicked. (20:13)

I'm reminded of the account in Acts 16 when Paul and Silas were beaten and thrown into a dungeon in Philippi and, like Jeremiah, fastened into stocks. At midnight, they began singing praises to God because their faith was focused on the greatness and glory of God and not on their circumstances. This is what Jeremiah had to learn to do—to sing praises to God in those "midnight" times of life.

It's only natural to sink into despair when people turn against us, when we are beaten and bloody, when everything we do meets with opposition. But God calls us to move from a *natural* reaction to a *supernatural* reaction. He calls us to sing praises to Him as we place our trust in Him. And let's not pretend this is easy to do.

In this passage, we see Jeremiah vacillating between a natural reaction to his circumstances (bitterness and despair) and a supernatural reaction (praise and trust in God). And in the next few verses, he sinks back into an even deeper despair than before:

> Cursed be the day I was born!
> May the day my mother bore me not be blessed!
> Cursed be the man who brought my father the news,
> who made him very glad, saying,
> "A child is born to you—a son!"
> May that man be like the towns
> the LORD overthrew without pity.
> May he hear wailing in the morning,
> a battle cry at noon.
> For he did not kill me in the womb,
> with my mother as my grave,
> her womb enlarged forever.
> Why did I ever come out of the womb
> to see trouble and sorrow
> and to end my days in shame? (20:14–18)

I believe Jeremiah has recorded for us the thoughts that went through his mind at about three in the morning, during his imprisonment in the stocks. He had been doing fine until around midnight, but his faith began to fade and his despair began to grow from midnight until three a.m. I can't prove this is true from the text; I'm just reading between the lines. But I think this is a likely interpretation of Jeremiah's state of mind.

A sixteenth-century Christian mystic, St. John of the Cross, once wrote about an experience Christians often go through, which he described as "the dark night of the soul through which the soul passes on its way to the Divine Light." He suggested that a time of deep despair often precedes a breakthrough to a deeper faith. Novelist F. Scott Fitzgerald, in his essay collection *The Crack-Up*, offered a commentary on this observation by St. John of the Cross: "In the real dark night of the soul, it is always three o'clock in the morning."

I think Jeremiah had reached his dark night of the soul, and it was either literally or figuratively three o'clock in the morning, the darkest hour of the night. In that hour, he cursed the day he was born, cursed the man who brought his father the news that he was born, and cursed the fact that he ever came out of the womb to live a life of trouble, sorrow, and shame. Clearly, Jeremiah has see-sawed from praising God to cursing the day of his birth in the space of a few hours.

I am not criticizing this great prophet of God. I doubt that I would have handled such an ordeal more nobly than he did. His physical pain was undoubtedly excruciating. His mental and emotional anguish were beyond imagining. And he had to endure these sufferings completely alone. That experience would try your soul and test your faith to the breaking point.

And it is there, in that extreme frame of mind, that Jeremiah ends this part of the narrative. Perhaps he was able to get a few hours of fitful sleep before the sun came up. We don't know. He doesn't say.

GOD WATCHES OVER HIS WORD

But if we turn back in the narrative to verses 3 through 6, we see what Jeremiah did in the morning:

The next day, when Pashhur released him from the stocks, Jeremiah said to him, "The LORD's name for you is not Pashhur, but Terror on Every Side. For this is what the LORD says: 'I will make you a terror to yourself and to all your friends; with your own eyes you will see them fall by the sword of their enemies. I will give all Judah into the hands of the king of Babylon, who will carry them away to Babylon or put them to the sword. I will deliver all the wealth of this city into the hands of their enemies—all its products, all its valuables and all the treasures of the kings of Judah. They will take it away as plunder and carry it off to Babylon. And you, Pashhur, and all who live in your house will go into exile to Babylon. There you will die and be buried, you and all your friends to whom you have prophesied lies.'" (20:3–6)

The name *Pashhur* means a "cleaver" or "splitter" or "divider." The name fits. Pashhur was always dividing people up, stirring up animosity, and creating opposing factions. Jeremiah said, "The LORD's name for you is not Pashhur, but Terror on Every Side" (v. 3). In other words, he was a man who generated fear all around, who made one side distrustful of the other. He would divide and conquer by playing on people's fears and pitting people against each other.

During the night, Jeremiah was consumed with bitterness and despair. By morning, he was as steady as a rock. What happened to change his attitude? Jeremiah doesn't say. He only leaves hints. But I have a guess.

I think it's likely that sometime during his dark night of the soul Jeremiah felt the word of God burning in his bones. The word of God triumphed over his trembling heart. The word proved true.

Jeremiah discovered what many of us have had to learn during long hours of anxiety and despair: "The one who is in you is greater than the one who is in the world" (see 1 John 4:4). God is greater than our enemy.

Jeremiah thought back about the word and its power and about what God's word had accomplished in the past. Something happened in the heart and soul of this struggling prophet, who was beaten and bloodied and bound hand and foot in wooden stocks. Somehow, strength seeped into his depleted soul. His ebbing faith rebounded. His failing courage came roaring back.

In the morning, when Pashhur the Divider showed up with the keys in his hand and a smirk on his face, the prophet Jeremiah looked Pashhur in the eye with a gleam of ferocity and boldness. Jeremiah told the temple official the message God had given him: "The LORD's name for you is not Pashhur, but Terror on Every Side. . . ."

Perhaps, as Jeremiah eyed Pashhur while rubbing the circulation back into his wrists and ankles, he recalled the words God spoke to him years earlier, recorded in the first chapter of the book of Jeremiah: "I am watching to see that my word is fulfilled" (1:12).

Even though it may take some time, even though God's timetable is not our timetable, even though we may have to endure suffering and injustice and mockery for the sake of God's message and God's glory, we can know that God is watching over His Word to see that it will be fulfilled. In our pain, in those dark, three a.m. nights of the soul, we may be tempted to doubt God or blame Him, but the morning always comes . . .

And with the morning, comes new light, a new day, new strength, and new blessings from our heavenly Father.

8

WHY THE
LAND MOURNS

Jeremiah 21–25

Of all the operations and strategies of war, one of the cruelest is the siege. In a siege, a military force surrounds a city or fortress, cutting essential supply lines, causing suffering and starvation within the city. The goal is to force the inhabitants to capitulate. The history of siege warfare is a history of misery, death, and devastation.

One of the most famous sieges in history was the siege of the ancient island city of Tyre in 332 BC. Tyre presented a unique problem to Alexander the Great and his Macedonian army. The city walls, standing 150 feet high, were built up to the sea, leaving no shore where Alexander could land his ships.

So Alexander sealed off the island with a seven-month-long naval blockade. During this time, Alexander's men built a causeway (land bridge) from the mainland almost to the walls of Tyre. Then he brought catapults and battering rams out onto the causeway to attack the city. Once the walls were breached, Alexander's forces poured into the city and slaughtered thousands of malnourished soldiers and civilians. Alexander ordered hundreds crucified, and he sold 30,000 people, mostly women and children, into slavery. Over the centuries, Alexander's causeway collected sand and silt, turning the island into a peninsula. The Siege of Tyre not only changed history but it changed geography as well.

One of the few cities ever besieged on American soil was Vicksburg, Mississippi, in 1863. In May of that year, Union Major General Ulysses S. Grant surrounded Confederate forces commanded by Lt. General John C. Pemberton at Vicksburg. Grant had his men dig trenches and cut off supply lines to keep the Confederates bottled up. Grant even had his men dig a tunnel and detonate a bomb under the city's fortifications, but the Confederates quickly sealed the breach.

After a siege of about six weeks, Pemberton surrendered. The defeat of the Confederates at Vicksburg gave the Union control of the Mississippi River and effectively cut the Confederacy in half. It was a major turning point in the Civil War.

One of the cruelest siege operations in history was the Babylonian siege of Jerusalem. The siege began after years of conflict between the kingdom of Judah and the Babylonian Empire. Here is a brief timeline of that period:

Babylon first invaded Judah in 605 BC, the year Nebuchadnezzar became king of Babylon. At that time, Jehoiakim was king of Judah. In that invasion, Nebuchadnezzar seized treasures from the royal palace and the temple of Solomon. A number of young princes of Judah were deported to Babylon—the first wave of deportations. Among them was a young man named Daniel and three of his friends: Hananiah, Azariah, and Mishael (better known by their Babylonian names: Shadrach, Meshach, and Abednego).

The next invasion of Judah by the Babylonians took place in 597 BC, when Jehoiachin became king of Judah. The Babylonians captured Jerusalem and forced a second deportation of Jews to Babylon. Among those deported was King Jehoiachin, who had only reigned for a little more than three months after the death of Jehoiakim. Nebuchadnezzar installed Jehoachim's uncle, Zedekiah, as a vassal king under the control of the Babylonian Empire.

But King Zedekiah was foolish and arrogant. In the ninth year of his reign, he revolted against Babylon and aligned himself with Pharaoh Hophra of Egypt, the sworn enemy of King Nebuchadnezzar of Babylon. Enraged, Nebuchadnezzar responded by again invading Judah (see 2 Kings 25:1).

Nebuchadnezzar laid siege to Jerusalem in December 589 BC. As related in 2 Kings 25 and Lamentations 4, Nebuchadnezzar's forces surrounded the walls of the city, and the people within were driven to cannibalism by the scourge of starvation. The siege lasted thirty months and ended with the complete destruction of the city and the temple of Solomon in 586 BC. The Babylonians plundered the city's wealth, including all of the bronze, silver, and gold utensils of the temple. They slaughtered most of the city's population, and they led thousands of Jews into captivity in Babylon. The Babylonians left only a few people behind to tend the land on behalf of their Babylonian overlords.

HE WILL DESTROY THE CITY WITH FIRE

As we come to Jeremiah 21, we are seeing the beginning stages of the siege of Babylon in 589 BC. King Zedekiah is on the throne—the last and weakest of all the kings of Judah. The royal house of Israel, which began with King Saul and King David, is now coming to an end. Nebuchadnezzar's army is marching toward Jerusalem, and King Zedekiah sends a hasty, panic-stricken message to Jeremiah, asking him to intercede with God on behalf of the kingdom:

> The word came to Jeremiah from the LORD when King Zedekiah sent to him Pashhur son of Malkijah and the priest Zephaniah son of Maaseiah. They said: "Inquire now of the LORD for us because Nebuchadnezzar king of Babylon is attacking us. Perhaps the LORD will perform wonders for us as in times past so that he will withdraw from us." (21:1–2)

King Zedekiah sounds very pious, doesn't he? He asks Jeremiah to intercede with God, hoping that after all of the sins of the nation and all of the ignored warnings God will simply let bygones be bygones, and He will miraculously rescue Judah from the advancing Babylonians. The king of Judah is not very different from people today who think God exists only to get them out of trouble and rescue them from the consequences of their sins. They imagine that they can go on living as sinfully as they please, ignoring God's Word, pretending their actions have no consequences, and God will make everything come out okay. The moment they realize their sin is about to be exposed or their sin has brought a disease into their lives or they are about to lose their marriage or job or reputation, they pray desperately for God to work a miracle on their behalf.

But why should God work a miracle on behalf of the disobedient? He has already given plenty of warnings. At some point, it's time to reap what we have sown.

Many seem to view God as the genie from Aladdin's lamp. You rub the lamp, and the genie appears and says, "Your wish is my command." But God is not our personal genie who exists to grant our wishes. We are not His master; He is ours. God is gracious. God is patient. But He is sovereign, and He will not be mocked.

After leading the nation deeper into sin, idolatry, and disrespect toward God, King Zedekiah wanted God to miraculously pull his fat out of the fire. To the king's dismay, Jeremiah told him that not only would God *not* help Judah but that He was also going to help Babylon fight *against* Judah:

> But Jeremiah answered them, "Tell Zedekiah, 'This is what the LORD, the God of Israel, says: I am about to turn against you the weapons of war that are in your hands, which you are using to fight the king of Babylon and the Babylonians who are outside the wall besieging you. And I will gather them inside this city. I myself will fight against you with an outstretched hand and a mighty arm in furious anger and in great wrath. I will strike down those who live

in this city—both man and beast—and they will die of a terrible plague. After that, declares the LORD, I will give Zedekiah king of Judah, his officials and the people in this city who survive the plague, sword and famine, into the hands of Nebuchadnezzar king of Babylon and to their enemies who want to kill them. He will put them to the sword; he will show them no mercy or pity or compassion.'" (21:3–7)

Why did God tell King Zedekiah, "I will fight against you"? Had Zedekiah reached the point of no return with God? No. There is a way King Zedekiah could have found mercy and grace from God, and even at that late hour—as the Babylonians were marching toward Jerusalem to destroy the city—God would have saved Jerusalem from destruction. What could Zedekiah have done? He could have knelt before God, confessed his evil deeds, and called upon God for mercy. If he had sought God with a heart of genuine contrition and repentance, God would have turned aside from His wrath, and He would have responded to his plea for help.

God sees the heart. He would know if Zedekiah was sincere or not. He would know if the king was trying to bargain with God and manipulate Him—or if he was crying out to God in genuine contrition and repentance.

The theme of Jeremiah's message to the king is summarized in verse 10: "I have determined to do this city harm and not good, declares the LORD. It will be given into the hands of the king of Babylon, and he will destroy it with fire." This message from God, delivered through the prophet Jeremiah, should have been enough to terrify the king into genuine repentance. But it was not.

Up to this point, Jeremiah has been delivering his messages through the king's subordinates and advisors. In Jeremiah 22, however, God tells the prophet to go and speak to King Zedekiah in person:

This is what the LORD says: "Go down to the palace of the king of Judah and proclaim this message there: 'Hear the word of the LORD to you, king of Judah, you who sit on David's throne—you, your officials and your people who come through these gates.'" (22:1–2)

Jeremiah chapters 22 through 25 record the message Jeremiah delivered directly and personally to King Zedekiah. In this message, Jeremiah traces the recent history of Judah's disobedience. As you read through these chapters, you can't help being struck by the similarity between the sins of Judah and the sins of our world today. If God warned Judah of the coming day of judgment for its sin and rebellion against God, can we expect God to permit our sin and rebellion to go on forever?

THE FIRST RESPONSIBILITY OF LEADERS: SHEPHERD THE FLOCK

The heart of Jeremiah's message is that the leaders of the nation—the king and the elders of the kingdom—have failed God and failed His people in two important areas of their leadership responsibilities. Jeremiah confronts the king with these two failures in a powerful way. He summarizes the first failing of Judah's leaders in chapter 23:

> "Woe to the shepherds who are destroying and scattering the sheep of my pasture!" declares the LORD. Therefore this is what the LORD, the God of Israel, says to the shepherds who tend my people: "Because you have scattered my flock and driven them away and have not bestowed care on them, I will bestow punishment on you for the evil you have done," declares the LORD. (23:1–2)

Who are the "shepherds" that God, through Jeremiah, speaks of here? They are the kings and elders of the nation. Throughout the Old and the New Testaments, God uses the imagery of sheep and shepherds when speaking of His concept of government. Leaders are to view themselves as shepherds of the people, watching over them, defending their rights, and protecting their lives, well-being, and property.

The first failure Judah's leaders are guilty of is this: They have not been good shepherds. Instead of guarding God's flock, they have scattered the flock. They have neglected and mistreated the flock. The people do not belong to the leaders; they belong to God, and the leaders are to be good stewards of His flock.

In chapter 22, Jeremiah sets forth the rightful responsibilities of government. What are presidents, prime ministers, representatives, governors, and so forth expected to do, in God's view?

> This is what the LORD says: Do what is just and right. Rescue from the hand of the oppressor the one who has been robbed. Do no wrong or violence to the foreigner, the fatherless or the widow, and do not shed innocent blood in this place. (22:3)

The king, his counselors and advisors, the elders of the city, the priests of the temple—all the leaders of the nation of Judah and the city of Jerusalem—had failed in their duty to the people. Through their faithlessness, they had led the people into idolatry and apostasy. Through their corruption, they had oppressed and robbed the people. Through their injustice, they had committed violence against foreigners and denied justice to widows and orphans. Through their cruelty and greed, they had murdered the innocent.

These same kinds of injustices are committed in our own nations today. We see it in our nations' capitals, in state and provincial legislatures, and at the local level. People elect representatives, expecting their leaders to work on behalf of the people. But leaders sometimes end up serving special interests instead of serving the people.

Often we see greed even in our religious leaders, those who are supposed to be spiritual shepherds to God's sheep. Many have become fabulously wealthy, flying around in private jets while preaching a "prosperity gospel" or some other false gospel. Like the priests of ancient Judah, they are polluting the truth of God's Word with false philosophies and leading the people into error and idolatry.

God will hold all leaders responsible for the way they have led. Rulers and leaders who set an example of righteousness, justice, integrity, and godliness, whether in the arena of government or the realm of religion, will have God's blessings. But "shepherds" who lead the "sheep" astray or take advantage of the "sheep" for their own dishonest gain will face the judgment of God.

In Romans 13, the apostle Paul sets forth a principle that might surprise you: Every government leader, every elected or appointed official, from the chief executive on down, is a minister of God. This is true whether that person is a believer or not, and whether that person knows it or not. It's true whether or not that person is a good and godly steward of that government office. It's true even if that person is a crook, a cheat, a money-grubbing thief, or a cruel tyrant. If that leader is guilty of wrongdoing in office, then he or she has much more guilt to answer to God for than an ordinary citizen would.

THE SECOND RESPONSIBILITY OF LEADERS: DO NO WRONG

The second responsibility of government leaders is: "Do no wrong." Do not mistreat the foreigners among you. Do not exploit or abuse the widows and orphans. In other words, leaders need to defend those in our society who are least able to defend themselves.

There have been times in the past when the United States has mistreated foreigners and minorities in America. Native Americans (American Indians) have been cheated, exploited, and forced off their land. African Americans have been enslaved and subjected to segregation. Asian immigrants worked for starvation wages to build America's railroads. Japanese Americans were place in internment camps during World War II, and they often lost their homes, businesses, and property for good. Latin American immigrants have been exploited in low-wage jobs for many years. The Jews, Arabs, Poles, and Irish have been exploited, denied rights, vilified, and discriminated against over the years. The list goes on and on.

Both legal and illegal immigrants to America have been exploited because immigrants tend to be vulnerable and powerless. They don't always know their rights, and they often don't understand the language. Although every nation has a right and an obligation to secure its borders and manage immigration in a way that protects national security, no immigrant, legal or illegal, should ever be treated with disrespect or violence. All governments have a responsibility to protect the weakest people within its borders against abuse and humiliation—from immigrants and foreigners to widows and orphans.

In order for a country to protect its weakest residents, its laws and our courts must be honest and just. "Do not shed innocent blood in this place," God says through Jeremiah. "Justice" should not mean that those who can afford the best lawyer can get away with anything, although, all too often, that's exactly what it has come to mean. A nation's laws and court decisions should not merely be about following procedures, but about truly determining innocence or guilt, right or wrong, just or unjust. When people begin to see the laws as being rigged to favor one group over another, respect for the law vanishes, and people begin to despise and ignore the law.

The divinely ordained task of government is to see that justice is meted out fairly in the courtroom, that the law truly makes no distinction between rich and poor or powerful and powerless, that the guilty are punished and the innocent are freed, and that victims are defended from the oppressors. King Zedekiah and his royal administration had failed in meeting this standard, and the prophet detailed the shocking depths of his failure:

> "Woe to him who builds his palace by unrighteousness,
>   his upper rooms by injustice,
> making his own people work for nothing,
>   not paying them for their labor.
> He says, 'I will build myself a great palace

with spacious upper rooms.'
So he makes large windows in it,
panels it with cedar
and decorates it in red." (22:13–14)

Throughout history, kings have always felt entitled to live like—
well, like kings! They want the best of everything—the biggest homes,
the grandest furnishings, solid gold plumbing fixtures, and cedar-
paneled rooms with red-velvet drapes. Even as the nation was going
bankrupt, even as a hostile enemy was marching toward the city gates,
King Zedekiah was redecorating the palace in high style. Yet he was
building his palace on a foundation of unrighteousness and injustice.

Jeremiah goes on to compare the lavish and exploitative lifestyle of
Zedekiah with that of Israel's last righteous king, Zedekiah's father,
Josiah. Zedekiah was the third son of Josiah, and his name at birth was
Mattaniah, meaning "Gift of God." However, King Nebuchadnezzar
of Babylon renamed him Zedekiah when installing him as a puppet
king, according to 2 Kings 24:17. Jeremiah describes the moral and
ethical standard set by righteous Josiah:

"Does it make you a king
to have more and more cedar?
Did not your father have food and drink?
He did what was right and just,
so all went well with him.
He defended the cause of the poor and needy,
and so all went well.
Is that not what it means to know me?"
declares the LORD. (22:15–16)

Isn't that an insightful question? This is what it means to know
God—to let your actions be controlled by your love of righteousness
and justice, by your concern for the poor and needy. If you demonstrate
the love and mercy of God, doesn't that indicate that you truly know
God in a personal way? Josiah was a king who loved his people and

knew his God. Josiah's son Zedekiah showed by his actions that he loved only himself, and he didn't know God at all.

THREE EVIL KINGS

The prophet Jeremiah cites three evil kings of Judah. First, he speaks of Shallum, which is another name of Jehoahaz, who went down to Egypt:

> For this is what the LORD says about Shallum son of Josiah, who succeeded his father as king of Judah but has gone from this place: "He will never return. He will die in the place where they have led him captive; he will not see this land again." (22:11–12)

Jeremiah also cites the example of Jehoiakim, one of the sons of Josiah:

> Therefore this is what the LORD says about Jehoiakim son of Josiah king of Judah:
>
> "They will not mourn for him:
>   'Alas, my brother! Alas, my sister!'
> They will not mourn for him:
>   'Alas, my master! Alas, his splendor!'
> He will have the burial of a donkey—
>   dragged away and thrown
>   outside the gates of Jerusalem." (22:18–19)

A third evil king listed is Coniah, another name for Jehoiachin, son of Jehoiakim:

> "As surely as I live," declares the LORD, "even if you, Jehoiachin son of Jehoiakim king of Judah, were a signet ring on my right hand, I would still pull you off. I will deliver you into the hands of those who want to kill you, those you fear—Nebuchadnezzar king of Babylon and the Babylonians." (22:24–25)

Coniah was just twenty-three years old when he became king. After a reign of only three months and ten days, he was deposed by the Babylonians and led away to spend the rest of his life in captivity in Babylon. God makes an amazing statement about him:

> This is what the LORD says:
> "Record this man as if childless,
>   a man who will not prosper in his lifetime,
> for none of his offspring will prosper,
>   none will sit on the throne of David
>   or rule anymore in Judah." (22:30)

This is a verse with prophetic significance, because it means the end of the Solomonic line of succession. Up to this time, all the kings of Judah had been descendants of King Solomon, the son of David. But the line of succession ended with Coniah. No man of that line would ever rule on the throne of Judah again.

The prophetic significance of this verse lies in the fact that the messianic prophecies state that Jesus the Messiah will be descended from the house of David. The New Testament genealogies of Jesus show that Joseph, the stepfather of Jesus, was the son of David through Coniah (or Jehoiachin). A biological son of Joseph could not sit on the throne of Judah. Had Jesus been Joseph's natural son, he would not have had the right to be king of Judah. But because he was the birth son of Mary, who was also a descendant of David through Nathan, a brother of Solomon, Jesus had the right to rule from the throne of David. It's amazing how God ties history together and works in ways we cannot anticipate.

Next, Jeremiah describes a vision of the true Shepherd. For the first time in this great prophecy, Jeremiah looks down through the centuries and foresees the coming of the One who would fulfill God's ideal of a Shepherd-King—the one who would carry out all of God's requirements for justice and godly leadership:

"The days are coming," declares the LORD,
  "when I will raise up for David a righteous Branch,
a King who will reign wisely
  and do what is just and right in the land.
In his days Judah will be saved
  and Israel will live in safety.
This is the name by which he will be called:
  The LORD Our Righteous Savior." (23:5–6)

The apostle Paul completed this prophecy of Jeremiah when he applied the title "Our Righteous Savior" to Jesus in 1 Corinthians 1:30: "It is because of him that you are in Christ Jesus, who has become for us wisdom from God—that is, our righteousness, holiness and redemption." Jesus is our righteousness, our holiness, our redemption—in other words, He is our Righteous Savior.

Jeremiah foresaw the Messiah coming as the rightful and righteous King, and through him, "Judah will be saved and Israel will live in safety" (Jeremiah 23:6). The fulfillment of this part of the prophecy still lies in the future, because for now, Judah is not saved and Israel lives in a state of constant peril and threat of war with neighboring nations.

But one day the Messiah will establish His reign on the throne of David. On that day Judah will be saved. On that day, Israel will dwell securely forevermore.

WHEN THE CHURCH FAILS THE NATION

Corruption in the government of Judah is bad enough, but Jeremiah now turns his attention to an even more troubling issue:

Concerning the prophets:

My heart is broken within me;
  all my bones tremble.
I am like a drunken man,

like a strong man overcome by wine,
because of the LORD
and his holy words.
The land is full of adulterers;
because of the curse the land lies parched
and the pastures in the wilderness are withered.
The prophets follow an evil course
and use their power unjustly. (23:9–10)

Behind the king stands the prophet. When the heart of the king goes astray, it is the job of the prophet, the preacher, to confront and correct the king. But if the heart of the prophet is evil, there is no one to hold the king accountable—and there is no hope for that land or its people.

There was a cancer at the heart of the nation of Judah, a terminal condition that could not be cured. This too required God's judgment. Jeremiah said:

Therefore this is what the LORD Almighty says concerning the prophets:

"I will make them eat bitter food
and drink poisoned water,
because from the prophets of Jerusalem
ungodliness has spread throughout the land." (23:15)

If we equate the prophets of Jeremiah's day to pastors and other religious leaders of our day, we can sense a challenge that needs to be heeded. The church is supposed to be a good example in the world, raising moral standards, proclaiming God's truth, and holding the government accountable for its actions, just as Jeremiah held the government of Judah accountable. Perhaps our nations would be improved if the church were to stand strong on the essential values and teachings of God's Word.

What is Jeremiah's accusation against the priests of Jerusalem (who were the "church" of that day)?

This is what the LORD Almighty says:

> "Do not listen to what the prophets are prophesying to you;
>   they fill you with false hopes.
> They speak visions from their own minds,
>   not from the mouth of the LORD." (22:16)

If the nation is growing weaker instead of stronger, it's because the religious establishment is not living in obedience to God. The prophets of Judah were not speaking the words of God, but they were proclaiming lies and made-up visions from their own imaginations. Instead of speaking the truth about God's coming judgment against sin, they preached pious-sounding platitudes, claiming that everything was going to work out. There was no need for confession of sin, no need for national repentance. There was nothing to worry about, nothing at all.

The prophets of Judah were filling the people with false hopes. Meanwhile, the Babylonians were coming to shatter the walls of the city and drench the streets with blood. Soon the air would ring with the screams of the dying and the wailing of mourners. But the prophets were assuring the people that everything was going to be just fine. Jeremiah warns:

> They keep saying to those who despise me,
>   'The LORD says: You will have peace.'
> And to all who follow the stubbornness of their hearts
>   they say, 'No harm will come to you.'
> But which of them has stood in the council of the LORD
>   to see or to hear his word?
> Who has listened and heard his word? (23:17–18)

The prophets were preaching their own message from their own imaginations, not God's truth. We can see this as a reminder that Bible-teaching churches throughout the world today must stick closely to the clear teaching of God's word based on strong, biblical hermeneutics—not on concepts, new or old, that veer from orthodox faith.

Over the years, we regularly held workshops for pastors at our church. During those workshops, we would study the Word of God together. At the close of each workshop, we would ask our participants to evaluate the sessions, and there were always a few pastors who would express anger—not at me or the workshop but at the seminary where they trained for the ministry.

They would say, "Why didn't my seminary teach me how to study and teach the Scriptures? The things I've learned in these sessions have been so practical and powerful—yet I've never heard these things before! The seminaries should be teaching pastors how to dig deeply into God's Word and expound it to their congregations, but I was never taught how to do this."

I'm not suggesting that all or most seminaries are deficient in this regard, but I do know that some seminaries teach new pastors how to preach their own opinions from the pulpit instead of the Word of God. Some seminaries turn out pastors who have never been trained to "correctly [handle] the Word of truth" (2 Timothy 2:15). And that means the congregations of these pastors are being starved for truth. And when those who are called to be shepherds of God's flock do not stand in the council of God, nor do they see and hear His Word, there is no one left to hold the government and society accountable for its sins.

Like the prophets and priests of Judah, the church sometimes fails to hold forth the truth of God's Word. When that happens, the church can no longer be effective in helping any nation that is in crisis.

FALSE PROPHETS, FALSE ASSURANCES

Jeremiah condemns those who falsely speak for God, those who claim, "The LORD says: You will have peace. No harm will come to you." We hear many such voices today—gurus of godless religions that preach an amoral morality:

- All you need is love.
- To live a good life, just think good thoughts.
- Don't worry about the moral rules contained in some old book—think freely and live freely.
- God didn't create man in His image, man created God in his image.
- God is whatever you want Him (or Her) to be.
- You are God, if you choose to be.
- There is no sin, only unhealthy thinking.
- There is no such thing as sexual sin or cheating on your marriage—there is just love, love, love in all its many forms.
- Live as you please, do whatever makes you happy in the moment, and there will be no consequences.

These are dangerous philosophies, but they are the teachings of some religious groups today. These ideas were also the religion of Judah in Jeremiah's day: "The LORD says: You will have peace. No harm will come to you." That is why Judah was destroyed, and that is why any nation, including our own, will inevitably lose its strength and fall apart. When teachers claim God's authority to say what God didn't tell them to say, when prophets and preachers lie in God's name, the heart of the nation will be eaten away. The people will starve for truth because they are not being fed from the Word of God.

God, speaking through Jeremiah, draws a contrast between the false prophets of Judah and a true prophet from God:

> "I did not send these prophets,
>   yet they have run with their message;
> I did not speak to them,
>   yet they have prophesied.
> But if they had stood in my council,
>   they would have proclaimed my words to my people
> and would have turned them from their evil ways
>   and from their evil deeds." (23:21–22)

To speak *for* God, a man must first speak *to* God. He has to stand in the *council* of God before he can speak the *counsel* of God to a congregation or a nation.

When I was a young pastor, lacking both experience and confidence, I preached sermons that I had more or less borrowed from great Bible teachers. Oh, I didn't plagiarize. I didn't borrow from them verbatim. But I leaned heavily on the insights of men I admired. I think every young man in ministry does so at the beginning.

But I gradually learned that God had to speak to my heart first before I could speak to a congregation. It wasn't enough to borrow someone else's fire. I had to have God's fire in my own soul, or I could never ignite the hearts of other people. I realized I had to stand in God's council and hear His words, or I would have nothing to share with my congregation.

God's indictment of the false prophets continues:

"I have heard what the prophets say who prophesy lies in my name. They say, 'I had a dream! I had a dream!' How long will this continue in the hearts of these lying prophets, who prophesy the delusions of their own minds? They think the dreams they tell one another will make my people forget my name, just as their ancestors forgot my name through Baal worship. Let the prophet who has a dream recount the dream, but let the one who has my word speak it faithfully. For what has straw to do with grain?" declares the LORD. "Is not my word like fire," declares the LORD, "and like a hammer that breaks a rock in pieces?

"Therefore," declares the LORD, "I am against the prophets who steal from one another words supposedly from me. Yes," declares the LORD, "I am against the prophets who wag their own tongues and yet declare, 'The LORD declares.' Indeed, I am against those who prophesy false dreams," declares the LORD. "They tell them and lead my people astray with their reckless lies, yet I did not send or appoint them. They do not benefit these people in the least," declares the LORD. (23:25–32)

The business of a preacher is to take what God has said in the Bible and to place it before the people faithfully, fully, and without diluting or polluting it. The truth of God's Word, honestly expounded to the people, is what will transform individuals and eventually save a nation from delusion and preserve it from destruction. God's ministry, He says, is like a fire that burns out impurities, or like a hammer that shatters falsehoods and illusions. So-called "prophets" can talk all they want about the dreams they've dreamed, but God's Word pounds away with honesty and realism, showing people the world as it really is.

GRACE IN HARDSHIP

Jeremiah concludes his great confrontational message to King Zedekiah in chapters 24 and 25. There he recalls how God dealt with Zedekiah's predecessor, Jehoiachin, the son of Jehoiakim, also known as Coniah. He was the king who only reigned for three months and ten days before being dethroned and taken captive by the Babylonians. Babylonian court records have been found in Iraq confirming that Coniah was held captive in Babylon and that he and his family were allowed a daily ration of food. These records, inscribed in clay tablets in cuneiform writing, were discovered in the ruins of Babylon by German archaeologist Robert Johann Koldewey in the early twentieth century.

Coniah was one of about three thousand Jews who were deported to Babylon. Nebuchadnezzar wanted to bring the best-educated and most highly skilled Jews to Babylon, where they would contribute to making the Babylon Empire great. Of Coniah and the other exiles, Jeremiah says:

> After Jehoiachin son of Jehoiakim king of Judah and the officials, the skilled workers and the artisans of Judah were carried into exile from Jerusalem to Babylon by Nebuchadnezzar king of Babylon, the LORD showed me two baskets of figs placed in front of the temple of the LORD. One basket had very good figs, like those that ripen early; the other basket had very bad figs, so bad they could not be eaten.
>
> Then the LORD asked me, "What do you see, Jeremiah?"
>
> "Figs," I answered. "The good ones are very good, but the bad ones are so bad they cannot be eaten."

Then the word of the LORD came to me: "This is what the LORD, the God of Israel, says: 'Like these good figs, I regard as good the exiles from Judah, whom I sent away from this place to the land of the Babylonians. My eyes will watch over them for their good, and I will bring them back to this land. I will build them up and not tear them down; I will plant them and not uproot them. I will give them a heart to know me, that I am the LORD. They will be my people, and I will be their God, for they will return to me with all their heart. (24:1–7)

How do you react when you are under the disciplining hand of God, when the only way He can get through to you is by allowing trouble into your life? What are you to do? Jeremiah sets before King Zedekiah three things he was to remember.

First, *accept the disciplining hand of God as the very best hope for you.* God gave Jeremiah a vision of two baskets of figs. One was a basket of good figs, the other of rotting, inedible figs. God told him that the figs were like people. The good figs represented people who had been carried captive to Babylon.

Now, this is astonishing. If you had lived in Judah in those days, you would have said, "The worst thing that could happen would be a lifetime of exile in Babylon." But God was saying, in effect, "No, captivity in Babylon is a sign of My grace and mercy toward you." In fact, He says, "My eyes will watch over them for their good, and I will bring them back to this land. I will build them up and not tear them down.... They will be my people, and I will be their God, for they will return to me with all their heart."

Of course, the deposed king, Coniah, was not being exiled for his good. He was not a "good fig." He was going to be dealt with harshly in Babylon because he had dared to defy King Nebuchadnezzar.

But the rest of the exiles were beneficiaries of God's grace. God was telling them, in effect, "This time of exile is going to be painful and unpleasant, but it will cure you, heal you, and set you straight. This is actually the best thing that could happen to you, because if you had still been living in Judah when the final destruction comes, you would experience more horrors and sufferings than you can imagine."

GOOD FIGS AND BAD

The real horrors that are to come are reserved for King Zedekiah and the other city elders and citizens who remain in Jerusalem during the final, awful siege that Nebuchadnezzar will impose on the city. Inspired by God, Jeremiah tells King Zedekiah what is about to happen to the "bad figs" like the king himself:

> "'But like the bad figs, which are so bad they cannot be eaten,' says the LORD, 'so will I deal with Zedekiah king of Judah, his officials and the survivors from Jerusalem, whether they remain in this land or live in Egypt. I will make them abhorrent and an offense to all the kingdoms of the earth, a reproach and a byword, a curse and an object of ridicule, wherever I banish them. I will send the sword, famine and plague against them until they are destroyed from the land I gave to them and their ancestors.'" (24:8–10)

God's admonition is to accept what He is doing as His best for you. If you are walking in His will, if you are seeking to obey Him, then you can know that His love and grace will triumph in your life, no matter what your circumstances may be.

Second, *wait for the measured end that God has planned*. Jeremiah said to King Zedekiah:

> Therefore the LORD Almighty says this: "Because you have not listened to my words, I will summon all the peoples of the north and my servant Nebuchadnezzar king of Babylon," declares the LORD, "and I will bring them against this land and its inhabitants and against all the surrounding nations. I will completely destroy them and make them an object of horror and scorn, and an everlasting ruin. I will banish from them the sounds of joy and gladness, the voices of bride and bridegroom, the sound of millstones and the light of the lamp. This

whole country will become a desolate wasteland, and these nations will serve the king of Babylon seventy years.

"But when the seventy years are fulfilled, I will punish the king of Babylon and his nation, the land of the Babylonians, for their guilt," declares the LORD, "and will make it desolate forever." (25:8–12)

For a time, God was going to allow Babylon to discipline and restore the "good figs" of Judah and destroy the "bad figs" of Judah. But Babylon's oppression of the land of Judah would be limited to seventy years. Why did God choose that specific length of time for the exile of the remnant of Judah? We know from other passages of Scripture that this was the length of time that Israel had failed to allow the land to enjoy its sabbath, as God had commanded (see Leviticus 26 and 2 Chronicles 36:21). For four hundred and ninety years, the people had worked the land, and not once had they observed the sabbatical year and allowed the land to lie fallow for one year.

The people of Judah owed the land seventy sabbatical years. So God sent the people to Babylon for seventy years to allow the land to enjoy its sabbath.

God always sets a time limit on His discipline toward us. It's painful to undergo a time of God's discipline, but it's a comfort to know that His chastening only lasts for a while, and then it's over. It will pass. Therefore, while you are under the hand of God's disciplining love, wait for the measured end that God has planned.

Third, *expect a widening circle of cleansing*. God told Jeremiah to expect a widening circle of cleansing beginning with Judah and spreading out to all the nations around. "But when the seventy years are fulfilled," God says, "I will punish the king of Babylon and his nation, the land of the Babylonians, for their guilt, and will make it desolate forever." When God has finished cleansing Judah, He will widen that circle and He will cleanse the Babylonians for their cruelty and violence toward His chosen people.

God uses the image of a cup of wine. First one nation will drink from it, then it will pass the cup to its neighbor—and so the circle of cleansing and discipline will widen as the nations become drunk with the judgment of God. Jeremiah writes:

> This is what the LORD, the God of Israel, said to me: "Take from my hand this cup filled with the wine of my wrath and make all the nations to whom I send you drink it. When they drink it, they will stagger and go mad because of the sword I will send among them."
>
> So I took the cup from the LORD's hand and made all the nations to whom he sent me drink it: Jerusalem and the towns of Judah, its kings and officials, to make them a ruin and an object of horror and scorn, a curse—as they are today; Pharaoh king of Egypt, his attendants, his officials and all his people, and all the foreign people there; all the kings of Uz; all the kings of the Philistines (those of Ashkelon, Gaza, Ekron, and the people left at Ashdod); Edom, Moab and Ammon; all the kings of Tyre and Sidon; the kings of the coastlands across the sea; Dedan, Tema, Buz and all who are in distant places; all the kings of Arabia and all the kings of the foreign people who live in the wilderness; all the kings of Zimri, Elam and Media; and all the kings of the north, near and far, one after the other—all the kingdoms on the face of the earth. And after all of them, the king of Sheshak will drink it too. . . .
>
> "See, I am beginning to bring disaster on the city that bears my Name, and will you indeed go unpunished? You will not go unpunished, for I am calling down a sword on all who live on the earth, declares the LORD Almighty." (25:15–26, 29)

When God begins a work in your life, He may use other people and the harm they do to teach you to rely on Him and cling to Him all the more. He will turn the harm they intended for you into blessing, deeper faith, and stronger character. Then God will turn to those who set out to harm you, and He will deal with their sin and disobedience.

As you demonstrate Christlike character and faith in those times of trial, those who tried to hurt you will learn from your example. Some may even come to repentance and faith in Christ. Whether they choose disobedience and God's judgment or repentance and God's mercy, God's cleansing hand will keep widening the circle; and He will redeem your sufferings in a beautiful way.

Finally, God describes himself as a mighty storm:

> This is what the Lord Almighty says:
> "Look! Disaster is spreading
>   from nation to nation;
> a mighty storm is rising
>   from the ends of the earth." (25:32)

God is stirring up a great and mighty storm, increasing in intensity century by century, which will in the end bring about the final day of judgment.

"For it is time for judgment to begin with God's household," said Peter, "and if it begins with us, what will the outcome be for those who do not obey the gospel of God?" (1 Peter 4:17). As we are subjected to God's judgment, as He searches our hearts and minds and we come to confession and repentance and we turn from our sin, we have to acknowledge that there is much within us to be judged: evil thoughts and evil speech, sinful habits, greed and coveting, lust and faithlessness, lies, and gossip.

God's judgment begins with us and it will reach beyond us, throughout our neighborhoods, across our states, throughout our nation, and around the world. God's storm of judgment is passing among men and women like a cyclone, bringing the cleansing of repentance and the cleansing of judgment. This truth should fill us with urgency in our witness to the people around us: "Don't wait, turn to Christ for forgiveness and mercy. Call on the name of the Lord and be saved!"

A time will come when all the frightening, soul-destroying scenes of Revelation come to pass, when this old world passes away, and when a new heaven and a new earth come into view. As the circle of cleansing spreads around the globe, I want all the people I know and love to hear the good news of Jesus Christ. I want them to escape God's judgment and take refuge in His mercy.

Don't think, "There will always be more time. God is in no hurry. Judgment will wait." For twenty-three years, Jeremiah begged the people of Judah to turn to God before it was too late. The people of Jerusalem always thought there would be more time. Then one day they looked out over the city walls, and they saw the vast army of Babylon camped before the gates.

The time of delaying had ended. The time of cleansing had come. The siege had begun.

A time of cleansing is coming for the whole world. Let's spread the good news of Jesus Christ while there is still time.

9

WHO KNOWS?

Jeremiah 26–29

Aleksandr Solzhenitsyn (1918–2008) was a Russian writer and a devout Christian who spoke with a prophetic voice in the tradition of Jeremiah. His books *One Day in the Life of Ivan Denisovich*, *Cancer Ward*, and *The Gulag Archipelago* exposed the horrors of the forced labor camp system in the Soviet Union. He was awarded the Nobel Prize for Literature in 1970.

For speaking out against the corrupt and abusive Soviet system, Solzhenitsyn was imprisoned or exiled from his home from 1945 to 1956, and he miraculously survived cancer during that time. He was threatened, reviled, and slandered by the government, and his work was banned. He was expelled from the Soviet Union and stripped of his Russian citizenship in 1974.

In 1978, Harvard University conferred an honorary degree in literature on Solzhenitsyn, and he gave the commencement address, entitled "A World Split Apart." His speech shocked the nation. Political liberals and political conservatives alike were outraged because the

Soviet dissident spoke out—*not* against the moral bankruptcy of the Soviet Union, as most people expected he would, but against the spiritual bankruptcy and corrupt materialism of America and Western civilization.

He excoriated the worldview of those in America who taught that there was no God, no battle between good and evil in the world, and no higher goal then attaining "happiness" through materialism. The world, Solzhenitsyn declared, was divided between two contrasting worldviews: democratic capitalism in the West and totalitarian communism in the East. Yet these two opposing worldviews had one thing in common that was leading the human race toward destruction: godless materialism. Both the East and West had rejected moral absolutes and the authority of God over the affairs of men.

"Is it true that man is above everything?" Solzhenitsyn asked. "Is there no Superior Spirit above him?" Godlessness—the absence of any sense of human responsibility or accountability to God—had become as pervasive in American culture and American entertainment media as it was in the officially atheist society of the Soviet Union. Godlessness had become the prevailing worldview of Western media, Western politics, and Western culture.

Solzhenitsyn's speech ignited a firestorm of controversy. James Reston of *The New York Times* called the speech "the wanderings of a mind split apart." Former presidential speechwriter Arthur Schlesinger, Jr., complained that Solzhenitsyn was advocating "a Christian authoritarianism governed by God-fearing despots."

Of course, Solzhenitsyn was not advocating anything of the kind. He was simply reminding the world that humanity must one day be judged by God, and if human society, whether in the democratic West or the communist East, continued to treat God as an irrelevant myth rather than our Creator and Judge, civilization is doomed.

Persecuted and imprisoned by Soviet despots, misunderstood and condemned by the American media elites, Solzhenitsyn could be buoyed by only one group that cheered his prophetic speech:

Bible-believing Christians. We Christians knew that Solzhenitsyn spoke the truth, because he issued essentially the same warning that Jeremiah delivered to the nation of Judah: Godlessness will destroy a nation, whether that nation is a communist evil empire or a lust-crazed, hedonistic, materialistic America. Jeremiah stood alone against a godless world, and so did Aleksandr Solzhenitsyn. The result, for both of these thundering prophets, was censure and persecution. As Solzhenitsyn said (and Jeremiah would have agreed), "Truth seldom is sweet; it is almost invariably bitter."

We are about to witness Jeremiah delivering yet another bitter dose of truth to the godless government of Judah. However, the head of the government he confronts is not Zedekiah, but a different godless king.

THREATENED WITH DEATH

The prophet Jeremiah didn't write his book in chronological order but rather as a series of themes. The narrative jumps back and forth in time. In Jeremiah 26, the prophet gives us a flashback to the beginning of the reign of King Jehoiakim, the son of King Josiah. He looks back to the days when Jehoiakim first came to the throne—years before the reign of Zedekiah.

God had sent Jeremiah to weak, vain, godless King Jehoiakim. Jeremiah was commissioned by God to deliver a message of warning about the destruction that awaited Judah, a nation steeped in idolatry, a nation that refused to repent.

Yet embedded within that stern warning is God's heartbeat of love and mercy. He longs to see people turn to him in repentance, to be delivered from sin and judgment. Jeremiah writes:

> Early in the reign of Jehoiakim son of Josiah king of Judah, this word came from the LORD: "This is what the LORD says: Stand in the court-yard of the LORD's house and speak to all the people of the towns of Judah who come to worship in the house of the LORD. Tell them everything I command you; do not omit a word. Perhaps they will

listen and each will turn from their evil ways. Then I will relent and not inflict on them the disaster I was planning because of the evil they have done. (26:1–3)

Again and again throughout Scripture, we see that God does not delight in judgment. He longs to see His people turn and listen and repent, so that He may sigh with relief and not have to deal harshly with them. God goes on to tell Jeremiah:

> "Say to them, 'This is what the LORD says: If you do not listen to me and follow my law, which I have set before you, and if you do not listen to the words of my servants the prophets, whom I have sent to you again and again (though you have not listened), then I will make this house like Shiloh and this city a curse among all the nations of the earth.'" (26:4–6)

These are not empty threats. God means what He says. God is sovereign over the affairs of men. He lifts one nation up and brings another down. It's reassuring to remember that God is in control of the nations. Whether the leader of a nation is a godly believer or a godless atheist, that leader cannot resist the sovereign will of God. Ungodly leaders like King Nebuchadnezzar of Babylon, King Cyrus of Persia, and the pharaohs of Egypt didn't love God, didn't serve God, didn't believe in God, but they did what God told them to do, like it or not. So-called "sovereign nations" are only sovereign where human affairs are concerned. God is sovereign over the nations.

Next, we come to a scene I call "The Impeachment of Jeremiah." The prophet Jeremiah has just delivered God's message to the leaders of the nation, and as Aleksandr Solzhenitsyn observed, truth is not sweet, but bitter. By speaking God's truth, Jeremiah had poked the hornets' nest:

> The priests, the prophets and all the people heard Jeremiah speak these words in the house of the LORD. But as soon as Jeremiah finished telling all the people everything the LORD had commanded him to say,

the priests, the prophets and all the people seized him and said, "You must die! Why do you prophesy in the LORD's name that this house will be like Shiloh and this city will be desolate and deserted?" And all the people crowded around Jeremiah in the house of the LORD. (26:7–9)

This is an official gathering at the temple, a trial at which Jeremiah has been accused, impeached, and convicted by the people. The religious authorities in the nation, the false prophets and the priests, are behind the plot against Jeremiah. The charge is serious—nothing less than treason, the crime of betraying his own nation.

Jeremiah had prophesied that the city of Jerusalem would be left desolate and the great temple of Solomon would be destroyed. This was an outrage to the people. They believed that because the temple was God's house, God would defend it and preserve it—even if they had comingled the worship of God with the worship of idols. They smugly thought themselves invulnerable to attack, because they thought God would never let anything happen to His temple and His holy city.

When Jeremiah prophesied the destruction of the city and the temple, the people were infuriated, and they charged him with blasphemy and treason. The rest of Jeremiah 26, beginning with verse 10, gives us an account of the trial of Jeremiah before the officials of the nation:

> When the officials of Judah heard about these things, they went up from the royal palace to the house of the LORD and took their places at the entrance of the New Gate of the LORD's house. Then the priests and the prophets said to the officials and all the people, "This man should be sentenced to death because he has prophesied against this city. You have heard it with your own ears!" (26:10–11)

The entrance of the New Gate of the temple was the judgment chamber where the trial was held. It's possible that among the officials of the nation were Daniel and his three friends, Mishael, Hananiah, and Azariah, because they were young noblemen of the house of Judah.

This scene took place before the first wave of captives were led away to Babylon. So there may have been a few godly men among the ungodly officials of the nation.

Although Jeremiah was on trial for his life, he made no attempt to defend himself or soft-pedal his message. Instead, he pressed ahead, intensified his warnings, and dared the officials to add the murder of God's prophet to their long list of sins:

> Then Jeremiah said to all the officials and all the people: "The LORD sent me to prophesy against this house and this city all the things you have heard. Now reform your ways and your actions and obey the LORD your God. Then the LORD will relent and not bring the disaster he has pronounced against you. As for me, I am in your hands; do with me whatever you think is good and right. Be assured, however, that if you put me to death, you will bring the guilt of innocent blood on yourselves and on this city and on those who live in it, for in truth the LORD has sent me to you to speak all these words in your hearing." (26:12–15)

This is godly courage on display. Jeremiah cares only about delivering God's message, loudly and clearly. He leaves his fate in God's hands. He is an excellent role model for you and me.

If you are doing God's will and someone accuses you falsely and unjustly, entrust the battle to God. Let Him be your Defender and Shield. This does not mean God will necessarily rescue you from your accusers and attackers. Down through the centuries, many Christians have fearlessly spoken God's truth—and have been martyred for it. But we are called to speak the truth whether we live or die.

Jesus spoke the truth regardless of the cost to himself. As the apostle Peter reminds us, "When they hurled their insults at him, he did not retaliate; when he suffered, he made no threats. Instead, he entrusted himself to him who judges justly" (1 Peter 2:23). That is what Jeremiah does here.

What does it take to silence a prophet of the Lord? The officials of Judah threatened Jeremiah with death, yet they could not shut him up.

What does it take to silence you? What does it take to silence me? If we are honest, we have to admit that there have been times when we have feared to speak up for Christ and His gospel. Are we afraid of being killed for our faith? No. We fear what others might think of us, we fear being thought "uncool," we fear being considered a "fanatic." If we are afraid to speak God's truth because of what others might think of us, how will we ever take a stand for Christ when our lives are on the line?

THE VERDICT

Next, Jeremiah reveals the outcome of the trial:

Then the officials and all the people said to the priests and the prophets, "This man should not be sentenced to death! He has spoken to us in the name of the LORD our God."

Some of the elders of the land stepped forward and said to the entire assembly of people, "Micah of Moresheth prophesied in the days of Hezekiah king of Judah. He told all the people of Judah, 'This is what the LORD Almighty says:

"'Zion will be plowed like a field,
Jerusalem will become a heap of rubble,
the temple hill a mound overgrown with thickets.'

"Did Hezekiah king of Judah or anyone else in Judah put him to death? Did not Hezekiah fear the LORD and seek his favor? And did not the LORD relent, so that he did not bring the disaster he pronounced against them? We are about to bring a terrible disaster on ourselves!"

(Now Uriah son of Shemaiah from Kiriath Jearim was another man who prophesied in the name of the LORD; he prophesied the same things against this city and this land as Jeremiah did. When King Jehoiakim and all his officers and officials heard his words, the king was determined to put him to death. But Uriah heard of it and fled in fear to Egypt. King Jehoiakim, however, sent Elnathan son of

Akbor to Egypt, along with some other men. They brought Uriah out of Egypt and took him to King Jehoiakim, who had him struck down with a sword and his body thrown into the burial place of the common people.)

Furthermore, Ahikam son of Shaphan supported Jeremiah, and so he was not handed over to the people to be put to death. (26:16–24)

The official verdict of this trial: not guilty. God moved in the hearts of the officials of the nation. I'm sure that if Daniel and his godly friends were among those officials, they may well have had an important role in seeing that God's will was done.

It was a tradition in the Jewish culture of that day that once the sentence had been pronounced by the court, certain elders of the people would stand up and confirm the sentence by recalling God's actions in the past. Therefore, some of the elders stood and spoke about two incidents in the history of the nation—one from the distant past and one from recent history.

The incident from the past concerned the prophet Micah. He had stood before King Hezekiah and predicted that God's judgment would fall against Jerusalem and the nation. Hezekiah repented, and God spared the nation.

The more recent incident concerned a prophet named Uriah, who is not mentioned anywhere else in Scripture. He stood before King Jehoiakim himself and predicted destruction for the nation. (This shows that Jeremiah was not the only prophet who preached a message of repentance in Judah. In addition to Jeremiah and Uriah, the prophet Habakkuk was also calling for the nation of Judah to repent at this time.) King Jehoiakim was enraged and ordered Uriah to be put to death, so Uriah fled to Egypt. However, the king had him brought back and executed him with a sword.

The elders concluded that if they had Jeremiah killed, they would bring destruction upon themselves by God's own hand. They confirmed the verdict of the court; Jeremiah was not guilty and would not be executed.

THE YOKE OF OPPRESSION

In Jeremiah 27, we leap over a period of about a dozen years to the time of Zedekiah, the last king of Judah. Nebuchadnezzar has made Zedekiah a vassal-king, subservient to the authority and power of the Babylonian Empire. Now a council of nations surrounding Israel has sent ambassadors to Jerusalem to plot a rebellion against Nebuchadnezzar. So God has a word for Jeremiah to give to King Zedekiah, and it is accompanied by another visual aid to heighten the impact of the message: "Early in the reign of Zedekiah son of Josiah king of Judah, this word came to Jeremiah from the LORD: This is what the LORD said to me: 'Make a yoke out of straps and crossbars and put it on your neck'" (27:1–2).

God told Jeremiah to go to the carpenter's shop and have a large wooden yoke made—two wooden crossbars, hand-carved to fit around the neck, held together with straps, like those used to yoke a team of oxen together. Jeremiah wore this yoke around his neck, probably for a number of months, to lend visual and symbolic impact to his message from the Lord.

Next, God told Jeremiah what his message would be. The prophet Jeremiah was to direct his message to all the surrounding nations, and it would be an unpleasant and unwelcome prophetic word. God said:

> "Then send word to the kings of Edom, Moab, Ammon, Tyre and Sidon through the envoys who have come to Jerusalem to Zedekiah king of Judah. Give them a message for their masters and say, 'This is what the LORD Almighty, the God of Israel, says: "Tell this to your masters: With my great power and outstretched arm I made the earth and its people and the animals that are on it, and I give it to anyone I please. Now I will give all your countries into the hands of my servant Nebuchadnezzar king of Babylon; I will make even the wild animals subject to him. All nations will serve him and his son and his grandson until the time for his land comes; then many nations and great kings will subjugate him." (27:3–7)

It is instructive to read this section of Jeremiah alongside Daniel 2. By the time God gave Jeremiah these prophetic instructions, Daniel had been a captive in Babylon for a number of years. Daniel tells of a dream Nebuchadnezzar had one night. The Babylonian wise men, enchanters, magicians, and diviners were unable to interpret it. Only Daniel, God's captive prophet in Babylon, was able to tell Nebuchadnezzar his dream and the interpretation of it, because God himself revealed the dream to Daniel. In that dream, King Nebuchadnezzar saw a towering statue made of different metals: gold, silver, bronze, iron, and iron mingled with clay. The statue depicted Nebuchadnezzar as the head of all the nations of the day, just as God declares to Jeremiah in chapter 27.

Here in Jeremiah's prophecy, God says that all the surrounding nations will become subject and subservient to King Nebuchadnezzar of Babylon and his successors until the Babylonian Empire is defeated and subjugated. If you read through the book of Daniel, you will see that Daniel serves Nebuchadnezzar and his successors until Cyrus, King of Persia, conquers and subjugates Babylon—exactly as God foretold to Jeremiah.

Many people are puzzled by God's actions in history. Why does God raise up a godless people—the cruel and arrogant Babylonians? Why does God call the king of Babylon "My servant Nebuchadnezzar"? Why does God give this godless nation authority and power that no other nation can resist? Why does God give the godless Babylonians the right and the power to punish His own chosen people, to destroy Jerusalem and the great Temple of Solomon, and to uproot His people and carry them off into captivity in an alien land?

Down through the centuries we have seen nations rise and fall. We have seen godless nations ride a wave of violent conquest. One of the most recent such occurrences was the rise of godless communism in the twentieth century. We wonder why God permits millions of people to come under the brutal authority of Stalin, Mao, Pol Pot, Ho Chi Minh, or Fidel Castro. The church comes under cruel, relentless persecution in those nations. Yet we often find that the church that suffers persecution is a church that is refined and purified.

One of the great lessons of history, and of the book of Jeremiah, is that God is in control of history. He does not *cause* the wickedness and oppression that men do, but He can take human evil, the result of human choices and human free will, and weave it into His eternal plan. No actions of a wicked despot ever take God by surprise. Dictators think they are the most powerful pieces on the chessboard, but they are pawns in the hand of our sovereign Lord.

Nebuchadnezzar's ascendancy to world supremacy was the beginning of what Jesus called "the times of the Gentiles." In Luke 21:24, He said, "Jerusalem will be trampled on by the Gentiles until the times of the Gentiles are fulfilled." In June 1967, the old city of Jerusalem was recaptured by the army of Israel. For the first time since Nebuchadnezzar's day, the old city was once again under Jewish control, under sovereign authority of the government of Israel. I believe this marks the end of the times of the Gentiles, the last of those strange periods of history that God has marked out in which His people would be subservient to the nations around them. We are seeing God's purposes being fulfilled in our own lifetime.

Under God's direction, the prophet Jeremiah goes on to tell the kings of the nations:

> "If, however, any nation or kingdom will not serve Nebuchadnezzar king of Babylon or bow its neck under his yoke, I will punish that nation with the sword, famine and plague, declares the LORD, until I destroy it by his hand. So do not listen to your prophets, your diviners, your interpreters of dreams, your mediums or your sorcerers who tell you, 'You will not serve the king of Babylon.' They prophesy lies to you that will only serve to remove you far from your lands; I will banish you and you will perish. But if any nation will bow its neck under the yoke of the king of Babylon and serve him, I will let that nation remain in its own land to till it and to live there, declares the LORD." (27:8–11)

When a nation becomes unstable and begins to disintegrate, false prophets invariably arise to confuse the people with lying words. God, through the prophet Jeremiah, warns the nations not to listen to false prophets, diviners (fortune tellers), interpreters of dreams, mediums (those who channel the spirits of the dead), and sorcerers (those who seek hidden knowledge and mystic powers from the demonic world). The rise of the occult, the prevalence of soothsayers and sorcerers, is evidence of moral and social disintegration. The prophecies of false prophets are nothing but lies that lead the people away from God and His will.

God, through Jeremiah, sends this same warning specifically and personally to King Zedekiah:

> "I gave the same message to Zedekiah king of Judah. I said, "Bow your neck under the yoke of the king of Babylon; serve him and his people, and you will live. Why will you and your people die by the sword, famine and plague with which the LORD has threatened any nation that will not serve the king of Babylon? Do not listen to the words of the prophets who say to you, 'You will not serve the king of Babylon,' for they are prophesying lies to you. 'I have not sent them,' declares the LORD. 'They are prophesying lies in my name. Therefore, I will banish you and you will perish, both you and the prophets who prophesy to you.'"
>
> Then I said to the priests and all these people, "This is what the LORD says: Do not listen to the prophets who say, 'Very soon now the articles from the LORD's house will be brought back from Babylon.' They are prophesying lies to you. Do not listen to them. Serve the king of Babylon, and you will live. Why should this city become a ruin?" (27:12–17)

Imagine the courage it took for Jeremiah to stand up to all the kings of the known world, including King Zedekiah, and say, "Surrender to the king of Babylon. Serve him, and you will survive. Oppose him, and you will be destroyed." To these kings, it must have seemed as if Jeremiah was a traitor and a spy, employed by the Babylonians to undermine their authority. No wonder they charged him with treason.

Yet Jeremiah is announcing the word of God concerning the nation of Judah and all the surrounding nations. He is courageously and faithfully warning these nations of the fatal results of unbelief.

CHALLENGED BY A FALSE PROPHET

Jeremiah 28 zooms in on one particular false prophet, Hananiah, and shows us the corrosive effect these lying charlatans can have on a society. As the scene opens, we are in the temple of Solomon, and there, in front of many witnesses, the false prophet challenges Jeremiah:

> In the fifth month of that same year, the fourth year, early in the reign of Zedekiah king of Judah, the prophet Hananiah son of Azzur, who was from Gibeon, said to me in the house of the LORD in the presence of the priests and all the people: "This is what the LORD Almighty, the God of Israel, says: 'I will break the yoke of the king of Babylon. Within two years I will bring back to this place all the articles of the LORD's house that Nebuchadnezzar king of Babylon removed from here and took to Babylon. I will also bring back to this place Jehoiachin son of Jehoiakim king of Judah and all the other exiles from Judah who went to Babylon,' declares the LORD, 'for I will break the yoke of the king of Babylon.'" (28:1–4)

Hananiah is a sly and clever liar. He knew exactly what the people wanted to hear, and that's the kind of optimistic message he delivered. Hananiah uses the same wording as Jeremiah, trying to confuse the people as to which man—Hananiah or Jeremiah—speaks for God. He uses Jeremiah's phrase: "This is what the LORD Almighty, the God of Israel, says." He is claiming to wear the mantle of a true prophet of God.

Imagine the confusion among the people as they hear both Hananiah and Jeremiah claiming to speak for God, yet speaking two diametrically opposed messages. Jeremiah predicted the fall of Jerusalem and captivity in Babylon for seventy years, and Hananiah predicted that God would break the yoke of Babylon within just two years.

Hananiah carefully chooses his words in an effort to humiliate Jeremiah. The prophet Jeremiah has been wearing a wooden yoke as a symbol of the yoke of bondage that Babylon would impose on the Jewish people. Hananiah was using Jeremiah's visual symbol against him, saying that God was going to break the yoke of the king of Babylon, return all the captives home, return all the precious ornaments and utensils of worship that had been taken from the temple, and even return Jehoiachin, Judah's former king who was captured and taken to Babylon in disgrace.

How should the people determine which prophet speaks the truth and which is a liar? Jeremiah offers a fascinating response to the false prophecy of Hananiah:

> Then the prophet Jeremiah replied to the prophet Hananiah before the priests and all the people who were standing in the house of the LORD. He said, "Amen! May the LORD do so! May the LORD fulfill the words you have prophesied by bringing the articles of the LORD's house and all the exiles back to this place from Babylon. Nevertheless, listen to what I have to say in your hearing and in the hearing of all the people: From early times the prophets who preceded you and me have prophesied war, disaster and plague against many countries and great kingdoms. But the prophet who prophesies peace will be recognized as one truly sent by the LORD only if his prediction comes true." (28:5–9)

Jeremiah says, in effect, that there is nothing he'd like better than for Hananiah's claim to be true. Hananiah offers a bright vision of the future, unlike the gloom and doom that Jeremiah predicts. Jeremiah wishes that Hananiah's happy-days-are-here-again scenario were true. But he knows it's all a lie.

Here, Jeremiah does what all true prophets of God have done. He says that the only way you can tell if a messenger is from God or not is to measure the accuracy of his prophecies. If everything he says comes true, 100 percent, no exceptions, then he is a prophet from God. There is no margin for error or guesswork. If a prophet's predictions are ever wrong, don't listen to him again. He does not speak for God.

This is an important precept to learn from Jeremiah. He says, in effect, "Fine, you say your prophecy will be fulfilled within two years. That's not long to wait. If, after two years, the exiles are not returned, the temple utensils are not returned, and the yoke of Babylon is still on our necks, then we'll know that Hananiah is not a true prophet and does not speak for God."

Hananiah has been challenging the prophetic authority of Jeremiah and flatly contradicting Jeremiah's message from the Lord. Jeremiah doesn't respond with anger or defensiveness. He very calmly and rationally exposes the weakness in Hananiah's challenge: Within two years, we will know who is lying and who is speaking God's truth.

Next, notice the arrogance of the false prophet Hananiah:

> Then the prophet Hananiah took the yoke off the neck of the prophet Jeremiah and broke it, and he said before all the people, "This is what the LORD says: 'In the same way I will break the yoke of Nebuchadnezzar king of Babylon off the neck of all the nations within two years.'" At this, the prophet Jeremiah went on his way. (28:10–11)

The text doesn't tell us in detail how Hananiah removed the yoke from Jeremiah's neck. But we know the yoke was fastened together by leather straps, and it could not be easily slipped off. Either Jeremiah willingly submitted to its removal—or Hananiah removed it by force. Jeremiah, under God's direction, had used the vivid imagery of the yoke to underscore God's message about the nation's coming enslavement by Babylon.

Hananiah chose to use an act of destruction to drive his own point home: he seized Jeremiah's yoke and broke it in two. Then he announced that contrary to what the prophet Jeremiah claimed, God would break the yoke of Babylon. The people would not need to repent. They could remain in their sin and idolatry, and God would rescue them from the consequences of their sin. Hananiah's false prophecy did not make rational sense, but he was saying what the people wanted to hear.

As for Jeremiah, the text tells us that he "went on his way." He didn't argue with Hananiah. He didn't protest Hananiah's act of destruction. He left the matter in God's hands. It was God's problem, not Jeremiah's. The prophet Jeremiah is an excellent role model for you and me whenever we are attacked or criticized for our faith. We do not need to defend ourselves. God is our defender.

Hananiah's actions turn out to have dire consequences, as we are about to see:

> After the prophet Hananiah had broken the yoke off the neck of the prophet Jeremiah, the word of the LORD came to Jeremiah: "Go and tell Hananiah, 'This is what the LORD says: You have broken a wooden yoke, but in its place you will get a yoke of iron. This is what the LORD Almighty, the God of Israel, says: I will put an iron yoke on the necks of all these nations to make them serve Nebuchadnezzar king of Babylon, and they will serve him. I will even give him control over the wild animals.'" (28:12–14)

It appears that God is responding to Hananiah's provocation by increasing the weight and strength of the yoke that will be on the necks of Judah and the other nations. Hananiah has broken the yoke of wood, only to see it replaced by a yoke of iron. God is going to give Nebuchadnezzar even more power and authority than before, and what God does, no man can contravene. Any attempt to avoid or evade God's judgment will only make matters worse. It is impossible to manipulate God or make Him a liar.

Next, God delivers a stern and frightening prophecy to Hananiah from the lips of the prophet:

> Then the prophet Jeremiah said to Hananiah the prophet, "Listen, Hananiah! The LORD has not sent you, yet you have persuaded this nation to trust in lies. Therefore this is what the LORD says: 'I am about to remove you from the face of the earth. This very year you are going to die, because you have preached rebellion against the LORD.'"
>
> In the seventh month of that same year, Hananiah the prophet died. (28:15–17)

It didn't take long for this prophecy to be fulfilled. Hananiah publicly challenged Jeremiah and broke Jeremiah's wooden yoke in the fifth month of the year. Two months later, Hananiah was dead, exactly as

Jeremiah had predicted. The word of God, spoken through Jeremiah, was proved true, and Hananiah, the false prophet, was proved to be a liar.

God honored and sustained the prophet Jeremiah through this difficult and challenging test. It's a dangerous business, challenging the Word of God.

GOD'S PLAN FOR YOUR FUTURE

In Jeremiah 29, the prophet writes a letter to the four thousand or more Jewish exiles in Babylon. False prophets are spreading confusion among the exiles, just as they have been doing in Judah. The false prophets are telling the people that their captivity will soon be over and that God is going to restore them to their homeland. God has told Jeremiah that not only will the captives who are already in Babylon remain there but also that Babylon will ultimately take even more captives and destroy the city of Jerusalem if the nation remains unrepentant. So Jeremiah writes this letter to the exiles in Babylon to end their confusion and set the record straight:

> This is what the LORD Almighty, the God of Israel, says to all those I carried into exile from Jerusalem to Babylon: "Build houses and settle down; plant gardens and eat what they produce. Marry and have sons and daughters; find wives for your sons and give your daughters in marriage, so that they too may have sons and daughters. Increase in number there; do not decrease. Also, seek the peace and prosperity of the city to which I have carried you into exile. Pray to the LORD for it, because if it prospers, you too will prosper." Yes, this is what the LORD Almighty, the God of Israel, says: "Do not let the prophets and diviners among you deceive you. Do not listen to the dreams you encourage them to have. They are prophesying lies to you in my name. I have not sent them," declares the LORD. (29:4–9)

God is telling the Jewish exiles, in effect, "You are going to be in Babylon for a long time. Accept it and make the most of it. Live your lives, marry and have families, be good citizens and for the sake of your own prosperity, seek the prosperity of the people around you. Pray and maintain your close and loving relationship with Me. And don't listen to the false prophets who tell you otherwise. They are all lying to you."

You and I are very much like these exiles in Babylon. This Earth is not our home. We are citizens of heaven, temporarily exiled on this planet. While we're here, we're to make the most of it, live our lives, and be good citizens. But we are surrounded by false prophets with lying messages, deceptive philosophies, and godless religions. There are even false prophets in the church. We need to listen for God's voice and screen out the deceptive babble of the false teachers all around us.

You may find yourself in a situation where you're enduring the consequences of some poor decisions or sinful choices in the past. You have regrets. Your life is unpleasant. There's nothing you can do to change it. What does God say to you about those circumstances? He says to you what He said to the exiled Jews in Babylon: Accept what you cannot change. Make the best of what you can change. Do good to the people around you. Be patient, wait for God, and He will deliver you when the time is right.

Jeremiah goes on in this letter to give a timeline for exile of the Jews in Babylon:

> This is what the LORD says: "When seventy years are completed for Babylon, I will come to you and fulfill my good promise to bring you back to this place. For I know the plans I have for you," declares the LORD, "plans to prosper you and not to harm you, plans to give you hope and a future. Then you will call on me and come and pray to me, and I will listen to you. You will seek me and find me when you seek me with all your heart. I will be found by you," declares the LORD, "and will bring you back from captivity. I will gather you from all the nations and places where I have banished you," declares the LORD, "and will bring you back to the place from which I carried you into exile." (29:10–14)

God had set a time limit on the exile of the Jews in Babylon: seventy years. In the closing chapters of the book of Daniel, you find that when Daniel was an old man, he took the scroll of the book of Jeremiah and read these very words. He realized that the seventy years of captivity were nearly fulfilled. He had been a young man when he was taken into captivity, and now the time of captivity was nearly over. So Daniel obeyed this word and prayed to God, and God gave Daniel a great vision of future history. That vision extended from Daniel's day to the coming of Jesus the Messiah, then down to our own era and the approaching time of tribulation, the Antichrist, and the end of the world. It's all laid out in startling detail in Daniel 9 through 12.

Embedded in this message to the exiles in Babylon is a promise that we can claim for our lives today. It's a promise of God's love to us and His desire to fill our lives with blessings and hope. Inspired by God, Jeremiah writes, "'For I know the plans I have for you,' declares the LORD, 'plans to prosper you and not to harm you, plans to give you hope and a future. Then you will call on me and come and pray to me, and I will listen to you. You will seek me and find me when you seek me with all your heart'" (vv. 11–13). While the primary recipients of this message were the exiles, we can see a secondary application. We can also see this as God's love letter to us, His promise to us, His message of encouragement to us for the trials and difficulties we're going through.

If you're undergoing a time of exile or trial in your life, even if it is the consequence of some past sin or failure, take these words that the Lord gave to Jeremiah and post them on your refrigerator or the lamp beside your bed or the dashboard of your car. Meditate on these words and internalize them. Read them every morning and every evening, and listen to the voice of God as He speaks peace and encouragement to your heart.

WHAT SHOULD YOU BELIEVE?

Jeremiah's letter to the exiles closes with a curse upon the false prophets in Babylon and with a warning to the people not to listen to them. Jeremiah mentions three false prophets by name: Ahab, Zedekiah, and Shemaiah. Jeremiah writes:

> You may say, "The LORD has raised up prophets for us in Babylon," but this is what the LORD says about the king who sits on David's throne and all the people who remain in this city, your fellow citizens who did not go with you into exile—yes, this is what the LORD Almighty says: "I will send the sword, famine and plague against them and I will make them like figs that are so bad they cannot be eaten. I will pursue them with the sword, famine and plague and will make them abhorrent to all the kingdoms of the earth, a curse and an object of horror, of scorn and reproach, among all the nations where I drive them. For they have not listened to my words," declares the LORD, "words that I sent to them again and again by my servants the prophets. And you exiles have not listened either," declares the LORD.
>
> Therefore, hear the word of the LORD, all you exiles whom I have sent away from Jerusalem to Babylon. This is what the LORD Almighty, the God of Israel, says about Ahab son of Kolaiah and Zedekiah son of Maaseiah, who are prophesying lies to you in my name: "I will deliver them into the hands of Nebuchadnezzar king of Babylon, and he will put them to death before your very eyes. Because of them, all the exiles from Judah who are in Babylon will use this curse: 'May the LORD treat you like Zedekiah and Ahab, whom the king of Babylon burned in the fire.' For they have done outrageous things in Israel; they have committed adultery with their neighbors' wives, and in my name they have uttered lies—which I did not authorize. I know it and am a witness to it," declares the LORD. (29:15–23)

This was a time of terrible uncertainty. People were confused by the torrent of conflicting voices and rival factions, all claiming to speak for God. The people desperately needed to know that the truth *could* be known, that God *was* speaking to the nation, including the exiled nation, with clarity. God was saying, in effect, "I am going to punish these false prophets for spreading confusion among the people. They have not listened to Me, and you have not listened to Me. I will punish them with the sword, famine, and plague. I will turn them over to Nebuchadnezzar for torture and execution. If you don't want to share their fate, listen to Me, not them. Trust My voice, not theirs."

God makes His way, His will, and His truth known to us in three ways: (1) through past history, which He has revealed through Scripture; (2) through current events, bringing His truth to light as He controls events in the world around us; and (3) through the direct revelation of His Word, the Bible, and the Word made flesh, Jesus Christ.

In these days of confusion and uncertainty, which voice will you listen to? The voices of the occult world? The voices of false prophets who claim to have visions or new revelations from God? The secular voices that tell us not to believe God's Word? The voices that preach a new gospel, a "prosperity gospel" or a "social gospel" or a "gospel of universalism"? Whose voice are you listening to today? The voice of God, who rules in the affairs of humanity, or the voice of the false prophets?

You cannot afford to be confused or uncertain about this question. Your freedom, your future, and your eternal life depend on your answer.

10

THE SECRET OF STRENGTH

Jeremiah 30–31

On August 28, 1963, Dr. Martin Luther King Jr. stood on the steps of the Lincoln Memorial in Washington, D.C. Facing a crowd of more than 250,000 fellow Americans, Dr. King delivered one of the most important speeches in American history, the "I Have a Dream" speech. He began with a celebration of Abraham Lincoln's Emancipation Proclamation, which freed the slaves in 1863. But, he noted sadly, "one hundred years later, the Negro still is not free."

As he neared the close of the speech, his friend, gospel singer Mahalia Jackson, called out to him, "Tell them about the dream, Martin!" In previous speeches, Dr. King had spoken about a dream he had of a brighter future, a better America. He had not planned to talk about the dream that day. The dream was not included in the notes of his speech.

But in response to Mahalia Jackson's urging, Dr. King made a decision, right then and there, to depart from his prepared remarks.

Looking out upon that vast crowd, he pushed the notes of his prepared speech aside and began to speak straight from his heart. He began to talk about the dream.

In cadences reminiscent of an Old Testament prophet, Dr. King spoke of the crisis of inequality that America faced at that moment in history, adding, "Now is the time to make justice a reality for all of God's children." Then he said those historic words, "I have a dream . . . ." Eight times he repeated that phrase, describing his vision of a unified and integrated America, including the statement, "I still have a dream, a dream deeply rooted in the American dream, that one day this nation will rise up and live up to its creed, 'We hold these truths to be self-evident, that all men are created equal.'"

As we come to Jeremiah chapters 30 through 33, we find another nation in crisis, and we hear another prophetic voice raised with a sense of urgency and hope, describing a dream of a brighter future. That nation is Judah, and that prophetic voice belongs to God's man of the hour, Jeremiah. We are about to explore a section of Scripture I call "The Dream of Jeremiah."

AN AS-YET-UNFULFILLED PROMISE

In Jeremiah 32, the prophet tells us that this section of the story takes place in the tenth year of King Zedekiah. The final destruction of Jerusalem and the ultimate captivity of Judah by Babylon occurred during the eleventh year of Zedekiah's reign, so these events take place very close to the end.

Jeremiah has been awaiting trial, indicted by the government for allegedly treasonous activities against the king and the country. What did Jeremiah do that was allegedly treasonous? He urged the people to surrender to the Babylonians.

Jeremiah is now being held prisoner. King Nebuchadnezzar and the armies of Babylon are at the gates of Jerusalem. This is the third time the Babylonians have surrounded the capital of Judah, and this time, the siege has lasted more than a year. Famine has set in. The people have no bread. It's only a matter of weeks before the city must capitulate. There is no relief in sight. The cavalry will not come galloping over the horizon to rescue the people of Judah. It is the nation's darkest hour—so far. Soon, events will turn even darker—and bloodier.

This is the setting for what I call "The Dream of Jeremiah." Though Jeremiah does not, at first, tell us that he is describing a dream, we know it was a dream, because in Jeremiah 31:26, the prophet makes this unusual statement: "At this I awoke and looked around. My sleep had been pleasant to me." Then he goes right back to describing his vision. It was evidently a dream that came to Jeremiah in the night, a vision of the future restoration of the Jewish people and the Jewish nation, and the glory God had promised to His people.

As we read this account, we should notice that God still works in our lives today. God shows the same care He showed in Jeremiah's day. The revelation of His great purposes and programs in the Old Testament serve to show us how God continues to love us and care for us today.

There are four themes in this song, and they are intertwined, though they are clearly distinguishable. The dominant theme is a note of the certainty of joy. A mood of joy is interwoven throughout The Dream of Jeremiah. Here's one sample passage to illustrate this theme:

> See, I will bring them from the land of the north
> and gather them from the ends of the earth.
> Among them will be the blind and the lame,
> expectant mothers and women in labor;
> a great throng will return.
> They will come with weeping;
> they will pray as I bring them back.
> I will lead them beside streams of water
> on a level path where they will not stumble,
> because I am Israel's father,
> and Ephraim is my firstborn son. (31:8–9)

In this passage of Jeremiah's dream, the prophet looks far beyond the return of the Jews from captivity in Babylon, and even beyond our own day. He looks to the time when God promises to restore the fortunes of Israel and to raise up King David to rule over the people once more. It is a promise as yet unfulfilled.

Here is another beautiful expression of Israel's future joy:

> "'But all who devour you will be devoured;
>   all your enemies will go into exile.
> Those who plunder you will be plundered;
>   all who make spoil of you I will despoil.
> But I will restore you to health
>   and heal your wounds,'
> declares the LORD,
> 'because you are called an outcast,
>   Zion for whom no one cares.'
> "This is what the LORD says:
> "'I will restore the fortunes of Jacob's tents
>   and have compassion on his dwellings;
> the city will be rebuilt on her ruins,
>   and the palace will stand in its proper place.
> From them will come songs of thanksgiving
>   and the sound of rejoicing.
> I will add to their numbers,
>   and they will not be decreased;
> I will bring them honor,
>   and they will not be disdained.
> Their children will be as in days of old,
>   and their community will be established before me;
>   I will punish all who oppress them.
> Their leader will be one of their own;
>   their ruler will arise from among them.
> I will bring him near and he will come close to me—
>   for who is he who will devote himself
>   to be close to me?'
> declares the LORD.

> "'So you will be my people,
> and I will be your God.'" (30:16–22)

All through the record of history, every nation that has ever attacked the Jewish people has suffered as a result. God promises to watch over His people and to return evil to any who harm His people.

The nation of Israel has suffered oppression, subjugation, captivity, exile, and even dispersion around the world, and it has also enjoyed numerous restorations. But Israel has never experienced a restoration like the one described here in Jeremiah's dream. The vision that Jeremiah describes in these verses awaits future fulfillment.

A DREAM OF HOPE AND JOY

Moving to chapter 31, we encounter another glorious passage of Jeremiah's dream of the future:

This is what the LORD says:

> "Sing with joy for Jacob;
>   shout for the foremost of the nations.
> Make your praises heard, and say,
>   'LORD, save your people,
>   the remnant of Israel.'
> See, I will bring them from the land of the north
>   and gather them from the ends of the earth.
> Among them will be the blind and the lame,
>   expectant mothers and women in labor;
>   a great throng will return.
> They will come with weeping;
>   they will pray as I bring them back.
> I will lead them beside streams of water
>   on a level path where they will not stumble,
> because I am Israel's father,
>   and Ephraim is my firstborn son.

"Hear the word of the LORD, you nations;
    proclaim it in distant coastlands:
'He who scattered Israel will gather them
    and will watch over his flock like a shepherd.'
For the LORD will deliver Jacob
    and redeem them from the hand of those stronger than
    they.
They will come and shout for joy on the heights of Zion;
    they will rejoice in the bounty of the LORD—
the grain, the new wine and the olive oil,
    the young of the flocks and herds.
They will be like a well-watered garden,
    and they will sorrow no more. (31:7–12)

Many Bible scholars believe that this passage of prophetic Scripture was fulfilled when the state of Israel declared its independence in May 1948. Jews from all over the world returned to their ancestral homeland, the land that was promised by God to Abraham and his descendants.

But I don't believe this passage of Scripture refers to the founding of the modern state of Israel. In my view, the state of Israel is a foreshadowing of the fully restored nation of Israel that is yet to come, but this passage has not yet been fulfilled. The people of Israel do not live in that nation in a state of belief and joy and worship, as described in these verses. They live in a state of unbelief, surrounded by enemies, in constant peril of being wiped off the map by yet another sneak attack.

Jeremiah's dream describes a golden age of peace and security, when the Lord himself will defend the city of Jerusalem and the nation of Israel:

"The days are coming," declares the LORD, "when I will plant the kingdoms of Israel and Judah with the offspring of people and of animals. Just as I watched over them to uproot and tear down, and to overthrow, destroy and bring disaster, so I will watch over them to build and to plant," declares the LORD....

"The days are coming," declares the LORD, "when this city will be rebuilt for me from the Tower of Hananel to the Corner Gate. The measuring line will stretch from there straight to the hill of Gareb and then turn to Goah. The whole valley where dead bodies and ashes are thrown, and all the terraces out to the Kidron Valley on the east as far as the corner of the Horse Gate, will be holy to the LORD. The city will never again be uprooted or demolished." (31:27–28, 38–40)

This description encompasses practically the entire city of old Jerusalem at the present time. Clearly, this prophecy is yet to be fulfilled. But what a scene of beauty and glory, what a promise of joy and gladness after the Jewish people have endured centuries of wandering and sorrow!

Remember too that this promise was given when the people of Judah had reached the lowest stage of national life. They were a wicked and idolatrous people, stubborn and rebellious toward God, even as the Babylonian armies had surrounded the city and the people were starving to death. God had dealt faithfully with the Jewish people for centuries, trying to bring them to repentance. It had been four hundred years since the halcyon days of the kingdom of David, when the nation reached unmatched heights of power and glory.

Despite occasional reforms, the people of Judah have sunk steadily lower and lower until, in a stubborn determination to have their own way, they are on the verge of being carried away into captivity in Babylon—at least, those that are not cut down with swords and left to die in their own blood. Jerusalem will be leveled by the Babylonians, and all the glory of the great capital city of King David and King Solomon will be turned to ashes and rubble in a day.

Humanly speaking, the situation is hopeless. Nothing can be done to rescue the nation. Yet, amid all this darkness and despair, the prophet Jeremiah—famed for his doom-and-gloom prophecies—relates a beautiful dream of hope for the future. Darkness is falling, but a beautiful and glorious morning is coming someday. Hope and joy are the dominant emotions woven throughout this dream of Jeremiah. It is one of the most beautiful and inspiring sections in all of Scripture.

AGONY AND TERROR

Alongside the themes of hope and joy in this section of Jeremiah's prophecy, there is a contrasting theme of a future time of agony and terror. Jeremiah writes:

These are the words the LORD spoke concerning Israel and Judah: "This is what the LORD says:

> "'Cries of fear are heard—
> terror, not peace.
> Ask and see:
> Can a man bear children?
> Then why do I see every strong man
> with his hands on his stomach like a woman in labor,
> every face turned deathly pale?
> How awful that day will be!
> No other will be like it.
> It will be a time of trouble for Jacob,
> but he will be saved out of it.'" (30:4–7)

These words remind us of the prophecy of Jesus: "For then there will be great distress, unequaled from the beginning of the world until now—and never to be equaled again" (Matthew 24:21). Jeremiah vividly describes men gripping themselves like women in labor, but these men are writhing in agony and terror instead of labor pains. I believe Jeremiah is describing a time yet to come—"a time of trouble for Jacob." I believe this is the time that the Bible calls the Great Tribulation.

The Bible tells us, and history has made clear, that any peace Israel makes with its neighbors is temporary at best. Sooner or later, that peace is broken. But a time is coming in Israel's future that is unlike any other time in history. It will be a time of distress and terror and suffering like the world has never seen before. When you think of the Holocaust during World War II, when the Nazis murdered six million Jews in concentration camps, it is hard to imagine anything worse. Yet Jeremiah relates these words from the Lord: "How awful that day will be! No other will be like it. It will be a time of trouble for Jacob, but he will be saved out of it."

God goes on to say:

> Why do you cry out over your wound,
> your pain that has no cure?
> Because of your great guilt and many sins
> I have done these things to you. (30:15)

God takes the full responsibility for the suffering and travail of Israel. He says that these sufferings are the consequences for their flagrant sins.

When we read the Bible, we tend to cling to the passages about blessings—and we skip past the warnings. We say, "Oh, it's too bad what happened to Israel way back in the past. It's too bad that God used to deal with people so harshly back then."

We need to remember that the story of this wayward kingdom is *our* story. God does not change. He still appeals to us to repent. He still disciplines the children He loves. There is a scriptural principle reflected here that we must not forget, as Paul told the Galatian Christians: "Do not be deceived: God cannot be mocked. A man reaps what he sows. Whoever sows to please their flesh, from the flesh will reap destruction; whoever sows to please the Spirit, from the Spirit will reap eternal life" (Galatians 6:7–8).

We tend to think that since judgment hasn't fallen immediately after we sinned, God must be okay with our sin. He winks at our sin and pretends it didn't happen. But no, the fact that God doesn't immediately punish our sin does not mean there are no consequences to pay. Don't kid yourself. If we plant seeds of sin in our lives, we should not be surprised if we one day harvest a crop of sorrow, destruction, and death.

Sin has consequences, and forgiveness does not cancel the consequences of sin. God will forgive us, but we may still have to deal with the broken marriage, the sexually transmitted disease, the lung cancer, the prison term, the humiliating loss of reputation that is a natural consequence of our sin.

These natural consequences are sometimes referred to as "the temporal judgment of the Lord." God doesn't always have to *actively* punish us for our sins. Many of our sins have natural consequences that cannot be avoided. As someone once said, you can pull the nail out of the wall, but you can't pull out the nail hole. And Rudyard Kipling put it this way: "The sin they do by two and two they must pay for one by one."[10]

But if we plant seeds of godliness in our lives, the Spirit of God will enable us to reap a harvest of eternal life. When we walk in the Spirit, the joy and glory of life are a natural consequence of living in fellowship with Him.

These principles operate invariably and inevitably in the life of the nation of Judah. But let's not deceive ourselves. They operate in our lives as well.

LOVE TO THE VANISHING POINT

Another theme woven throughout Jeremiah's dream is the theme of the faithfulness of God's love. We see it in the first few verses of chapter 31:

"At that time," declares the LORD, "I will be the God of all the families of Israel, and they will be my people."

This is what the LORD says:
"The people who survive the sword
will find favor in the wilderness;
I will come to give rest to Israel."
The LORD appeared to us in the past, saying:
"I have loved you with an everlasting love;
I have drawn you with unfailing kindness." (31:1–3)

God is with His people in the midst of trouble. Yes, we still have to go through trouble, but we don't have to go through it alone. God is with us, giving us His grace and love to sustain us. God goes on to speak about His people in loving, fatherly terms:

> Is not Ephraim my dear son,
>   the child in whom I delight?
> Though I often speak against him,
>   I still remember him.
> Therefore my heart yearns for him;
>   I have great compassion for him,"
> declares the LORD. (31:20)

A father must sometimes reprimand his son—not because he hates his son but because he loves his son so dearly. He wants his son to grow up with strong character, strong values, and a strong sense of right and wrong. A father's heart is tender toward his son, regardless of how sharply he must sometimes reprimand and discipline him. God, like a father, tenderly loves His people.

Behind the darkness, agony, and terror of the Babylonian invasion is the everlasting love of God. In His great love, He has patiently, persistently begged the people to turn away from their idols and turn back to Him—but to no avail. So the hand of discipline now falls, not because God hates His people, but because He loves them so much. He loves them too much to let them submit themselves to the blasphemous, hideous demon-gods of the Canaanites and other pagan peoples.

God says, "I have loved you with an everlasting love." You might think you know what God is saying here, but unless you understand the Hebrew language, you probably don't realize the richness of these words. The word translated "everlasting" connotes more than an infinite duration of time. It contains an element of mystery, and it refers literally to a concept called "the vanishing point."

If you stand in the middle of a perfectly straight road that runs across a perfectly flat stretch of land, you can look toward the end of that road and the lines of the road will seem to converge and meet in the distance. The point at which they meet is the "vanishing point." Now imagine that the road is time. Look down one direction, and that is the past. Look down the other direction, and that is the future. We can remember a certain distance into the past. We can imagine a certain distance into the future. But ultimately, there is a vanishing point where our memories of the past and our imaginings of the future can go no further. We come up against a vanishing point of comprehension, where time and duration seem meaningless.

That is what God is saying to us when He says, "I have loved you with an everlasting love." He is saying that His love for us surpasses our comprehension. It transcends our imagination. The apostle Paul speaks of the same transcendent love in his letter to the Ephesians:

> And I pray that you, being rooted and established in love, may have power, together with all the Lord's holy people, to grasp how wide and long and high and deep is the love of Christ, and to know *this love that surpasses knowledge*—that you may be filled to the measure of all the fullness of God. (Ephesians 3:17–19, emphasis added)

Jeremiah and the apostle Paul are speaking in similar terms of the very same quality of love—love that reaches to the vanishing point of our comprehension, love that is wider and longer and higher and deeper than we can possibly imagine.

There will be times when the sins of the past and the consequences of the present take a seemingly intolerable toll on our lives. We are tempted to cry out, "Why? Why is God allowing this to happen to me? What have I done to deserve this?" We are tempted to think that God is unjust or uncaring or unloving. But God wants us to understand that the things that happen in our lives don't always feel warm and pleasant and loving, yet God has loved us with an everlasting, all-transcending love. The Christian life is a journey of learning to trust His love even in painful circumstances.

God is saying, in effect, "I know this hurts you, but I won't let it damage you. The very hurt you are going through is producing proven character in you. I know you want stronger character, and you know that's what I want for you. These painful circumstances are refining you, removing the imperfections and impurities from your life, so that you will be more and more like Christ."

This sounds strange to us. We want to have good character, but we don't want the painful growth process that produces it. We would much rather continue in sin and selfishness, but we want to escape the consequences of sin. God leads us through these difficult circumstances because of His everlasting love for us.

A NEW MOTIVE, A NEW POWER, A NEW FAMILY

Another theme God introduces through Jeremiah's dream is the idea that He is doing something new. He is giving His people a new motive and new power. Jeremiah writes:

> "The days are coming," declares the LORD,
>   "when I will make a new covenant
> with the people of Israel
>   and with the people of Judah.
> It will not be like the covenant
>   I made with their ancestors
> when I took them by the hand
>   to lead them out of Egypt,
> because they broke my covenant,
>   though I was a husband to them,"
> declares the LORD.
> "This is the covenant I will make with the people of Israel
>   after that time," declares the LORD.
> "I will put my law in their minds
>   and write it on their hearts.
> I will be their God,
>   and they will be my people.

No longer will they teach their neighbor,
    or say to one another, 'Know the LORD,'
because they will all know me,
    from the least of them to the greatest,"
declares the LORD.
"For I will forgive their wickedness
    and will remember their sins no more." (31:31–34)

God has promised to do something *new* in our lives. He is going to make a *new* covenant with us, and out of that new covenant will flow a *new* motivation for living, a *new* power for living, and a *new* family in which to live.

The first manifestation of this new covenant is a *new motivation* for living. God says, "I will put my law in their minds and write it on their hearts." He is going to transform the very motivation that compels us to get up each day and live our lives. This new motivation will come from within instead of without. The old covenant, the Law, is a demand made on us from without. "If you do this, then I'll do that," God says to us through the Law. But it is impossible for us to live up to our side of the bargain.

But this new covenant that God announces here in Jeremiah 31 is something that God places within us. And what is that? Answer: *Love!* Love is the motive at the heart of the new covenant. Love is our new motive for living. We respond to God out of love and gratitude for all He has done in our lives and hearts. As our love for God grows, we realize the glory and blessing of experiencing a relationship with the God who created us. As a result, our love for Him grows.

Where does obedience come in? Instead of obeying God out of fear of judgment, we obey Him out of a heart filled with love. And love is the fulfillment of the Law. Under the old covenant, we would obey the Law out of fear of punishment. But under the new covenant, we replace fear of punishment with love. The Law tells you not to harm your neighbor—or else. But the new covenant law of love enables you to fulfill the Law without being afraid of the Law. After all, if you love your neighbor, you don't have to be told not to steal from him, lie about him, or murder him. Love means you would never think of harming him.

The second manifestation of this new covenant is new *power* for living. God says, "I will be their God, and they will be my people." God himself becomes our strength for living. He supplies the power to act, the power to love, the power to live. Everything comes from God; nothing comes from us. God is at work in us, and that gives us the power we need to accomplish His will for our lives.

The third manifestation of this new covenant is a new *family*. God says, "No longer will they teach their neighbor, or say to one another, 'Know the LORD,' because they will all know me, from the least of them to the greatest" (v. 34). Isn't that amazing? God says, "They will all know me." We will all have one Father, because we will all be one family. We will all know each other. We will know each other's hopes and dreams and passions, because we will all have the same passion in life—a passion to know the Lord better and become like Him.

That's why, when Christians meet one another, they always feel as if they know each other, even if they have never met before. This is true of Christians who come from opposite sides of the globe and from different cultures. This is true of Christians who don't even speak the same language; their shared love for Christ speaks louder and more clearly than words. They share the same life and the same love for God. They are part of the same family, and they know each other, they help each other, and they love each other.

I once taught at a Bible conference in northern Minnesota. It was a beautiful setting, among the birch trees along the lake, not far from the Canadian border. I led a small group session of pastors and their wives. I had been teaching all week about the new covenant, and my goal for this small group session was that we would apply the principles of the new covenant to our lives. I hoped that all of us in the group would feel free to share our authentic struggles, so we could pray for one another and find healing.

Unfortunately, the people in the group were inhibited and closed. They were pastors. They wanted to help their own congregations become more caring and authentic, yet they could not bring themselves to open up and share with each other.

The few problems they were willing to share were superficial, like the need for a new mimeograph machine in the office. Finally, I stopped them and said, "Look, you all told me you want to teach your congregations how to carry one another's burdens, yet you are not willing to share your own hurts and struggles. How can you motivate your church to do what you yourselves are unwilling to do?"

After a few moments of silence, one young man stood up and said that he and his wife had returned from Brazil after three years as missionaries. They had come back to the States with a deep sense of failure, and they resented the Christians they had encountered who had no empathy for their hurts.

Then a young woman stood and spoke in a shaking voice, telling how her young husband, a pastor, had died the previous year. She was lonely, and none of her Christian friends seemed to care about her, none of them called, none of them reached out. "I would just like you to remember me and pray for me," she said.

A pastor stood and shared about the death of his daughter, and how hard this loss had been for his wife.

A man stood and confessed before the group that he had been judgmental and critical of another woman in the group. He asked her forgiveness in front of everyone, and they forgave each other.

Again and again, people stood and shared from the depths of their souls. Tears ran down their faces. People prayed for each other and confessed their sins to each other.

I sat down. The Lord was running the meeting. He didn't need me to say anything else.

We ended with a Communion service. We all felt healed, forgiven, restored, and cleansed. As we passed the cup to one another, we said, "Your sins are forgiven you." It was the new covenant in action.

HOPE IN THE MIDST OF HOPELESSNESS

As God said through the prophet Jeremiah, "I will forgive their wickedness and will remember their sins no more" (31:34). The new covenant rests on that statement. That is how God proposes to win the battle against sin and death.

The Law, with its impossible demands of perfection, must inevitably fail. We cannot respond as we ought to. We cannot keep the law. We cannot win the battle against sin and death. Our situation is hopeless.

But God says, in effect, "In the midst of hopelessness, I bring you hope. I have already made provision for your failure. I will not hold your failure against you. My love will be with you and will sustain you, even through your times of sin and failure. I am for you, not against you. I will turn your failures into advantages, I will bring beauty out of your suffering. That is the new covenant in action."

God is going to heal and restore Israel—not the political entity we now call Israel but the true nation and people of Israel. God will bring them into an understanding of the new covenant relationship they have with Him.

A healing relationship with God has always been available to the human race—ever since the first man appeared on the earth. God had the new covenant of the shed blood of Jesus Christ in mind since before the foundation of the world. The entire Old Testament pointed to the coming of Jesus and His sacrifice on the cross. From Genesis to Revelation, there has only been one basis on which human beings can come to God and be forgiven: the blood of the new covenant. That's what the Old Testament sacrifices looked forward to. That's what the celebration of Communion looks back on.

The sacrifice of Jesus on the cross is the sole basis for our salvation. When God made coverings of animal skins for Adam and Eve, He was teaching them that innocent blood would have to be shed for the forgiveness of sin—the innocent blood of God's own Son. When the Old Testament priests spilled the blood of a lamb on a stone altar, they pictured the crucifixion of Christ. When God told Abraham to sacrifice his only son on Mount Moriah, God was showing Abraham what it was going to cost Him to sacrifice His only Son on Calvary.

Someday, the Jewish people will understand that the Hebrew Scriptures, what Christians call the Old Testament, are all about Jesus and the new covenant relationship He came to give us. God is going to bring Israel into this new covenant relationship, as He promised through the prophet Jeremiah:

> This is what the LORD says,
> > he who appoints the sun
> > > to shine by day,
> > who decrees the moon and stars
> > > to shine by night,
> > who stirs up the sea
> > > so that its waves roar—
> > > the LORD Almighty is his name:
> > "Only if these decrees vanish from my sight,"
> > > declares the LORD,
> > "will Israel ever cease
> > > being a nation before me."
>
> This is what the LORD says:
> "Only if the heavens above can be measured
> > and the foundations of the earth below be searched out
> will I reject all the descendants of Israel
> > because of all they have done,"
> declares the LORD. (31:35–37)

God absolutely, unconditionally guarantees that He will bring Israel into this new relationship, this new covenant relationship. Israel will never be destroyed, no matter what threats are arrayed against her. As long as the sun is in the sky, as long as the moon comes up at night, as long as the seasons change, God is with His people. They will never be wiped out. That promise is as strong as the natural order of the universe.

He guarantees that a day will come when His chosen people will open their eyes and turn to Him. Israel will fill the earth and be the leader of the nations. David shall rule over them, and Israel will again experience a golden age of power, glory, and joy.

As Paul tells us in Romans 11, if the temporary rejection of Israel meant riches and joy and grace to us, how much more will Israel's full inclusion mean when the nation comes at last into the fulfillment of that promise! And this is our promise too. Like Israel, we rest upon the new covenant.

When Jesus sat down with His disciples in the upper room the night before the crucifixion, He took the bread and the cup, and He passed the bread among them, saying, "This is My body which is given for you" (Luke 22:19 NKJV). Then he passed the cup and said, "This cup is the new covenant in My blood" (v. 20 NKJV).

God has made that covenant with you and me and anyone who is ready to come to Him, to any man who has reached the end of himself, to any woman who is ready to say, "Lord, save me! I'm at the end of my rope." That's why the Sermon on the Mount begins with a blessing for people who recognize their own moral and spiritual bankruptcy: "Blessed are the poor in spirit, for theirs is the kingdom of heaven" (Matthew 5:3).

Into our bankruptcy, God pours His rich, full supply. That is the new covenant.

11

IS ANYTHING TOO HARD FOR GOD?

Jeremiah 32–33

Your real estate agent calls you and says, "I've just found the perfect property for you. The owner is very motivated to sell, and I think you can have it for a fraction of the appraised value. There's only one small catch."

"A catch?" you say. "There's a problem with the property?"

"A *small* problem. Hardly worth mentioning."

"Go ahead and mention it."

"Well, it's sort of in a war zone."

"I think we have a bad connection. I thought you said it's in a—"

"A war zone. And to be honest, enemy forces are about to roll right over the property and enslave everybody and destroy everything in sight. But you really ought to keep an open mind about this property—it's a real steal!"

I ask you: Who would be foolish enough to conduct a real estate transaction in a war zone as enemy forces swarm across the land, killing people and turning houses into rubble?

The prophet Jeremiah, that's who.

What's more, as we come to Jeremiah 32 and 33, we find that God's prophet is not a free man. He is in prison for preaching that the nation is about to fall. In fact, he is in prison for predicting exactly what is now coming to pass. The Babylonians have surrounded the city and are knocking on the front gate with battering rams. Jeremiah's prophecy has been proven true, and still the king and the officials of the nation want to shut him up.

For the Jews huddled inside the city walls, it's the end of the world. Once the Babylonians break through the gates, the Jewish civilization will be crushed. The Babylonians have already taken thousands of Jews captive and led them away to Babylon in previous deportations. This time, Nebuchadnezzar's forces are going to finish the job.

As the Babylonian siege spreads hunger and panic throughout the city, as the Jewish people become cornered animals, willing to cannibalize their own children to stay alive for a few more days, God commands Jeremiah to . . .

Invest in real estate?

It seems like insanity. If so, it is madness with a purpose. Let's see what God's purpose for His prophet is this time.

Confirming a word from the Lord

Authentic faith is a paradox. If your faith is genuine, it will be both cautious and bold at the same time. It will be simultaneously patient and audacious, careful and adventurous. That's the paradox we will explore in Jeremiah 32 and 33. These chapters form the second part of the great dream of hope that Jeremiah expressed in song as he was imprisoned in the courtyard of the guard.

Here again, God instructs Jeremiah to use a series of visual aids to teach the people. In the process of obeying God's instructions, Jeremiah is being toughened and strengthened for the challenges ahead. God is in the business of preparing us for future trials. Often the trials we go through today are learning exercises for tomorrow.

Many Christians seem to feel entitled to a trouble-free life. I'm not sure where people get this idea, because you won't find it anywhere in Scripture. In fact, the Bible repeatedly tells us that in this broken world we will have trouble. We live in a fallen world filled with sinful people, a world under the domination of Satan, who is the god of this world. But God can take any trouble we suffer, any problem we face, any persecution we endure, and He can transform it into blessing. One of the greatest lessons in the book of Jeremiah is seeing God use the obstacles and opposition in Jeremiah's life to strengthen and prepare him for greater challenges ahead.

In Jeremiah 32, God asks Jeremiah to do something that makes no sense, and we will see if Jeremiah has the faith to be obedient to this strange instruction:

> Jeremiah said, "The word of the LORD came to me: Hanamel son of Shallum your uncle is going to come to you and say, 'Buy my field at Anathoth, because as nearest relative it is your right and duty to buy it.'
>
> "Then, just as the LORD had said, my cousin Hanamel came to me in the courtyard of the guard and said, 'Buy my field at Anathoth in the territory of Benjamin. Since it is your right to redeem it and possess it, buy it for yourself.'
>
> "I knew that this was the word of the LORD; so I bought the field at Anathoth from my cousin Hanamel and weighed out for him seventeen shekels of silver. I signed and sealed the deed, had it witnessed, and weighed out the silver on the scales. I took the deed of purchase—the sealed copy containing the terms and conditions, as well as the unsealed copy—and I gave this deed to Baruch son of Neriah, the son of Mahseiah, in the presence of my cousin Hanamel and of the witnesses who had signed the deed and of all the Jews sitting in the courtyard of the guard (32:6–12).

Jeremiah demonstrated remarkable faith. He bought real estate at the worst possible time. More than anyone else in Jerusalem, Jeremiah knew that the city would soon be captured and destroyed by the Babylonians. He had been preaching about the coming fall of

Jerusalem for some four decades. Soon, the Babylonian army would swarm over the land like locusts, and the entire land—including the field at Anathoth—would be rendered empty and desolate for seventy years. Real estate values during that time would be nil.

Yet God wanted Jeremiah to follow His instructions to the letter. While the prophet was imprisoned in the courtyard of the guard, his cousin Hanamel came to him, offering to sell him the field. Jeremiah faithfully and obediently agreed to the transaction, as God had instructed. Jeremiah is showing us, in practical terms, what it means to walk by faith. Each of us is called to live by faith, not by sight. When God tells us to do something that makes no logical sense, we are to follow faith, not logic.

This doesn't mean God calls us to live recklessly or irrationally. There are certain essential qualities of faith revealed in this passage, and one of those qualities is what I would call "the caution of faith." We will soon see the role of godly caution in the life of faith.

Notice how the story progresses. God speaks to Jeremiah in the loneliness of his prison, saying, "Hanamel son of Shallum your uncle is going to come to you and say, 'Buy my field'" (32:7). Later, when cousin Hanamel came to him exactly as God had said, Jeremiah records, "I knew that this was the word of the LORD" (v. 8).

It's important to see how God's message to Jeremiah unfolds. At first, Jeremiah receives an impression that he thinks is from the Lord, but he's not certain. Jeremiah must test this impression, and the way he tests it is to see if it comes true. If this impression from the Lord is later confirmed by an actual visit from his cousin, then Jeremiah will know that it was God speaking, not Jeremiah's imagination.

I have known a number of Christians who have been led far astray by their own imagination, thinking they were hearing a word from the Lord. They received this impression in a dream or during prayer or while going about their daily lives, but they didn't bother to test it as Jeremiah did. They simply accepted that impression as a word from God. So they quit their job or they moved to another country or they cashed in their life savings and gave it to a false teacher, thinking they had received a word from the Lord.

When the strange, spur-of-the-moment decision they made turns out disastrous, they ask, "Why did God tell me to do something so obviously wrong and stupid?" Answer: God didn't tell them anything of the sort. That impulse came from their subconscious mind, their own delusions, or perhaps a mood swing from a medication.

People often wonder how God spoke to the Old Testament prophets. Again and again in the Scriptures, we read a prophet saying, "The word of the LORD came to me." We have to wonder, how did that word come to the prophet? Did that prophet hear an audible voice—a thundering voice that shook the earth? Or did God speak to that prophet in the still, small voice of the Holy Spirit?

We have all felt that prompting, from time to time, of a silent voice within our thoughts—more of an impression than words. And it's always tempting to think that this *must* be God speaking to us. But the lesson of Jeremiah 32 is that the inner voice we sometimes hear is *not always the voice of God.* Jeremiah clearly understood this principle, so he tested the impression he received to make sure that it truly came from God himself.

Those impressions we receive that we easily mistake for the voice of God may be nothing more than our own inner urges. Then again, it could be the god of this world, Satan, speaking through that inner voice, imitating the voice of God. I've known a number of people who have been tremendously injured in their faith and have damaged the faith of others because they have acted impulsively on what that inner voice was prompting them to do.

Jeremiah demonstrates the importance of testing whether that impulse is the voice of God or not. This is what I call "the caution of faith." Authentic faith realizes that not every inner impulse comes from God, so these thoughts and motivations must be carefully put to the test.

Faith does not act fanatically or recklessly. Faith is cautious. Faith is not gullible, and it doesn't leap at every impulse, thinking it's the voice of God. Faith is willing to wait on God, knowing that He will confirm His word. In Jeremiah's case, God confirmed His word by fulfilling the prediction. At other times, He will confirm His word through Scripture or through the insight and counsel of other Christians.

CAUTIOUS AUDACITY

I'm acquainted with a young woman who sincerely, earnestly desired to know God and follow His leading. She sometimes thought God had spoken directly to her heart, and she would try to follow the leading she felt God had given her. On one occasion, she felt God was telling her she should marry a certain man. She didn't know this man very well, nor was she in love with him. But she felt certain that God was speaking to her, telling her He had planned for her to marry this man. So she began to think of ways they could become better acquainted so that they could eventually get married.

A few months after she experienced this impression, she learned that this man had become engaged to another young lady in the church. She was devastated—not because she had fallen in love with him; she hadn't—but because she was so certain she had heard the voice of God. She wondered how she could have been so misled.

Later, this young woman thought she received a message from God that involved her parents. But it later turned out that this impression too was mistaken. She felt confused in her faith and her understanding of God.

Eventually, she learned an important lesson in listening to God—the same lesson Jeremiah exemplifies for us here: Proceed with caution when you hear an inner voice, an inner impression that God is speaking to you. It may be the voice of God, but it may not be. God will confirm His word to us if that message is truly from Him. Before acting on that inner voice, wait for God to confirm His message. Be cautious, not impetuous, when it comes to listening for God's inner leading.

But here's the paradox of faith that I mentioned earlier. Alongside the caution of faith, we need another quality of faith that I would call "the audacity of faith." We need to be cautious in making sure that the inner voice truly comes from God. But once we have confirmed that God has truly spoken to us, we need to obey God instantly and completely, no matter how ridiculous His command may seem. Authentic faith often takes people in directions that seem irrational and illogical. If you live your entire life according to common sense and logic, then you are not living by faith. Faith often defies reason. Faith often means stepping out and taking a risk.

Hebrews 11 tells us that Noah built an ark. I'm sure the people of his day called him "Crazy Noah" because he was a nutty old man building a big boat on dry land.

And then there was Abraham, setting out on a journey without a map. People asked him, "Where are you going?" He said, "I don't know. I'm just going, that's all. God is leading me." "Poor old Abe," the people must have said, "he's lost his marbles!"

And don't forget Moses, raised in the household of Pharaoh to be a prince of Egypt. Yet he chose to identify with slaves and lead them out into the desert because God spoke to him from a burning bush. People must have said, "He's lost his ever-lovin' mind!"

But that's the audacity of faith. It acts in apparently irrational ways because it is based on a different kind of knowledge than reason and evidence. It is based on direct revelation from God, which has been carefully and cautiously confirmed. But once we have carefully confirmed God's word to us, we can dare to do great things, seemingly crazy things, for God, knowing that He will accomplish His will in our lives.

You might ask, "What about Hanamel? Was Jeremiah's cousin acting by faith when he asked him to buy that piece of land?" There's no indication in this passage that Hanamel was listening to the prompting of God. It appears that Hanamel was simply taking advantage of the situation. He saw a chance to unload his worthless property on

Jeremiah before the city fell. You can take money with you into captivity, but you can't take land. So he converted his real estate into cash. Hanamel appears to put pressure on Jeremiah. He says, "Buy my field at Anathoth, because as nearest relative it is your right *and duty* to buy it." Did Jeremiah really have an obligation to buy the property from Hanamel? In a way, yes. Leviticus 25:25–28 lays out a transaction by which someone can buy back (or redeem) a piece of property that a relative must sell because of financial difficulty. In ancient Israel, a piece of land that had been in the family for generations was considered an inheritance from God, and it was a tragic thing to lose that inheritance in the Promised Land. So the redemption of property was a family obligation when a relative got into financial trouble.

Shortly after the outbreak of World War II, I was one of about 2,000 young men on a troop transport sailing from San Francisco to Hawaii. We were in a convoy, protected against submarine attack by two American destroyers. One morning when we were about three-quarters of the way to our destination at Pearl Harbor, an alarm sounded. Everyone aboard had to go down into the hold. A submarine had been detected, and our destroyers started dropping depth charges.

Huddled in the belly of the transport, we could hear the terrible clang of the depth charges as the concussion banged the side of our vessel. About a thousand men were gathered in the hold where I was, and we wondered *what* would happen—and *when* it would happen. The atmosphere was tense, and no one said a word until one fellow called out, "Hey, does anybody here want to buy a good watch?"

I thought of that incident as I was reading this account of Hanamel selling his property to Jeremiah. That's how absurd Jeremiah's situation was. It made as much sense as buying a watch during a submarine attack.

In Judah, the world was collapsing around the people's ears, yet Hanamel wanted Cousin Jeremiah to invest in real estate. It was crazy, yet God was in the middle of this transaction, blessing it and confirming it. By faith, Jeremiah was willing to look ridiculous, willing even to be taken advantage of, and willing to buy a piece of worthless property because God had instructed him to do so.

THE COMMITMENT OF FAITH

In addition to the caution of faith and the audacity of faith, there is also an element that I would call "the commitment of faith." Jeremiah writes:

> "In their presence I gave Baruch these instructions: 'This is what the LORD Almighty, the God of Israel, says: Take these documents, both the sealed and unsealed copies of the deed of purchase, and put them in a clay jar so they will last a long time. For this is what the LORD Almighty, the God of Israel, says: Houses, fields and vineyards will again be bought in this land.'" (32:13–16)

This is a ringing testimony to the power and greatness of God. Jerusalem will soon fall, and the temple will be destroyed. The people will be slaughtered or taken captive to Babylon. It looks like the end of the world, but Jeremiah, by buying this field, offers a ray of hope to the dying nation. Houses will be bought, fields will be farmed, and vineyards will be tended once again in this land.

Jeremiah goes to great lengths to show how carefully the deed was drawn up, signed, and witnessed. Every "i" was dotted, every "t" was crossed in strict accordance with Hebrew law. The deed would be stored in a safe place, and seven decades later, when the Jews returned from their captivity in Babylon, that deed would still be valid. Jeremiah made sure that the legal documents conformed to the accepted procedures, and he made the entire transaction public and open to examination by anyone who was interested.

Once the documents were properly executed, Jeremiah explained that this was far more than a mere real estate transaction. This was a visual representation of God's promise to restore the people after seventy years of captivity.

Authentic faith does not take halfway measures. When it begins to act, it acts completely, consistently, and it goes all the way. Jeremiah does not hedge his bets. He does not tell the people, "Well, first, I'm illustrating a message from God, and second, I'm buying this property on speculation, hoping it will increase in value after the Babylonians go away, and third, I'm helping out my cousin, who's in a bit of a financial bind." No, Jeremiah offers one explanation, and it is a prophecy, based on what God has told him—a prophecy that the disgrace and desolation of the land of Judah will come to an end. The nation will be restored, and real estate will have value in Judah once again.

Faith is committed. Jeremiah demonstrated a complete commitment to the message God had given him.

The doubting prophet

So far, we have seen that faith is audacious, but faith is also cautious, waiting upon the word of God. And faith is consistent and committed in its actions. But there is one more quality of faith to be discovered in Jeremiah's account. He records a remarkably honest prayer.

When Jeremiah stands before kings and judges and priests who have the power to take his life, he is resolute and bold. He is a thundering Old Testament prophet. But in this prayer before God, he freely confesses his doubts that all these events will play out as they should. I'm grateful for this account, which reveals the humanness of Jeremiah. Here he reveals what I call "the doubtings of faith."

Faith always has its doubts. I think we do a disservice to fellow Christians when we suggest that doubting is a sin or that doubting is a sign of spiritual immaturity. As a young Christian, I thought faith and doubt were mutually incompatible. If you had faith, you had no doubts. And if you had doubts, you had no faith. Over time, I gradually began to realize that this is not true.

Doubt is the proof of faith, because doubt is an attack on faith. If you have doubts, it shows that you have a faith that can be attacked by doubts. You cannot have doubts unless you have faith. God works through our faith, so it should come as no surprise that the enemy seeks to attack our faith, and he does so by inflicting doubts on us. So doubts will arise, sometimes because of the normal thinking and questioning process we all go through, and sometimes because Satan is deliberately trying to overthrow our faith.

But let's not pretend that people of faith never doubt.

It may surprise you to know that our Lord Jesus himself, though He lived by faith in everything He did, was sometimes subject to attacks of doubt. If that were not so, then this statement in Hebrews would not be true: "For we do not have a high priest who is unable to empathize with our weaknesses, but we have one who has been tempted *in every way*, just as we are—yet he did not sin" (Hebrews 4:15, emphasis added).

In the garden of Gethsemane, Jesus doubted His mission. In the daylight, He had told His disciples again and again that He had come to Earth to die. But in the dark night before He went to the cross, He experienced doubts about going through with that awful mission. He prayed three times that God would take the "cup" of the cross from Him and not make Him drink it—though He was willing to accept the cross as the Father's will if there was no other way (see Matthew 26:36–46). And while He was on the cross, dying for our sins, He prayed the words of Psalm 22:1: "My God, my God, why have you forsaken me?" This was the cry of a soul engulfed in anguish, loneliness, and doubt.

God understands our doubts, and He accepts them. When we struggle and doubt, we should pray the prayer of the man who asked Jesus to heal his demon-possessed son: "I do believe; help me overcome my unbelief!" (Mark 9:24). Don't let your doubts overthrow you. Work through your doubts by praying honestly and clinging to the Lord for dear life.

Let's look at the prayer of Jeremiah. He begins by reminding himself of the nature and character of God:

> "After I had given the deed of purchase to Baruch son of Neriah, I prayed to the LORD:

"Ah, Sovereign LORD, you have made the heavens and the earth by your great power and outstretched arm. Nothing is too hard for you. You show love to thousands but bring the punishment for the parents' sins into the laps of their children after them. Great and mighty God, whose name is the LORD Almighty, great are your purposes and mighty are your deeds. Your eyes are open to the ways of all mankind; you reward each person according to their conduct and as their deeds deserve. You performed signs and wonders in Egypt and have continued them to this day, in Israel and among all mankind, and have gained the renown that is still yours. You brought your people Israel out of Egypt with signs and wonders, by a mighty hand and an outstretched arm and with great terror. You gave them this land you had sworn to give their ancestors, a land flowing with milk and honey. They came in and took possession of it, but they did not obey you or follow your law; they did not do what you commanded them to do. So you brought all this disaster on them." (32:16–23)

Jeremiah is following the pattern of prayer that Jesus taught us: "This, then, is how you should pray: 'Our Father in heaven, hallowed be your name'" (Matthew 6:9). Begin by reminding yourself of the name of God, the greatness of His being, and the faithfulness of His character. That's what Jeremiah is doing here. He starts off by reminding himself that the Lord is the God of power who made the heavens and the earth. Nothing is too hard for Him. He is the God of faithful love, who saves us and judges us. He is the God of wisdom and truth, whom history reveals, and who has done great wonders among us down through the ages.

Jeremiah was strengthening himself by reminding himself of the greatness of God. Why? Because his faith was under a ferocious attack. Jeremiah went on to recount the history of Israel and to remember how God had worked among His people. Jeremiah also remarked on the unfailing accuracy of God's predictions. Whatever He promised invariably came to pass.

Then Jeremiah prayed about what was really troubling him at that moment; the destruction of Jerusalem was at hand. He said:

"See how the siege ramps are built up to take the city. Because of the sword, famine and plague, the city will be given into the hands of the Babylonians who are attacking it. What you said has happened, as you now see. And though the city will be given into the hands of the Babylonians, you, Sovereign LORD, say to me, 'Buy the field with silver and have the transaction witnessed.'" (32:24–25)

Here, Jeremiah looks at his circumstances. The enemy is at the gate—an enemy with a reputation for unspeakable cruelty. The city was about to fall, just as the Lord had predicted. In the past, God did mighty works of rescue and salvation for His people, and Jeremiah concludes, "Nothing is too hard for the Lord" (See 32:17). Yet as Jeremiah looks at his city under siege, with starvation and panic in every house and in every street, his faith trembles and waivers.

Jeremiah has a great faith. He knows the great things God has done in the past. But as the Babylonians encircle the city, preparing to launch a bloody invasion, what has God asked His prophet to do? Buy a worthless field. Why does God make Jeremiah perform trivial tasks when the end of civilization is at hand?

Knowing the city is about to be destroyed, Jeremiah sees his faith go wobbly. He is focused on the desolation of the city, not the degradation of the people. Until now, Jeremiah has preached vehemently, calling the people to repentance. For forty years, the prophet has poured out his heart to his people, and for forty years the people have rejected his message. Now the day of judgment is coming, and Jeremiah has begun to doubt the Lord. So God replies:

Then the word of the LORD came to Jeremiah: "I am the LORD, the God of all mankind. Is anything too hard for me? Therefore this is what the LORD says: I am about to give this city into the hands of the Babylonians and to Nebuchadnezzar king of Babylon, who will capture it. The Babylonians who are attacking this city will come in and set it on fire; they will burn it down, along with the houses where the people aroused my anger by burning incense on the roofs to Baal and by pouring out drink offerings to other gods." (32:26–29)

"Nothing is too hard for you," Jeremiah said. God now turns Jeremiah's statement into a rhetorical question: "Is anything too hard for me?"

This is also what God said to Abraham's wife Sarah when she laughed at God's promise to give Abraham a son. Knowing that her own body was past the years of childbearing, she laughed at the thought of bearing a son. The Lord responded, "Why did Sarah laugh and say, 'Will I really have a child, now that I am old?' Is anything too hard for the LORD?" (See Genesis 18:13–14). The New Testament tells us that Sarah was a woman of faith. When her baby was born, she named him Isaac, meaning "Laughter," because she had laughed when God said she would have a son.

Now God says to Jeremiah, "I am the Lord, the God of all mankind. Is anything too hard for me?" I don't know about you, but my doubt issue is that I often find it hard to believe that God can change the hearts and minds of unbelievers. I'm confident that God can work on the conscience of Christians, but non-Christians seem so stubborn and resistant to God that sometimes I think He can't do much with them. I think this was also Jeremiah's problem. He found it hard to believe that God could do much to influence unbelieving Jews and unbelieving Babylonians.

So God replied, "I am the LORD, the God of *all* mankind"—both believers and unbelievers. "Is anything too hard for me?" God, in his reply to Jeremiah, zeroed in on the source of Jeremiah's doubts, and He assured the prophet that no force on earth, not even a stubborn and sinful human will, could thwart God's eternal purpose.

GOD WELCOMES OUR DOUBTS

Jeremiah closes chapter 32 with God's review of Israel's long history of sin, idolatry, and waywardness:

> "The people of Israel and Judah have done nothing but evil in my sight from their youth; indeed, the people of Israel have done nothing but arouse my anger with what their hands have made, declares the LORD. From the day it was built until now, this city has so aroused my anger and wrath that I must remove it from my sight. The people

of Israel and Judah have provoked me by all the evil they have done—they, their kings and officials, their priests and prophets, the people of Judah and those living in Jerusalem. They turned their backs to me and not their faces; though I taught them again and again, they would not listen or respond to discipline. They set up their vile images in the house that bears my Name and defiled it. They built high places for Baal in the Valley of Ben Hinnom to sacrifice their sons and daughters to Molek, though I never commanded—nor did it enter my mind—that they should do such a detestable thing and so make Judah sin." (32:30–35)

Then the Lord reaffirms, in a passage of poignant beauty, His plan to heal the wounds of Jerusalem:

"I will surely gather them from all the lands where I banish them in my furious anger and great wrath; I will bring them back to this place and let them live in safety. They will be my people, and I will be their God. I will give them singleness of heart and action, so that they will always fear me and that all will then go well for them and for their children after them. I will make an everlasting covenant with them: I will never stop doing good to them, and I will inspire them to fear me, so that they will never turn away from me. I will rejoice in doing them good and will assuredly plant them in this land with all my heart and soul.

"This is what the LORD says: As I have brought all this great calamity on this people, so I will give them all the prosperity I have promised them. Once more fields will be bought in this land of which you say, 'It is a desolate waste, without people or animals, for it has been given into the hands of the Babylonians.' Fields will be bought for silver, and deeds will be signed, sealed and witnessed in the territory of Benjamin, in the villages around Jerusalem, in the towns of Judah and in the towns of the hill country, of the western foothills and of the Negev, because I will restore their fortunes, declares the LORD." (32:37–44)

God is saying to Jeremiah, "I will heal this city and restore it to life again." But Jeremiah still struggled with doubt, so the opening lines of chapter 33 tell us that God spoke to Jeremiah a second time. He came to the troubled prophet with some additional insights into His purposes, and He invited Jeremiah to inquire further:

> While Jeremiah was still confined in the courtyard of the guard, the word of the LORD came to him a second time: "This is what the LORD says, he who made the earth, the LORD who formed it and established it—the LORD is his name: 'Call to me and I will answer you and tell you great and unsearchable things you do not know.'" (33:1–3)

This is a great promise for all who doubt and cling tightly to God throughout their time of doubt. God is saying that if we take our questions and doubts to Him, if we call on Him and ask Him for wisdom to deal with our doubts, He will answer and unlock the door to the secrets of the Almighty. This is similar to the promise Jesus made: "If you hold to my teaching, you are really my disciples. Then you will know the truth, and the truth will set you free" (see John 8:31–32).

During times of doubt, many people either retreat from God or hide from Him. They think God will be angry with them because of their doubts. Not true! He welcomes your questions, and He wants to tell you great and unsearchable things you do not know. He wants you to know the truth that will set you free from anxiety and uncertainty. Run to Him. Climb into His lap, and ask Him all your questions.

Unfortunately, we tend to take our doubts and unbelief to each other instead of to God. We complain that God doesn't keep His word. We may not put it that way, but that's what we are really saying. "I've tried praying, but it doesn't work for me." In other words, prayer only works for the people God favors. Even though God says He does not play favorites, we convince ourselves that He does. In different ways, in different words, we take our unbelief to each other instead of directly to God, and that's why our faith is stunted and immature.

But the man or woman who takes those doubts straight to God will not be turned away. God honors the prayer that says, "Lord, this is what I'm struggling with. I know nothing is too hard for you, but I can't see how you're going to solve this problem." The Scriptures contain story after story of men and women who have struggled in this way—people who have honestly spread their doubts out before God and have pleaded for understanding and wisdom.

When Jeremiah brought his honest questions and doubts to the Lord, God welcomed Jeremiah's questions, saying, "Call to me and I will answer you and tell you great and unsearchable things you do not know" (33:3).

TRUE JOY AND TRUE PROSPERITY

Next, God outlines the process by which He will fulfill His promises. First, *destruction leads to cleansing*:

> "For this is what the LORD, the God of Israel, says about the houses in this city and the royal palaces of Judah that have been torn down to be used against the siege ramps and the sword in the fight with the Babylonians: 'They will be filled with the dead bodies of the people I will slay in my anger and wrath. I will hide my face from this city because of all its wickedness.'" (33:4–5)

Destruction is often God's first step to cleansing. Why? Because we have been building on a false foundation, and God knows He must destroy the false foundation before He can build a new and true foundation for our lives. You may have experienced this process in your own life. There may have been something in your life that you were counting on: a relationship, a job, a goal, a dream. And suddenly it was shattered. It felt as if your life was over, as if you had nothing left to live for. Yet that was the moment God began to cleanse and restore your life. He was removing the false foundation so you could discover *His* foundation for your life. Cleansing is an essential step in restoration, but destruction is often necessary for cleansing to take place.

The next step God reveals to Jeremiah is that *cleansing leads to joy*:

> "'Nevertheless, I will bring health and healing to it; I will heal my people and will let them enjoy abundant peace and security. I will bring Judah

and Israel back from captivity and will rebuild them as they were before. I will cleanse them from all the sin they have committed against me and will forgive all their sins of rebellion against me. Then this city will bring me renown, joy, praise and honor before all nations on earth that hear of all the good things I do for it; and they will be in awe and will tremble at the abundant prosperity and peace I provide for it.'" (33:6–9)

We easily forget that one of God's great purposes for humanity is *joy*. Satan has succeeded in slandering God's reputation so that people see God as a cosmic killjoy, an angry and vindictive deity who seeks to stamp out pleasure and fun wherever it may be found. The God we serve, the God of the Bible, is the exact opposite of that deceptive image. God's purpose for our lives is that, in everything we experience—even as we endure hardships—our joy would increase. And He knows the steps we must take to bring that joy about.

As human beings, we all want to experience joy. But in our fallenness, we seek joy the wrong way. We look for joy in hedonistic pleasures, in drugs and alcohol, in mindless entertainment, and in all sorts of pursuits that seem to promise joy but never fulfill the promise. From the time of Moses to the time of Jeremiah, the Hebrew people repeatedly sought their spiritual joy in false religions, in worshiping a golden calf while Moses was on the mountain receiving the Law, or by sacrificing their children on the fiery altars of Baal and Molek (which is not unlike what we still do today in sacrificing unborn children on the altars of abortion).

So, while unbelieving human beings hate God, resent God, and resist God, thinking He only wants to destroy their pleasure and fun, God is lovingly, patiently pleading with them to receive the true, deep, lasting *joy* He wants to give them. It is one of the great ironies of life that human beings stubbornly reject the One who offers the joy they so desperately seek in all the wrong places.

Finally, God tells us that *joy permits prosperity*:

"This is what the LORD Almighty says: 'In this place, desolate and without people or animals—in all its towns there will again be pastures for shepherds to rest their flocks. In the towns of the hill country, of the western foothills and of the Negev, in the territory of Benjamin, in the villages around Jerusalem and in the towns of Judah, flocks will again pass under the hand of the one who counts them,' says the LORD." (33:12–13)

Here God pictures the prosperity that will accompany the unparalleled joy of that coming day. The picture of many pastures with shepherds and their flocks is an idyllic representation of prosperous conditions. God is telling us that the only time a society can be secure in its prosperity is when the people have been cleansed and filled with authentic, godly joy. So many seek prosperity the wrong way, which is why people rob, steal, cheat, and embezzle. It's also why people gamble, buy lottery tickets, and enter sweepstakes.

True prosperity comes to a society when joyful people live together in love, each using his or her skills to create financial security for the benefit of his or her family, neighbors, customers, and community. One day, when Jesus returns to reign over the earth, the world will realize that unimaginable prosperity comes from living together in love. Until that day, God withholds ultimate prosperity because the fallen human race is unable to achieve it, sustain it, or even comprehend it.

THE CITY OF GOD

God again opens a window on future history and reveals to the prophet Jeremiah a magnificent vision of a golden age that lies in our future. God reveals the power that will turn this vision into a reality:

"'The days are coming,' declares the LORD, 'when I will fulfill the good promise I made to the people of Israel and Judah.

"In those days and at that time
  I will make a righteous Branch sprout from David's line;
  he will do what is just and right in the land.
In those days Judah will be saved
  and Jerusalem will live in safety.

This is the name by which it will be called:
The Lord Our Righteous Savior.'" (33:14–16)

It has always been God's plan to establish Israel as a land ruled by a King of the line of David, who is also a Priest of the order of Melchizedek. In the fullness of time, that Ruler was born—Jesus, the King who is our righteousness, whose righteousness is imputed to us. Earlier in this book, Jeremiah related a similar prophecy:

> "The days are coming," declares the Lord,
>   "when I will raise up for David a righteous Branch,
> a King who will reign wisely
>   and do what is just and right in the land.
> In his days Judah will be saved
>   and Israel will live in safety.
> This is the name by which he will be called:
>   The Lord Our Righteous Savior." (23:5–6)

By this prophecy, God tells us that we, who will become the city of God, the new Jerusalem, partake of the very righteousness of Christ our Lord. The restoration of our world, the revelation of the new heaven and the new earth, the appearance of the new Jerusalem—these will all be characterized by one word: *righteousness*.

Righteousness consists, first of all, of truth. But it is more than that. It is also love—truth operating out of love. Man's righteousness, at best, can only be truth. But the righteousness of God is truth that operates lovingly, with forgiveness and understanding, yet utterly consistent with truth. These are the essential characteristics of that coming city, because these are the essential traits of our God.

Jeremiah 33 closes with God's statement that His covenant with the Jewish people is as steadfast and reliable as His covenant with the heavens. The day and the night come at their appointed times in accordance with God's covenant with the heavens and the laws of celestial mechanics that He has ordained. His covenant with His people is as sure as the law of gravity and the other physical laws that rule the universe. There could be no more ironclad guarantee than that.

When you come to the Lord, when you commit yourself to trusting Him and walking by faith, you can know that all the problems and sorrows of your life, as well as all the crises and tragedies of this world, will ultimately find their solution in the Lord and His righteousness. He will establish what He has promised. You have His Word on that.

12

WHAT DOES GOD REQUIRE?

Jeremiah 34–39

What does God require for a nation to survive and thrive?

In times past, many Americans lived with the impression that their nation endured and thrived because it was founded on faith in Almighty God. There was a common understanding, from our national leaders to everyday citizens, that (as one of our presidents once put it) "if we ever forget that we are One Nation Under God, then we will be a nation gone under."

As I write these words, it seems that we're on our way toward fulfilling that dire prophecy. Many in our nation, including a large number of our leaders, seem to have forgotten that we are One Nation Under God, and they want the rest of us to forget it as well. But the history of America is the history of a people who earnestly wanted to follow God and worship Him, and the country's forebearers were willing to cross an ocean and endure hardships for the freedom to do so.

The Pilgrims arrived in what is now in Massachusetts in 1620, wanting only the freedom to worship God according to their conscience. Ten years later, the Puritans arrived in America with the same goal. Quaker William Penn began his "holy experiment" in Pennsylvania in 1682. In 1740, the evangelical Great Awakening began in England and quickly spread to America. In 1787, the Continental Congress drafted the United States Constitution, but the states refused to ratify it until 1791, when the Bill of Rights was added, guaranteeing freedom of worship.

Then, in 1947, a Supreme Court ruling invoked a now-famous phrase from a letter by Thomas Jefferson: "separation of church and state." Jefferson had intended that phrase to mean that the government should not interfere in the affairs of the church. Since then, however, anti-religious activists, legislators, and judges have invoked that phrase to mean that the church should not be permitted to speak about the affairs of the government.

The courts have been chipping away at the biblical foundation of America ever since. For example, in 1962, the Supreme Court ruled that even nonsectarian prayer in public schools is unconstitutional. In the years since then, America has been less and less One Nation Under God and more and more a nation gone under.

As we come to Jeremiah chapters 34 through 39, we see Jeremiah facing some of the same questions Christians in America face today. The key question of these chapters is this: What does God require for any nation to survive and thrive? What qualities does God look for in a nation when He is deciding to either bless that nation—or consign it to the ash heap of history?

The narrative of these chapters is not arranged in chronological order. Rather, we see a series of historical flashbacks as the prophet reviews his ministry and relates certain incidents not previously mentioned in the book. Even though the book of Jeremiah is not arranged chronologically, it is organized thematically. These chapters, 34 through 39, focus on the theme of what God requires of a nation.

The narrative in these chapters dramatizes the failure of Judah to meet God's requirements for the life of the nation.

HAVE WE PROFANED GOD'S NAME?

Chapter 34 deals with the time of the second invasion of Nebuchadnezzar, after Jehoiachin (also known as Coniah) was taken captive to Babylon, and Zedekiah, the last king of Judah, became a vassal subservient to Nebuchadnezzar. The Chaldean (Babylonian) army was approaching Jerusalem again, and God sent Jeremiah to King Zedekiah with a message, another prediction of defeat at the hands of the Babylonians. Fearing the approaching Babylonian army, Zedekiah was looking for ways to placate God so He would spare the nation of Judah.

King Zedekiah was like so many people who are too busy for God until a crisis strikes. Only when life seems to spin out of control do they suddenly take an interest in God. Then they start going to church for the first time in years, hoping to placate God. They start putting money in the collection plate. They try bargaining with God: "Lord, I'll stop swearing, or I'll stop drinking, or I'll stop cheating on my marriage—if you'll get me out of this crisis." That's the fix King Zedekiah was in. He wanted a favor from God, so he ordered that all the household slaves of Judah be released from bondage.

In Deuteronomy 15, the law of Moses provides that slaves, Jewish people who became indentured servants to work off their debts, could be required to work for six years but must be set free at the seventh year. No Jew could be kept in servitude more than six years, and no Jew could hold one of his Jewish brothers as a permanent slave.

Over the years, however, this provision of the law of Moses had fallen into disuse. The people had become accustomed to holding permanent slaves in their households, and the economy of the kingdom had become dependent on human slavery. King Zedekiah had allowed this practice to go on even though he knew that his kingdom and his people were violating God's law. So now that his back was against the wall, King Zedekiah issued an edict declaring that the slaves should be released.

In chapter 37, which deals with the same time period, we learn that Egypt sent an army to Jerusalem to do battle with the Babylonians. When the Babylonians heard that the Egyptians were coming up against them, they left the siege of Jerusalem and went out to meet the Egyptians in battle. When King Zedekiah saw the Babylonian army withdraw, he immediately went back on his promise to God and rescinded his proclamation to release the slaves. So God sent Jeremiah to confront King Zedekiah with a new message, which Jeremiah records in chapter 34:

> "Recently you repented and did what is right in my sight: Each of you proclaimed freedom to your own people. You even made a covenant before me in the house that bears my Name. But now you have turned around and profaned my name; each of you has taken back the male and female slaves you had set free to go where they wished. You have forced them to become your slaves again.
>
> "Therefore this is what the LORD says: You have not obeyed me; you have not proclaimed freedom to your own people. So I now proclaim 'freedom' for you, declares the LORD—'freedom' to fall by the sword, plague and famine. I will make you abhorrent to all the kingdoms of the earth." (34:15–17)

The remarkable phrase in this passage is, "you have . . . profaned my name" (v. 16)." This was a serious charge against any Jew. The Hebrew people were brought up to revere and honor the name of God. The scribes did not even dare to write the name of God without taking a bath and changing their clothes. They never pronounced His name aloud. The four Hebrew letters used for the name of God were called "the ineffable Tetragrammaton"—the unpronounceable or unspeakable four letters YHWH. They never spoke the name of God for fear of speaking it with sinful lips.

Yet God's charge against King Zedekiah was, "You have profaned my name." The Hebrew word translated *profane* means "wound," "pierce," or "deface." God's charge is, "You have defaced Me, you have polluted My name." How did Zedekiah do this? By willfully violating the human rights of slaves. When you treat another human being as less than fully human and made in the image of God, you commit blasphemy against God himself.

And when you agree, in a moment of crisis, to repent and follow God's Law, then reverse that decision the moment the pressure is off, you treat God as if He can be easily fooled and manipulated. That too is an act of blasphemy.

As those of us who are Americans think of the history of our land, we can see what a heavy charge must be leveled against us. White Americans, who originally emigrated from Europe and became the dominant culture in America, have had much to answer to God for. As we have already noted, the first immigrants from Europe came in the 1600s and 1700s in search of freedom to worship God according to their own conscience. But soon after these first immigrants arrived, people discovered there was enormous wealth to be made in this land, and the wealth could be multiplied many times over by pushing the original inhabitants off the land and by importing slave labor from Africa to work the land.

So, as an American nation, our forbearers have badly mistreated the Native Americans, the original inhabitants of this land, and the Africans we brought to this land by force. They mistreated the Chinese, Japanese, Mexican, Puerto Rican, and other peoples who came to this land, treating them as second-class human beings or worse. Those groups they didn't enslave, they paid slave wages to keep them subservient, to keep them doing the so-called "jobs Americans won't do." They have been segregated, had passed laws against them, kept out of our neighborhoods, and treated as less than human.

The God of all nations and all peoples of the world says, in effect, "You have profaned My name by the way you have treated fellow members of the human family."

It's always helpful to remember that God's view of our spiritual state is based not on how we treat our friends and family, but how we treat those who may be different from us—either ethnically or socially. Do we treat them as equals? Do we treat every person we encounter as human beings made in the image and likeness of God? That is the true test of our spirituality. If we fail that test, we profane the name of God.

TRUTH VERSUS TRADITION

In Jeremiah 35, we meet the Rekabites, a people group related to Israel by marriage. They were descendants of the Kenites, the tribe of Jethro, the father-in-law of Moses. Some three hundred years before Jeremiah's time, one of their number, Rekab, was an associate of Jehu, king of Israel during the time of Elisha. Rekab's son was Jehonadab, and this account tells us that Jehonadab grew tired of life in the city and longed for a simpler way of life. Many of us feel that way, wishing for a way to escape the rat race and get back to nature.

Jehonadab felt so strongly about honoring God and living close to nature that he commanded his sons to drink no wine, build no houses, and tend no vineyard or field, but to live in tents as nomads. The descendants of Jehonadab heeded his commands, and the Rekabites had followed his admonitions for almost 300 years. When Nebuchadnezzar invaded Judah, the Rekabites took refuge in the city of Jerusalem. So God sent Jeremiah to the Rekabites.

Jeremiah 35 opens with God's command to Jeremiah to go to the Rekabites, bring them into the temple, and offer them wine to drink. Jeremiah did as God commanded, and when he offered the Rekabites wine, they refused to drink it—exactly as God knew they would.

Please don't misunderstand the crucial theme of this chapter. Jeremiah is not teaching us about whether it is right to drink wine. Nor does this passage teach that God sometimes tempts people to sin— James 1:13 makes it clear that God never tempts anyone to sin. The Rekabites had made a commitment to keep the commandments of their ancestor Jehonadab, but these were human commandments, not the commandments of God.

After God sent Jeremiah to the Rekabites to offer them wine, He then sent Jeremiah to the nation of Judah with a message:

> Then the word of the LORD came to Jeremiah, saying: "This is what the LORD Almighty, the God of Israel, says: Go and tell the people of Judah and those living in Jerusalem, 'Will you not learn a lesson and obey my words?' declares the LORD. 'Jehonadab son of Rekab ordered his descendants not to drink wine and this command has been kept. To this day they do not drink wine, because they obey their forefather's command. But I have spoken to you again and again, yet you have not obeyed me. Again and again I sent all my servants the prophets to you. They said, "Each of you must turn from your wicked ways and reform your actions; do not follow other gods to serve them. Then you will live in the land I have given to you and your ancestors." But you have not paid attention or listened to me. The descendants of Jehonadab son of Rekab have carried out the command their forefather gave them, but these people have not obeyed me.'" (35:12–16)

It would be easy to misread this passage and think that God is commending the Rekabites for faithfully keeping Jehonadab's commands to abstain from wine and to live in tents. But God is not commending these people for refusing wine or for their nomadic lifestyle. He is commending them for their faithfulness and their commitment—qualities that the people of Judah utterly lack. Because the Rekabites have been faithful to their commitments, God gives Jeremiah a word of prophecy concerning these people at the end of this chapter: "Therefore this is what the LORD Almighty, the God of Israel, says: 'Jehonadab son of Rekab will never fail to have a descendant to serve me'" (35:19).

God always keeps His promises, so we can be certain that, somewhere in the world, there are Rekabites still living, still serving God in their own unique way.

The main point of this passage is not so much that God was commending the Rekabites, but that God was holding them up as an example of the kind of faithfulness, obedience, and commitment the people of Judah lacked. The Rekabites had demonstrated absolute fidelity to commandments that were purely human in origin, yet the people of Judah had received commandments directly from God, and they had repeatedly broken them.

The first two of the Ten Commandments relate to the sin of idolatry:

> And God spoke all these words:
> "I am the LORD your God, who brought you out of Egypt, out of the land of slavery.
> "You shall have no other gods before me.
> "You shall not make for yourself an image in the form of anything in heaven above or on the earth beneath or in the waters below. You shall not bow down to them or worship them; for I, the LORD your God, am a jealous God, punishing the children for the sin of the parents to the third and fourth generation of those who hate me, but showing love to a thousand generations of those who love me and keep my commandments." (Exodus 20:1–6)

The first commandment: "You shall have no other gods before me." The second commandment: "You shall not make for yourself an image" of another god. I believe these two commandments are number one and number two because they are first and second in order of importance. And what did the people of ancient Israel and Judah do that caused them to be disciplined by God? They broke the first and second commandments.

So to make His point with devastating logic, God used the Rekabites as an example, an object lesson. The Rekabites remained faithful to the commandments of an ancestor, a mere man, for three centuries. There is nothing sacred about the Rekabite tradition. In fact, it would be fair to say that tradition is nothing more than the dead hand of the past maintaining its vice grip on the future. Yet many people love tradition more than they love principles of right and wrong.

We in the church are easily seduced by the power of tradition. I have traveled across the country and have visited hundreds of churches. I have seen how easily Christians get so caught in the iron grip of the past that they cannot obey God in the present. Over the years, I've seen churches wither and die, and the epitaph on their tombstone should read, "We've never done it that way before." They are slaves to human tradition. Evangelist William Bell Riley observed:

> The past should instruct us without restraining us. We should draw upon the customs of our fathers for what they are worth; we should refuse to let those same customs run us into ruts. Thomas Dixon once said: "Tradition was the most constant, the most persistent, the most dogged, the most utterly devilish opposition the Master encountered. It openly attacked him on every hand. . . ."
>
> It was his departure from customs, in search of souls, that caused Christ to be crucified, and the same fact caused the great apostle Paul to be imprisoned. But without it there could have been no Christian church, no soul-winning endeavor worthy the name. To a certain extent the same is true today. The great soul-winners of the past have shaken off the shackles of overconservatism in methods. Witness Luther, Melancthon, Wesley, Edwards, Finney. . . . The church itself grows by iconoclasm; its first work was to set aside false gods; its permanent work is to set aside false ideals and dispense with obsolete customs.[11]

Jeremiah 35 reveals two essential actions God requires of a nation: First, God requires that a nation remove all false gods and worship the One True God alone. Second, God requires that a nation operate on the basis of God's truth and moral principles, not dead tradition and notions of "This is the way we've always done it." God's truth and God's moral principles are reliable and guaranteed to keep a nation strong and free, whether in Old Testament times or New Testament times or the age in which we live today. God's truth and God's principles were true yesterday, they are true today, and they will be true tomorrow. Traditions tend to maintain their grip on us long after they have become obsolete.

You cannot destroy God's Word

Jeremiah 36 contains another revelation of what God requires of a nation, and it tells us how the book of Jeremiah came to be written and how it was nearly destroyed. This chapter takes us back to the fourth year of Jehoiakim, the son of Josiah, king of Judah, at about the midpoint of Jeremiah's prophetic ministry. God commanded Jeremiah to write down in a book all the things He had been saying. Up to this point, Jeremiah had been delivering spoken messages to the people. Now God commands him to write these messages down in a book. So Jeremiah dictates the messages to his secretary, Baruch. Then, because Jeremiah was a prisoner at this time and unable to go himself, he sent Baruch to read the messages in the temple.

Baruch waited until all the people from the cities around Jerusalem had come to the temple on a day of fasting, and he read the words God had given to Jeremiah. The prophet hoped the people would repent so God would restore the nation. One of the government officials heard Baruch reading the book in the temple, and he told other government officials what he had heard. They gathered and sent for Baruch to read it again to them.

The account says that when the government officials heard God's words, they were afraid because of the prophecies of doom for the nation. They said to each other, "We must report this to the king." Next, we read the shocking response of King Jehoiakim:

> After they put the scroll in the room of Elishama the secretary, they went to the king in the courtyard and reported everything to him. The king sent Jehudi to get the scroll, and Jehudi brought it from the room of Elishama the secretary and read it to the king and all the officials standing beside him. It was the ninth month and the king was sitting in the winter apartment, with a fire burning in the firepot in front of him. Whenever Jehudi had read three or four columns of the scroll, the king cut them off with a scribe's knife and threw them into the firepot, until the entire scroll was burned in the fire. The king and all his attendants who heard all these words showed no fear, nor did they tear their clothes. Even though Elnathan, Delaiah and Gemariah urged the king not to burn the scroll, he would not listen to them. Instead, the king commanded Jerahmeel, a son of the king, Seraiah son of Azriel and Shelemiah son of Abdeel to arrest Baruch the scribe and Jeremiah the prophet. But the LORD had hidden them. (36:20–26)

The Scriptures have had many critics—the textual critics, the source critics, and the historical or so-called "higher" critics—but few critics have been as blunt as King Jehoiakim, who simply cut God's word into shreds, then burned the shreds. For his contemptuous act of defiance, God condemned this wicked king. Later in this chapter, we will see him condemned to death in disgrace. His body is cast out onto the ground to be eaten by wild dogs.

After the destruction of the first scroll of Jeremiah, God tells Jeremiah to write the words again:

> After the king burned the scroll containing the words that Baruch had written at Jeremiah's dictation, the word of the LORD came to Jeremiah: "Take another scroll and write on it all the words that were on the first scroll, which Jehoiakim king of Judah burned up. . . ."
>
> So Jeremiah took another scroll and gave it to the scribe Baruch son of Neriah, and as Jeremiah dictated, Baruch wrote on it all the words of the scroll that Jehoiakim king of Judah had burned in the fire. And many similar words were added to them. (36:27–28, 32)

King Jehoiakim had tried to eliminate God's message with a knife and a fire. Instead, his actions resulted in judgment upon himself, and even more words were added to the scroll of Jeremiah. You cannot thwart God's will, and you cannot destroy God's Word. The scroll King Jehoiakim tried to destroy is the very book we are studying here.

This wicked king was judged not only because he acted foolishly in burning God's Word but also because of the wicked and defiant condition of his heart. Not only was he willing to destroy the word of God but he also did so arrogantly, brazenly, without a hint of hesitation or fear. This man had lost the fear of God, and when a nation or an individual has no fear of God, destruction is sure to follow. The fear of God is based on a knowledge of God. Those who have no fear of God are worse than the merely senseless; they have completely lost touch with reality.

In history, in nature, and in Scripture, we see the operation of what is called "the law of retribution." It states that there are inevitable consequences for doing wrong, and those consequences cannot be escaped. Even an atheist must admit, when he examines the laws of nature, that if you violate the laws of nature, there are consequences to be paid. We human beings don't like to admit it, but we are subject to forces more powerful than we are. We disregard and disrespect the laws of gravity, motion, electricity, and so forth at our own peril. The law of retribution is woven into every aspect of life. The wise man or woman respects God's moral laws as much as God's physical laws. God always accomplishes what He says He is going to do. He requires that every nation recognize His sovereign government over all the nations. Therefore, the ability to ably and wisely rule a people begins with the fear of God and a respect for His Word.

King Jehoiakim had no fear of God, no respect for God's word, and no wisdom. He led the nation into sin and rebellion against God. And in the end, King Jehoiakim discovered that there is always a price to pay for a refusal to fear God. As King Solomon wisely observed, "The fear of the LORD is the beginning of wisdom, and knowledge of the Holy One is understanding" (Proverbs 9:10).

THE LOW POINT

Jeremiah 37 and 38 together form a single account, and once again, the theme is what God requires of nations. This is the story of the persecution of Jeremiah, which took place after the Babylonians withdrew from Jerusalem to confront Pharaoh's army. God sent Jeremiah to King Zedekiah to tell him that Nebuchadnezzar would return and that the army of Babylon would again lay siege to Jerusalem. Jeremiah writes the following:

> After the Babylonian army had withdrawn from Jerusalem because of Pharaoh's army, Jeremiah started to leave the city to go to the territory of Benjamin to get his share of the property among the people there. But when he reached the Benjamin Gate, the captain of the guard,

whose name was Irijah son of Shelemiah, the son of Hananiah, arrested him and said, "You are deserting to the Babylonians!"

"That's not true!" Jeremiah said. "I am not deserting to the Babylonians." But Irijah would not listen to him; instead, he arrested Jeremiah and brought him to the officials. They were angry with Jeremiah and had him beaten and imprisoned in the house of Jonathan the secretary, which they had made into a prison. (37:11–15)

This passage tells us how Jeremiah first became a prisoner. Later, at the request of King Zedekiah, Jeremiah was permitted the courtesy of house arrest instead of a dungeon cell, and he was permitted slightly more liberty. Chapter 38 tells us how the officials of the nation became angry as Jeremiah continued to urge the nation to surrender to the Babylonians. Jeremiah writes:

Then the officials said to the king, "This man should be put to death. He is discouraging the soldiers who are left in this city, as well as all the people, by the things he is saying to them. This man is not seeking the good of these people but their ruin."

"He is in your hands," King Zedekiah answered. "The king can do nothing to oppose you."

So they took Jeremiah and put him into the cistern of Malkijah, the king's son, which was in the courtyard of the guard. They lowered Jeremiah by ropes into the cistern; it had no water in it, only mud, and Jeremiah sank down into the mud. (38:4–6)

This is, literally and figuratively, the lowest point in Jeremiah's career. He is down in the mud and gloom of a dark cistern, without food or water and without adequate clothing. There his enemies left him alone to die of exposure and starvation.

But God had not forgotten His prophet. Christians who think that God has promised them a life without troubles, sufferings, or persecution would do well to remember the example of Jeremiah. Here was a man who was faithful and obedient to every command of the Lord, yet God allowed this suffering in his life. But God also had a rescuer in place to save Jeremiah's life.

In the court of King Zedekiah was a Cushite (Ethiopian), a black African eunuch whose name is given as Ebed-Melek, which in Hebrew means "the servant of the king." I think it's likely that this was not the man's name, but his designation, a description of his position in the king's palace. He was a servant, a nameless man, yet God knew his name, and God had placed him in that position for a purpose.

The king and the officials in the palace probably just called him, "Hey, you!" To them, he was a nonentity, and no name was needed. But God sent "Hey, you!" to deliver Jeremiah from the cistern. When Ebed-Melek the Cushite heard that Jeremiah's enemies had put him in the cistern, he went before the king and said this:

> "My lord the king, these men have acted wickedly in all they have done to Jeremiah the prophet. They have thrown him into a cistern, where he will starve to death when there is no longer any bread in the city." (38:9)

King Zedekiah is clearly a weak man. When Jeremiah's enemies came to him, demanding the prophet's death, Zedekiah said, "He is in your hands. The king can do nothing to oppose you." He seemed to be saying, in effect, "Do whatever you want to him, but leave me out of it. I don't want to know the details, but I'm not going to stop you."

Then, when his own servant arrives, telling King Zedekiah that some men have acted wickedly, throwing Jeremiah into a cistern to starve to death, King Zedekiah reverses himself. He tells Ebed-Melek the Cushite, "Take thirty men from here with you and lift Jeremiah the prophet out of the cistern before he dies" (v. 10).

With tender, compassionate care, this African servant carefully provides cushioning rags so Jeremiah won't be injured by the ropes used to lift him out of the cistern. So Jeremiah was permitted to be imprisoned in the courtyard of the guard, instead of the muck at the bottom of the cistern. There he would stay until the fall of Jerusalem.

While Jeremiah was in prison, God told him to tell Ebed-Melek that He was about to fulfill his judgment against Jerusalem, yet He would rescue Ebed-Melek from the sword of the Babylonians. Ebed-Melek would escape with his life because his trust was in the Lord (see 39:15–18).

GOD IDENTIFIES WITH HIS PEOPLE

King Zedekiah knew that Jeremiah was indeed a true man of God. It undoubtedly troubled this weak and vacillating king to realize that by fighting Jeremiah the prophet, he had been fighting against God. King Zedekiah sent for Jeremiah and asked him for a message from God. He finally wanted to hear what the prophet had to say.

After the king promised Jeremiah that he would neither kill the prophet nor hand him over to those who wanted him dead, Jeremiah agreed to give the king a message from God. Jeremiah records their conversation:

> Then Jeremiah said to Zedekiah, "This is what the LORD God Almighty, the God of Israel, says: 'If you surrender to the officers of the king of Babylon, your life will be spared and this city will not be burned down; you and your family will live. But if you will not surrender to the officers of the king of Babylon, this city will be given into the hands of the Babylonians and they will burn it down; you yourself will not escape from them.'"
>
> King Zedekiah said to Jeremiah, "I am afraid of the Jews who have gone over to the Babylonians, for the Babylonians may hand me over to them and they will mistreat me."
>
> "They will not hand you over," Jeremiah replied. "Obey the LORD by doing what I tell you. Then it will go well with you, and your life will be spared." (38:17–20)

Jeremiah assured the king he would be safe if he did what God commanded. But the king was not a courageous man. He feared the people around him, and he had no faith in God. So the king sent Jeremiah back to the courtyard of the guard.

What does God expect of a nation? He takes it personally when His people are attacked and persecuted.

Over and over in Scripture, we see God identifying with His people. In Matthew 10:40, Jesus tells His disciples, "Anyone who welcomes you welcomes me, and anyone who welcomes me welcomes the one who sent me." And in Acts 9:4, when Saul of Tarsus was on his way to round up Christians in Damascus, the voice of Jesus spoke to him, saying, "Saul, Saul, why do you persecute me?" He didn't say, "Why are you persecuting my followers?" He said that Saul was persecuting *Him* personally.

Although God was angry with the people of Judah for their idolatry, He still loved them and wanted them to turn back to Him. He identified with them regarding the calamity that was about to fall on them. King Zedekiah, in his cowardice and weakness, was making a decision that would seal the fate not only of himself but also of all the people in the land of Judah. Zedekiah was filling up the cup of wrath for himself and his people. God, who identified with His people, was anguished over the king's refusal to obey.

Zedekiah wanted to place a gag order on Jeremiah. There had been no witnesses—the king and the prophet had spoken together alone—and Zedekiah wanted to keep their conversation a secret. Jeremiah records what happened next:

> Then Zedekiah said to Jeremiah, "Do not let anyone know about this conversation, or you may die. If the officials hear that I talked with you, and they come to you and say, 'Tell us what you said to the king and what the king said to you; do not hide it from us or we will kill you,' then tell them, 'I was pleading with the king not to send me back to Jonathan's house to die there.'"
> All the officials did come to Jeremiah and question him, and he told them everything the king had ordered him to say. So they said no more to him, for no one had heard his conversation with the king.
> And Jeremiah remained in the courtyard of the guard until the day Jerusalem was captured. (38:24–28)

Jerusalem would soon fall to the Babylonians. God holds a nation accountable when it rejects the word of God and continues in disobedience.

Shortly after His triumphal entry into Jerusalem as the king of the Jews on Palm Sunday, Jesus wept over the city of Jerusalem, saying, "Jerusalem, Jerusalem, you who kill the prophets and stone those sent to you, how often I have longed to gather your children together, as a hen gathers her chicks under her wings, and you were not willing" (Matthew 23:37).

Jesus knew that Jerusalem was about to crucify God's authorized Messiah, and within a few years, the city would again be besieged by a Gentile nation, the Roman Empire. Once again, Jerusalem would be strangled and starved, then overthrown. Blood would flow in the streets, and again the temple would be destroyed. Jesus identified with the people of that city, but the people would pay the price for the actions of their corrupt leaders.

LEST WE FORGET

Jeremiah 39 opens with a brief account of the fall of Jerusalem:

> In the ninth year of Zedekiah king of Judah, in the tenth month, Nebuchadnezzar king of Babylon marched against Jerusalem with his whole army and laid siege to it. And on the ninth day of the fourth month of Zedekiah's eleventh year, the city wall was broken through. Then all the officials of the king of Babylon came and took seats in the Middle Gate: Nergal-Sharezer of Samgar, Nebo-Sarsekim a chief officer, Nergal-Sharezer a high official and all the other officials of the king of Babylon. When Zedekiah king of Judah and all the soldiers saw them, they fled; they left the city at night by way of the king's garden, through the gate between the two walls, and headed toward the Arabah.
>
> But the Babylonian army pursued them and overtook Zedekiah in the plains of Jericho. They captured him and took him to

Nebuchadnezzar king of Babylon at Riblah in the land of Hamath, where he pronounced sentence on him. There at Riblah the king of Babylon slaughtered the sons of Zedekiah before his eyes and also killed all the nobles of Judah. Then he put out Zedekiah's eyes and bound him with bronze shackles to take him to Babylon.

The Babylonians set fire to the royal palace and the houses of the people and broke down the walls of Jerusalem. (39:1–8)

The last chapter of Jeremiah offers additional details about the fall of Jerusalem. The temple of God was burned and destroyed. It was a scene of unbelievable, mind-shattering horror as people were put to the sword, as women were raped, as children and young people were dragged out of their homes to be led into captivity. The air was filled with flames, smoke, and the moans and screams of the dying and grieving.

King Zedekiah had rejected Jeremiah's warning, and he had many years to regret that decision. He was forced to watch the slaying of his own sons—the last sight he beheld before the Babylonians put out his eyes. Nebuchadnezzar wanted to make sure that the cruel memory would haunt Zedekiah for the rest of his life. Then the Babylonians shackled him and led him off to Babylon.

It's both ironic and fitting that the wealthy slave owners of Jerusalem became slaves themselves. Clearly, God gives you the judgment you ask for. Under the remorseless logic of "an eye for an eye," the man who enslaves others earns the fate of enslavement.

The last requirement God has for a nation is this: it must recognize that judgment will ultimately come. God is patient, and He is not willing that any should perish. But even though judgment is delayed, judgment always falls. God himself says in the book of Ezekiel, "A ruin! A ruin! I will make it a ruin! The crown will not be restored until he to whom it rightfully belongs shall come; to him I will give it" (Ezekiel 21:27).

Any nation that deliberately rejects the requirements of God's justice has forfeited its right to exist. The hand of doom rests upon godless and disobedient nations. Ultimately, judgment will come. No political manipulation or act of defiance can delay God's justice for even a second. For Jerusalem in Jeremiah's day, the moment of judgment arrived on the ninth day of the fourth month of Zedekiah's eleventh year.

God has a specific day, month, and year appointed for every nation that rejects His warning. Nothing but complete, heartfelt, sincere repentance can avert God's judgment when the appointed time arrives.

In this section of the book of Jeremiah, we have seen four key principles that still apply to our lives and our nations today—four ways individuals and nations reject the will of God. We see these principles in nations around the world—including the United States.

First, a nation can ignore God and refuse to listen to Him. People who do so usually give themselves over to actions and habits that help them forget that God will hold them accountable: sexual depravity, drugs, alcohol, gambling, every form of entertainment—anything to take their minds off of God's Word, the inevitability of death, and the swift approach of eternity. For example, we can see this in the United States. We are seeing out-of-control hedonism and an epidemic of wickedness throughout American society. In many ways, the US has become a nation that has shut its ears to God's Word and God's warnings.

Second, a nation can persecute the prophets of God and hinder the message of God. In the past, those who spoke God's Word in a prophetic way were only persecuted in totalitarian societies, such as Pastor Paul Schneider in Nazi Germany and Aleksandr Solzhenitsyn in Soviet Russia. Today, those who speak out for the gospel and Christian morality are persecuted, both in America and around the world.

Evangelist Billy Graham carefully guarded his marriage and his Christian witness by refusing to even enter an elevator alone with a woman who was not his wife, and he was praised for his moral stance. Today, though, leaders who follow his example are often criticized and ridiculed. In addition, Christian political leaders, teachers, and students are sometimes denied their First Amendment right to pray and profess Christ at public events. And we can expect anti-Christian persecution in America to intensify over time.

Third, a nation can seek to circumvent judgment through legal maneuvering, political manipulation, and silencing witnesses. King Zedekiah and his allies tried every political scheme in the book, and that ultimately resorted to throwing their chief accuser into a cistern. The political scandal in Jeremiah's day reminds me of the Watergate scandal of the 1970s, in which everyone involved, from hired burglars to the President and his top aides, tried to escape legal judgment through cover-ups, political scheming, and bribery. Human justice can sometimes be fooled for a while; but God's justice, never.

Finally, a nation can put on an outward show of morality and piousness, while inwardly rejecting God and refusing to submit to His will. People can become quite adept at saying all the right "God words," supporting all the right causes, and attending all the prayer breakfasts, commemorations, and observances to make others think they are sincere, godly people. But in many cases, inwardly their hearts can be far from God. This kind of public hypocrisy has been with us for thousands of years, and it is offensive to God. He looks upon the heart, not the outward appearance.

There is only one attitude that will avert the judgment of God: *repentance.* True repentance consists of a deep humility before God and an honest and searching acknowledgment of guilt. Repentance requires that we humbly cry to God for mercy we do not deserve, for healing that we cannot achieve ourselves, and for forgiveness that only God offers.

The night after King Solomon dedicated the great temple in Jerusalem (the same temple that would be utterly destroyed by the Babylonians in Jeremiah's day), God spoke to Solomon. He made certain promises to the king, and he also issued certain warnings. One of the beautiful promises God made to Solomon that night was this: "If my people, who are called by my name, will humble themselves and pray and seek my face and turn from their wicked ways, then I will hear from heaven, and I will forgive their sin and will heal their land" (2 Chronicles 7:14).

But God also gave Solomon this warning:

> "But if you turn away and forsake the decrees and commands I have given you and go off to serve other gods and worship them, then I will uproot Israel from my land, which I have given them, and will reject this temple I have consecrated for my Name. I will make it a byword and an object of ridicule among all peoples. This temple will become a heap of rubble. All who pass by will be appalled and say, 'Why has the LORD done such a thing to this land and to this temple?' People will answer, 'Because they have forsaken the LORD, the God of their ancestors, who brought them out of Egypt, and have embraced other gods, worshiping and serving them—that is why he brought all this disaster on them.'" (2 Chronicles 7:19–22)

This warning to Solomon was fulfilled to the letter in Jeremiah's day. This is the fate of any nation that ignores God. It becomes a heap of rubble. It is uprooted and cast aside, and it is remembered by history with either scorn or horror.

May this not be the epitaph of America: "They have forsaken the Lord, the God of their ancestors." May we come to our senses and turn back to the Lord in time. Let us pray and live out these lines of the poem "Recessional" (1897) by Rudyard Kipling, written during the twilight of the British Empire:

> Lord of Hosts, be with us yet,
> Lest we forget—lest we forget!

13

BACK TO EGYPT

Jeremiah 40–45

It took a lot of work and many miracles to liberate the people of Israel from their long bondage in Egypt. God first had to recruit a deliverer, Moses, by the miracle of a bush that burned without being consumed. When Pharaoh refused to let the people leave, God had to strike Egypt with a series of ten miraculous plagues—a river of blood, a swarm of frogs, the death of first-born Egyptian sons, and more. Then came the biggest miracle of all—the parting of the Red Sea.

After God went to all that trouble to get the people of Israel out of bondage in Egypt, you'd think the Israelites would want to *stay* out of Egypt—but no!

Even after the Babylonians had destroyed the temple, after the city was laid waste, after much of the population was killed and the rest led away to Babylon, some of those left behind wanted to go right back into the land of bondage, the land of Egypt, from which their ancestors had been delivered 900 years earlier.

As we come to Jeremiah chapters 40 through 45, Jerusalem is overthrown. The city walls are leveled. The great temple of Solomon is burned, its treasures ransacked, its columns toppled, its splendor reduced to dust and rubble. The streets are littered with corpses.

For forty years, Jeremiah has preached and pleaded with the kings and priests of Judah, trying with all his might to prevent this tragedy from falling upon the nation. Throughout those years, the specter of this event has hovered on the horizon of Jeremiah's ministry. God delayed His judgment while Jeremiah ministered among the people, trying to turn them back to God, trying to prevent, if he could, the death of this nation.

Now that the judgment against Judah has fallen, you would think that at long last the hearts of the people would turn back to God. But the people of Judah have still not reached bottom. They continue to be led by the deceitfulness of their fallen human nature. They continue to rebel against God, even in the depths of their downfall.

The New Testament tells us that all the Old Testament stories are recorded for our instruction, so that we would learn about ourselves. All the Old Testament stories have a double meaning. Not only are they reliable accounts of historical events but they also teach us about the nature and functioning of that strange tendency toward evil that the Bible calls "the flesh," the sin nature, which is our moral and spiritual inheritance from Adam.

One of the most important lessons we can learn as Christians is how to recognize the flesh and how it functions in our lives. Remember Jeremiah's statement as he was being instructed by the Lord, probably the most frequently quoted verse in the book: "The heart is deceitful above all things and beyond cure. Who can understand it?" (17:9).

This section of the book shows how our fallen nature deceives and misleads us. This is an account of the flesh at work. It demonstrates to us how our only hope to overcome the deceitfulness of the flesh is to place our trust in the living God. As we look at these chapters, we will see the various forms the flesh takes and the strategies it uses to deceive us.

This section of Jeremiah is a mirror in which you and I will find our self-deceptive sin nature reflected with startling clarity.

IS IT RIGHT TO DO WRONG
WITH RIGHT INTENTIONS?

Jeremiah 40 is the account of the prophet's experiences after the fall of Jerusalem. He was imprisoned in the courtyard of the guard when the Babylonians broke through the gates and invaded the city. During the overthrow of the city, the Babylonians broke into the prison, took all the prisoners out, and gathered them together with all the Jews who were to be exiled to Babylon. The Babylonians bound all the captives in chains, including Jeremiah.

As Jeremiah stood shackled and chained, Nebuzaradan, the captain of King Nebuchadnezzar's guard, set Jeremiah free and gave him a choice. The prophet could go to Babylon, where he would be treated with honor and respect, or he could stay in the land. If Jeremiah chose to stay, Nebuzaradan said, he could stay with Gedaliah, the man appointed by the king of Babylon as governor over the province of Judah. So Jeremiah chose to stay in the land and live near Gedaliah.

The fall of Jerusalem did not mean the end of Judean resistance against the Babylonian invaders. Bands of Judean warriors gathered in the hills as guerrilla fighters under the leadership of various captains—Ishmael, Johanan, Seraiah, and Jezaniah. They refused to surrender to the Babylonian conqueror. Jeremiah tells us that the guerrilla captains came to Governor Gedaliah at Mizpah to talk to him. Jeremiah doesn't tell us why they wanted to speak with the governor, but they probably hoped to enlist his help in undermining (and eventually overthrowing) the Babylonian overlords.

But Gedaliah refused to take part in any rebellion against the Babylonians. Jeremiah tells us that Gedaliah took an oath to reassure these guerrilla captains and their men. Reassure them of what? He probably wanted them to know that he would not report them to the Babylonians. Jeremiah tells us that Gedaliah also gave them some advice:

"Do not be afraid to serve the Babylonians," he said. "Settle down in the land and serve the king of Babylon, and it will go well with you.

I myself will stay at Mizpah to represent you before the Babylonians who come to us, but you are to harvest the wine, summer fruit and olive oil, and put them in your storage jars, and live in the towns you have taken over." (40:9–10)

Gedaliah had seen enough bloodshed. He wanted to bring peace to the land, and the only way to do that was through submission to their Babylonian masters. But these guerrilla captains wanted nothing to do with peace through submission. They were determined to continue their guerrilla war against Babylon, with or without the governor's help.

Jeremiah relates an incident that is instructive to us today:

> Johanan son of Kareah and all the army officers still in the open country came to Gedaliah at Mizpah and said to him, "Don't you know that Baalis king of the Ammonites has sent Ishmael son of Nethaniah to take your life?" But Gedaliah son of Ahikam did not believe them.
>
> Then Johanan son of Kareah said privately to Gedaliah in Mizpah, "Let me go and kill Ishmael son of Nethaniah, and no one will know it. Why should he take your life and cause all the Jews who are gathered around you to be scattered and the remnant of Judah to perish?"
>
> But Gedaliah son of Ahikam said to Johanan son of Kareah, "Don't do such a thing! What you are saying about Ishmael is not true." (40:13–16)

One of the most subtle and deceptive manifestations of our old sin nature is the tendency to be either overly trustful of others without discrimination or to be overly suspicious of others without cause. Either extreme is unrighteous, according to Scripture. It is a moral and spiritual weakness to be either gullible and naïve or automatically defensive and suspicious of everyone you meet. Gedaliah, unfortunately, gravitated to the extreme of being overly trusting where this man Ishmael son of Nethaniah was concerned.

Satan deceives us and tricks us into error by tempting us to one position or its extreme opposite. We tend to think that if one extreme position is wrong, then the opposite must be right. But the Christian life is a fence-walk, a balancing act between extremes. That godly balance is hard to find, and the wisdom to maintain our balance can only be found in God himself.

Gedaliah, unfortunately, had not found that balance. He was trusting and undiscerning with regard to Ishmael. No doubt, Ishmael made certain assurances that Gedaliah believed. A wiser and more godly man than Gedaliah would have at least suspected that Ishmael's word could not be trusted—and might have seen through Ishmael's deception.

But the fact that Gedaliah was wrong in being overly trusting does not mean that Johanan was right in the way he dealt with the matter. Johanan wanted to warn the governor about an assassination plot against him. So far, so good. But his solution to the assassination plot was an ungodly solution. He proposed that Gedaliah allow him to take preemptive action by murdering Ishmael.

I don't think it's an accident that the assassin's name is Ishmael. This was also the name of Abraham's son by his wife's servant Hagar, so Abraham's son Ishmael was Isaac's half-brother. The New Testament refers to Ishmael as a man of the flesh, a man who cannot be trusted (See Galatians 4:28–29). All the people in the Bible who bear the name Ishmael are people who cannot be trusted.

The Ishmael in the book of Jeremiah is no exception. He was bribed by the king of the Ammonites to assassinate Gedaliah. And Gedaliah, being too trusting, did not test the spirits—something God tells us to do in 1 John 4:1. So when Johanan told him the truth about Ishmael, he refused to believe it—and that refusal would cost him his life.

Johanan's plan was to take vengeance by murdering him in secret. This is yet another manifestation of the flesh—the belief that we can do the wrong thing for the right motive, and it will all turn out just fine. This is how deceptive the flesh is. We easily convince ourselves that wrong is right, that sin is justified, and that the end justifies the means.

I think every human being, at one time or another, has thought about how sweet it would be to secretly take vengeance against an enemy or a persecutor. I confess I have felt this way myself, even as a Christian and a pastor. I am ashamed of this impulse, but I hope that by confessing it, I can help you to face some of the shameful and secret impulses you struggle with.

Every now and then, I would receive a blistering letter of criticism that would take me apart and confront me with all my faults. Now, I do welcome criticism. These letter-writers were usually right, and they were only telling me what I already know too well. At the same time, these letters almost always contain a mistaken impression or two. While I cannot deny the accurate criticism, I would like to correct any misimpressions that exist—but I can't. In most cases, the letter of criticism is unsigned and anonymous.

An anonymous letter of criticism is like being shot by a sniper. You've been hit, you've been wounded, but the identity of your assailant is unknown. It leaves you feeling frustrated, vulnerable, defenseless—and angry. You think, "The coward! I'd be happy to talk about my failings with anyone face-to-face—but how can I respond to an anonymous letter?" And I confess that there were moments when I would have liked to have taken vengeance against my anonymous critic. But then I came to my senses, turned the matter over to the Lord, and asked Him to be my defender.

Johanan wanted to disrupt the assassination plot against Governor Gedaliah—but more than that, he wanted to take vengeance. He wanted to do a wrong thing for the right reasons, but good motives do not transform a sinful act into a righteous act.

The source of our unreasoning fears

Jeremiah 41 tells us the outcome of Gedaliah's misplaced trust:

> In the seventh month Ishmael son of Nethaniah, the son of Elishama, who was of royal blood and had been one of the king's officers, came with ten men to Gedaliah son of Ahikam at Mizpah. While they were eating together there, Ishmael son of Nethaniah and the ten men who

were with him got up and struck down Gedaliah son of Ahikam, the son of Shaphan, with the sword, killing the one whom the king of Babylon had appointed as governor over the land. Ishmael also killed all the men of Judah who were with Gedaliah at Mizpah, as well as the Babylonian soldiers who were there. (41:1–3)

This is a bloody account of treachery and jealousy. Ishmael was of the royal family, one of the chief officers of the king. Perhaps this accounts for Ishmael's jealousy of the man who, though of humble origin, was now governor of the land. In this scene, Ishmael and his allies are eating a meal with Gedaliah and his men. We can imagine them talking together pleasantly, smiling and treating each other as brothers—then, at some point in the meal, Ishmael rises from the table, draws his sword, and the slaughter begins.

This picture of treachery and murder reveals what lies hidden in our own hearts. Any time we become furiously angry, we feel this same murderous rage within. In that moment, given the opportunity, if we felt there would be no consequences to pay, we might even take somebody's life. Hating a brother is murder, the Scriptures say, and hate is a characteristic of the flesh we live with.

When Cain was disappointed that God had rejected his offering, God warned him: "Sin is crouching at your door; it desires to have you" (see Genesis 4:7). Cain rejected God's warning and went on to murder his brother Abel. The flesh, our fallen sin nature, makes this kind of horrifying violence possible for anyone, even Christians, under the right circumstances.

I recall with sadness a tragic incident that took place many years ago. A pastor and his wife had a son who grew up to be rebellious and hostile. This young man had once professed Christ as his Savior, but he later became involved in drugs and other criminal behavior. One day, he came to his parents' home and argued with them. Then, in a fit of rage, he killed his own mother.

As we read further in the story of Ishmael son of Nethaniah, the tale becomes even more tragic. Ishmael trapped eighty men who had come to Mizpah to bring their offerings to the Lord. Ishmael and his men ambushed and killed them, then dumped their bodies down a cistern. Then Ishmael took the rest of the people of Mizpah captive. Among the captives was Jeremiah. Ishmael planned to turn the captives over to the Ammonites, but a band of warriors led by Johanan rescued them. Even though the captives were freed, Ishmael and eight of his men escaped from Johanan and fled to safety among the Ammonites.

Jeremiah writes:

> Then Johanan son of Kareah and all the army officers who were with him led away all the people of Mizpah who had survived, whom Johanan had recovered from Ishmael son of Nethaniah after Ishmael had assassinated Gedaliah son of Ahikam—the soldiers, women, children and court officials he had recovered from Gibeon. And they went on, stopping at Geruth Kimham near Bethlehem on their way to Egypt to escape the Babylonians. They were afraid of them because Ishmael son of Nethaniah had killed Gedaliah son of Ahikam, whom the king of Babylon had appointed as governor over the land. (41:16–18)

Johanan and his men were innocent of any wrongdoing. They had rescued the people Ishmael had captured, and they had attacked and sent fleeing the men responsible for the murder of Governor Gedaliah. Yet these innocent men apparently feared that they would be blamed for the death of Gedaliah, so they fled.

Here is another manifestation of the flesh. An evil heart makes us afraid when there is nothing to fear. The flesh provokes all sorts of unreasonable fears within us. As Proverbs 28:1 says, "The wicked flee though no one pursues, but the righteous are as bold as a lion." Why would Johanan and his men flee when they had nothing to fear? Because their consciences were not right with God. Although they were innocent of the death of Gedaliah, they were not entirely innocent. Their consciences were stained—by what crimes or sins, we don't know—but I believe that's why they were afraid.

So they fled to Egypt, where they had no business going, and they took all of the people they had freed with them.

Once, when I was in the Navy in Hawaii, we had a barber at the naval base who was very emotional and excitable. When he talked, he spoke with big, sweeping gestures and wide eyes. My friends and I enjoyed taking him to the movies at the base because he would get completely swept up in the drama of the story. We enjoyed watching him more than we enjoyed watching the movie. If a villain attacked the hero on the screen, the barber would jump up and shake his fist and shout at the villain. Everyone in the audience would laugh.

On one occasion, something frightening happened on the screen, and the barber leaped out of his seat and ran screaming out of the theater. When I read this account of Johanan and his men fleeing to Egypt because of their needless fear of the Babylonians, I'm reminded of our friend the barber, running and screaming in terror out of the movie theater because of some flickering lights and shadows projected on a movie screen.

When our hearts are not right before God, we too often run from shadows. We become anxious and fearful, and we can't even name the thing we're afraid of. That's the flesh at work within us.

PUTTING ON A RELIGIOUS APPEARANCE

Jeremiah goes on to write:

Then all the army officers, including Johanan son of Kareah and Jezaniah son of Hoshaiah, and all the people from the least to the greatest approached Jeremiah the prophet and said to him, "Please hear our petition and pray to the LORD your God for this entire remnant. For as you now see, though we were once many, now only a few are left. Pray that the LORD your God will tell us where we should go and what we should do."

"I have heard you," replied Jeremiah the prophet. "I will certainly pray to the LORD your God as you have requested; I will tell you everything the LORD says and will keep nothing back from you."

Then they said to Jeremiah, "May the LORD be a true and faithful witness against us if we do not act in accordance with everything the LORD your God sends you to tell us. Whether it is favorable or unfavorable, we will obey the LORD our God, to whom we are sending you, so that it will go well with us, for we will obey the LORD our God." (42:1–6)

At last, after following their own flawed counsel and watching their numbers dwindle, Johanan and his men approach Jeremiah the prophet and ask him to consult with God on their behalf. They want Jeremiah to ask God where they should go and what they should do.

They already knew it was wrong to flee to Egypt, because the Scriptures say unequivocally that Israel was never to return to Egypt. Ever! As the prophet Isaiah wrote, "Woe to those who go down to Egypt for help, who rely on horses, who trust in the multitude of their chariots and in the great strength of their horsemen, but do not look to the Holy One of Israel, or seek help from the LORD" (Isaiah 31:1).

Finally, they had decided to ask Jeremiah for wisdom from God, and they promised to do whatever God said they should do. But there's an interesting detail in the way they phrased their request: "Please hear our petition and pray to the LORD your God for this entire remnant. . . . Pray that the LORD your God will tell us where we should go and what we should do" (vv. 2–3). They refer to God as "the LORD *your* God," Jeremiah's God. They have placed distance between themselves and God, as if He is not also their own God, the God of Israel, the God of Abraham, Isaac, and Jacob.

In replying to them, Jeremiah turns the tables on them, saying, "I will certainly pray to the LORD *your* God as you have requested" (v. 4). He refers to God as *their* God. Jeremiah wants them to know that the God of Israel is not some remote and foreign deity to them. He is every bit as much their God as He is Jeremiah's God. He will pray to God on their behalf, but they need to know that they are as accountable to the God of Israel as is Jeremiah. They need to view the Lord as *their* God, and they need to submit themselves to His will.

The words of Johanan and his men sounded pious enough, but their hearts were not right with God, as later events will prove. They didn't need a prophetic word from God telling them they should not go to Egypt. They knew what they were doing was wrong. But they wanted God to put His stamp of approval on their unrighteous actions, so they clothed their request to Jeremiah with pious-sounding words.

This too is a manifestation of the flesh. Fleshly, unrighteous people are often extremely religious. They love to sing in the choir and serve on the church board. They sometimes carry a big, heavy Bible so everyone will notice how "spiritual" they are. Many fleshly people are even preachers. They preach very sincere-sounding messages, but their words come from a heart of unbelief. That is what Johanan and his men were doing through their pious-sounding but insincere religious talk. Jeremiah was not fooled for a moment.

YOU CAN'T RUN AWAY FROM YOUR OWN HEART

Jeremiah placed the request of these men before the Lord in prayer. Then Jeremiah tells us how God responded:

> Ten days later the word of the LORD came to Jeremiah. So he called together Johanan son of Kareah and all the army officers who were with him and all the people from the least to the greatest. He said to them, "This is what the LORD, the God of Israel, to whom you sent me to present your petition, says: 'If you stay in this land, I will build you up and not tear you down; I will plant you and not uproot you, for I have relented concerning the disaster I have inflicted on you. Do not be afraid of the king of Babylon, whom you now fear. Do not be afraid of him, declares the LORD, for I am with you and will save you and deliver you from his hands. I will show you compassion so that he will have compassion on you and restore you to your land.'
>
> "However, if you say, 'We will not stay in this land,' and so disobey the LORD your God, and if you say, 'No, we will go and live in Egypt, where we will not see war or hear the trumpet or be hungry for bread,' then hear the word of the LORD, you remnant of Judah.

This is what the LORD Almighty, the God of Israel, says: 'If you are determined to go to Egypt and you do go to settle there, then the sword you fear will overtake you there, and the famine you dread will follow you into Egypt, and there you will die. Indeed, all who are determined to go to Egypt to settle there will die by the sword, famine and plague; not one of them will survive or escape the disaster I will bring on them.'" (42:7–17)

Do you see how thoroughly God knew their hearts? He knew their hidden motives and secret plans: "Ah, down in Egypt we'll have no trouble. If we go to Egypt, everything's going to be fine. There'll be no famine in Egypt, no war in Egypt, no draft, no drills. Everything will be fine in Egypt." This is another characteristic of the flesh. It not only arouses within us these unreasonable fears but it also leads us to trust in unrealistic hopes and to imagine that "everything's going to be all right" in some place other than in the center of God's will.

We so easily succumb to the temptation to run. What were these men hoping to escape by running to Egypt? The sword, famine, and pestilence. What did God say they would find if they went to Egypt? The sword, famine, and pestilence. You can't run away from God. Wherever you go, you bring your troubles with you. A change of scenery won't save you, because the problem is not the scenery; the problem is within you. Your heart is deceitful above all things and desperately corrupt. And you can't run away from your own heart.

Johanan and his men said they wanted to hear the word of the Lord and do it. But their actions are about to prove otherwise. Chapter 43 continues the account:

When Jeremiah had finished telling the people all the words of the LORD their God—everything the LORD had sent him to tell them—Azariah son of Hoshaiah and Johanan son of Kareah and all the arrogant men said to Jeremiah, "You are lying! The LORD our God has not sent you to say, 'You must not go to Egypt to settle there.' But Baruch son of Neriah is inciting you against us to hand us over to the Babylonians, so they may kill us or carry us into exile to Babylon."

So Johanan son of Kareah and all the army officers and all the people disobeyed the LORD's command to stay in the land of Judah. (43:1–4)

These men asked Jeremiah to pray for a word directly from the Lord, and they promised to obey whatever the Lord said through Jeremiah. Then, when Jeremiah brought God's message specifically for them, they called Jeremiah a liar. Jeremiah has spent forty years or more of his ministry demonstrating the highest integrity. Throughout that time, Jeremiah repeatedly predicted exactly what came to pass—the complete destruction of Jerusalem by the Babylonian Empire. His track record as a spokesman for God was 100 percent.

But these men accused Jeremiah of lying. It was they themselves who went back on their own word, refusing to honor their promise to follow whatever God said. Why? Because they didn't like God's answer. But they projected their own dishonesty onto a blameless man of God. They justified their own faithlessness by blaming Jeremiah's secretary, Baruch. They told Jeremiah, "Baruch put you up to this. He just wants us to be killed or exiled to Babylon. We don't believe God really spoke to you."

Here again, we see the flesh in action, the deceptive and desperately wicked human heart doing what it does best: transferring blame and leading people into self-destructive error. So these men, who truly had nothing to fear from the Babylonians, were fleeing from the Babylonians right into the very danger they feared most. God warned them that doom awaited them in Egypt, yet they were determined to defy God and follow their deceptive hearts into the land of their own doom.

Jeremiah was a captive of Johanan and his men. He didn't want to go to Egypt, but his captors gave him no choice. So Jeremiah was led down into Egypt by these disobedient men.

The word of the Lord came to Jeremiah at Tahpanhes in Egypt. The word of God is never bound, even if the people of God are. Jeremiah was bound, but he could still hear the voice of the Lord. God told Jeremiah to once again perform one of those memorable visual demonstrations of God's message.

In the past, God had told Jeremiah to take a clay jar and smash it against the trash heap outside the city to dramatize what God was going to do to the unrepentant nation of Judah. Later, God told Jeremiah to wear a wooden yoke to dramatize the yoke of bondage and oppression the Babylonian Empire was about to impose on the nation of Judah if the people did not repent.

Now, in Egypt, God tells Jeremiah to take large stones and hide them in the mortar of the pavement at the entrance to Pharaoh's house at Tahpanhes. This was a testimony to the prophecy that Nebuchadnezzar, the king of Babylon, would come to Egypt and spread his royal canopy over those stones. The tragic irony of Johanan and his men was that they were running to Egypt to escape the king of Babylon, but before long, the king of Babylon would arrive in Egypt as a conqueror.

In the late nineteenth century, discoverer and archaeologist William Flinders Petrie went to the site of Tahpanhes (known in modern times as Qasr Bint al-Yahudi, "the Castle of the Jew's Daughter"), located near what is now the northern end of the Suez Canal. There he discovered and excavated the platform of brickwork that paved the entry of Pharaoh's palace. Petrie later wrote:

> Here the ceremony described by Jeremiah took place before the chiefs of the fugitives assembled on the platform, and here Nebuchadnezzar "spread his royal pavilion." . . . Unhappily, the great denudation [erosion over time] which has gone on has swept away most of this platform, and we could not expect to find the stones whose hiding is described by Jeremiah. I turned over all that remained of the platform, but found no stones within it. Some blocks of limestone lay loose upon its surface, but they had evidently never been embedded in it, but had only fallen from the masonry of the fort, and were covered with burned earth and mud washed down from the destroyed walls. The site, however, is unmistakable.[12]

The winds and sands of time have erased the evidence of Jeremiah's stones, but the pavement that Jeremiah describes remains as confirmation of this account.

Rebellion and the loss of God's presence

Jeremiah 44 is a sequel to the preceding events. The people who have come down from Judah to the land of Egypt have spread across the region. After they have been in the land for a few months, Jeremiah calls them together and announces that they are still engaging in the same idolatry that brought down God's judgment in Judah.

The Jewish women were leaders in these idolatrous acts, offering incense to the Moon Goddess (or the Queen of Heaven, as Jeremiah calls her). The people also gave themselves in idolatrous ways to the other Egyptian gods that surrounded them. This is precisely what God had judged the nation of Judah for, as Jeremiah reminds them. The city of Jerusalem was destroyed just months earlier and the people carried off to Babylon in exile for the very sins they were now committing once again. Did they think that God's judgment wouldn't find them in Egypt? Jeremiah assures the people that God will judge them for the sin of idolatry wherever they are.

Jeremiah tells us how the people responded to his message:

> Then all the men who knew that their wives were burning incense to other gods, along with all the women who were present—a large assembly—and all the people living in Lower and Upper Egypt, said to Jeremiah, "We will not listen to the message you have spoken to us in the name of the LORD! We will certainly do everything we said we would: We will burn incense to the Queen of Heaven and will pour out drink offerings to her just as we and our ancestors, our kings and our officials did in the towns of Judah and in the streets of Jerusalem. At that time we had plenty of food and were well off and suffered no harm. But ever since we stopped burning incense to the Queen of Heaven and pouring out drink offerings to her, we have had nothing and have been perishing by sword and famine." (44:15–18)

The people were openly defiant toward both Jeremiah and the Lord. They said, in effect, "We don't care what you say and we don't care what God says. We will do what we want." They justified their defiance on the grounds that their sacrifices to the goddess protected them from harm, and failing to sacrifice to her brought them death and famine.

Another way the flesh leads us into error is by fogging our memory and making us forget the truth. These people look back on their days of idolatry and sin in Judah as a golden age, a utopia when false gods brought them prosperity, protection, and plenty of food. They forgot the lean times, the troubled times they experienced in Judah, and they remembered only the good times. They refused to acknowledge that those good times they had were the result of God withholding His judgment out of mercy toward the people. Now they took God's mercy for granted, and they felt they could return to their idolatry without any repercussions.

Amazingly, these people had learned nothing from the defeat of their nation, the overthrow of their city, and the exile of their fellow Jews to Babylon. The stubbornness of the flesh and the deceitfulness of the unregenerate human heart seemed practically limitless.

So these people, who have already experienced God's judgment in the loss of their nation, are about to experience God's judgment yet again. This marks the deepest level of the decay of the people and the nation of Judah. Jeremiah told the rebellious people:

> "But hear the word of the LORD, all you Jews living in Egypt: 'I swear by my great name,' says the LORD, 'that no one from Judah living anywhere in Egypt will ever again invoke my name or swear, "As surely as the Sovereign LORD lives." For I am watching over them for harm, not for good; the Jews in Egypt will perish by sword and famine until they are all destroyed. Those who escape the sword and return to the land of Judah from Egypt will be very few. Then the whole remnant of Judah who came to live in Egypt will know whose word will stand—mine or theirs.'" (44:26–28)

The people of Judah have thrown down a challenge to God, and God accepts the challenge. He says that the judgment that shall fall upon them is this: His name shall be removed from them. Though it's not clear exactly what this means in practical terms, it was a real and terrible judgment on these rebellious people. It probably meant they would lose all sense of a relationship with God, all sense of God's presence in the world.

We used to live in a world in which, generally speaking, even unbelievers had some vague sense of God's presence in the world. But that has changed. Today, people all around us live with a sense of being completely alone and lost in the universe. French biologist Jacques Monod expressed this sense of lostness and aloneness in his book *Chance and Necessity: An Essay on the Natural Philosophy of Modern Biology*: "The ancient covenant is in pieces; man knows at last that he is alone in the universe's unfeeling immensity, out of which he emerged only by chance. His destiny is nowhere spelled out, nor is his duty."[13]

The people around us, believing they live in a godless universe, are afflicted with cosmic loneliness. They feel abandoned to the random and terrifying forces of an uncaring cosmos. All the tremendously complex problems of the world—from solving the riddle of our own mortality to surviving the threat of nuclear annihilation—are a crushing burden, a baffling mystery that we are helpless to solve.

When people think they live in a godless universe, when they think they are morally unaccountable to anyone, they are capable of any horrifying behavior. The rapists, thugs, and mass murderers who stalk our society are almost entirely people who have no sense of God's presence in the world. The totalitarian dictators who terrify and murder their own people—Stalin, Hitler, Mao, Castro, Pol Pot—are always people who have no sense of God's presence in the world.

People tend to respond to the emptiness of a godless universe in one of two ways: (1) they seek to become a god themselves by controlling, terrorizing, or extinguishing the lives of other people; or (2) they yield to despair and suicide. That is the world we see around us. That is the world in which we live.

This is probably the despairing mindset God handed these people over to when He said, "I swear by my great name that no one from Judah living anywhere in Egypt will ever again invoke my name." He had removed His name from among them, and He had removed His presence from among them. You and I are prone to sin and error, but we always know that we can go back to God, confessing our sin and repenting, and God will be there to forgive us and receive us back. But for those who have lost all sense of God's presence in the world, there is no place to go but the place of despair.

ESCAPE IF YOU CAN!

Jeremiah 45, the briefest chapter of the book, gives us the final picture of the flesh in action. The five verses of this chapter cover the time when Jeremiah sent Baruch down to the temple to read the words he had dictated, as we saw earlier. Chronologically, chapter 45 should follow chapter 36. But Jeremiah has placed it here because it fits thematically with the preceding chapters dealing with the deceptive nature of the human heart. Jeremiah writes:

> When Baruch son of Neriah wrote on a scroll the words Jeremiah the prophet dictated in the fourth year of Jehoiakim son of Josiah king of Judah, Jeremiah said this to Baruch: "This is what the LORD, the God of Israel, says to you, Baruch: You said, 'Woe to me! The LORD has added sorrow to my pain; I am worn out with groaning and find no rest.'" (45:1–3)

Jeremiah had sent Baruch to the temple to read the words of the Lord. This passage reveals Baruch's emotional state. He expected that reading God's message to the people would impact them, and he would be exalted before them as God's spokesman. But it didn't work out that way. The people rejected Baruch and his message. He went home feeling discouraged and defeated. He cried out to God, "Woe to me! The LORD has added sorrow to my pain; I am worn out with groaning and find no rest." So God sent a message to Baruch through Jeremiah:

> "But the LORD has told me to say to you, 'This is what the LORD says: I will overthrow what I have built and uproot what I have planted, throughout the earth. Should you then seek great things for yourself?

Do not seek them. For I will bring disaster on all people, declares the LORD, but wherever you go I will let you escape with your life.'" (45:4–5)

What is the root of all our troubles with the flesh? It is the "almighty self." It is our self-seeking, self-important, self-centered obsession with ourselves. Baruch wanted to make a name for himself among these people, even though they would soon be judged by God. He was hoping to exalt himself, and when it didn't happen, he was dejected.

But God put everything in perspective for Baruch. He was about to uproot what he had planted—the kingdom of Judah, the city of Jerusalem, the great temple of Solomon, the people of Judah, everything. It was all about to be yanked out by the roots and tossed aside like so many useless weeds.

God told Baruch to keep his priorities straight, to stay focused on serving God, and to stop seeking fame among the people who are about to be uprooted. God promised that wherever Baruch would go, his life would be spared. Even in a time of disaster, God would protect him.

Baruch learned an important lesson about the deceitfulness of the heart. He learned that he was prone to the deceitfulness of pride and ego and ambition. He learned that his heart secretly craved the glory that belongs to God. So God taught him to seek humility rather than fame, and He would be Baruch's defender and protector.

As we look at our own lives in light of these lessons, it would be easy to sink into despair. It would be easy to say, "Who is capable of understanding and overcoming the deceitfulness of the human heart? How can I defeat this enemy within? How can I find victory over my own fallen flesh, my own deceitful heart?"

But God has provided an answer to these questions. The answer, of course, is the death and resurrection of the Lord Jesus Christ. Only the cross can put our fallen flesh to death. Only the resurrection can give us newness of life. Only Jesus himself, living His life through us, can give us victory over the flesh. That is the good news of the gospel.

Near Watsonville, California, there is a creek called Salsipuedes Creek. In Spanish, *Sal si puedes* means, "Escape if you can." The creek is lined with quicksand, and there is a legend that in the early days of California a laborer fell into the quicksand and was struggling to get out. A Spanish soldier riding by on horseback saw the unfortunate fellow and called out to him, "Sal si puedes! Escape if you can!" And the creek has borne that name ever since.

That is what our fallen flesh is like. We are sinking in the quicksand of our selves—our deceitful, fleshly selves. We struggle against our sinful tendencies, but we cannot escape them. Only God has the power to rescue us from the trap we have fallen into. That's why Jeremiah, earlier in his book, said: "LORD, I know that people's lives are not their own; it is not for them to direct their steps" (10:23).

And that's why King Solomon wrote:

> Trust in the LORD with all your heart
> > and lean not on your own understanding;
> in all your ways submit to him,
> > and he will make your paths straight. (Proverbs 3:5–6)

Your own heart will deceive you. Your own heart will entrap you like quicksand. Only the wisdom of God, the wisdom of the Word, can free you from the muck and mire of your own deceptive flesh.

Bring your deceptive heart to God and ask Him to put your flesh to death on the cross. Rely on His resurrection for the power and grace to lead you to truth and understanding. God knows your heart more deeply, fully, and completely than you could ever imagine. He knows your conscious thoughts and your unconscious drives and motivations. He knows the temptations you feel powerless against, and that's why He included that all-important little phrase in the Lord's prayer—a prayer I pray every day: "Lead us not into temptation."

Only God can free you from the lies of your deceptive heart. Trust Him. Lean on Him. Submit to Him. Then watch in awe and gratitude as He directs your steps and makes your paths straight.

14

NOW HEAR THIS!

Jeremiah 46–52

Seven months after Thomas Jefferson was inaugurated as the third president of the United States, the Danbury Baptist Association of Danbury, Connecticut, wrote a letter to the new president. The Baptists were a religious minority in the state of Connecticut, and they were concerned that a religious majority might influence the state legislature to establish an official state religion for Connecticut. In their letter, dated October 7, 1801, they asked President Jefferson for assurances that the First Amendment protected them against the establishment of a state religion.

President Jefferson replied to the Danbury Baptists in a letter dated January 1, 1802. He stated, "I contemplate with sovereign reverence that act of the whole American people which declared that their legislature would 'make no law respecting an establishment of religion, or prohibiting the free exercise thereof,' thus building a wall of separation between Church and State."

It's clear to anyone reading the correspondence between the Danbury Baptists and President Jefferson that this "wall of separation between church and state" was intended to prevent the state from interfering with the church. It was never intended to insulate the government from the moral and spiritual influence of the church.

The relationship between the realm of the church and the realm of the political state has always been uneasy. As Christians, we have acknowledged the principle of a separation between the sacred realm and the secular realm ever since Jesus told the Pharisees, "Give back to Caesar what is Caesar's, and to God what is God's" (Matthew 22:21).

Government should never interfere with the free exercise of religion, and the church should never try to use politics to increase the worldly power of the church. But Christians also have a right and a responsibility to hold the government accountable for acts of injustice. Jesus calls us to be salt and light—a savor, a preservative, a source of moral illumination and spiritual enlightenment—in a dark and decaying world (Matthew 5:13–16). This means that when the government sins against God and against humanity, God's people, no matter where they live, must speak out and hold the government accountable. As Christians, we have a *vote,* and we have a *voice* in our government.

Throughout the book of Jeremiah, we have seen this prophet living out these very principles, speaking out against the sins of the government and the people, living as salt and light in the decaying and darkening culture of the kingdom of Judah. For more than four decades, Jeremiah labored tirelessly, spoke boldly, and prayed unceasingly for the repentance and restoration of the nation. Now the kingdom of Judah was no more.

But Jeremiah's work was not done. Carried off into Egypt against his will, Jeremiah continued to preach a message of repentance to the refugees from fallen Judah. And he is about to take his message of repentance from a national stage to an international stage.

God is now calling Jeremiah to confront the nations of the world. Through this thundering message of Jeremiah, God addresses the world and shouts, "Now hear this!"

JEREMIAH'S AUTHORITY OVER NATIONS

The book of Jeremiah closes with a series of messages that the prophet addressed to the nations around Israel. God called him to be a prophet and promised that he would have authority over nations:

> Then the LORD reached out his hand and touched my mouth and said to me, "I have put my words in your mouth. See, today I appoint you over nations and kingdoms to uproot and tear down, to destroy and overthrow, to build and to plant." (1:9–10)

Now we come to the fulfillment of this promise. Beginning with Jeremiah 46, we see the prophet sending messages to the nations surrounding Israel regarding their destinies. Jeremiah is not the only prophet who delivers warnings to the Gentile nations. There are three collections of prophetic messages to the nations in the Old Testament—one series by Isaiah (chapters 13 through 17), another by Ezekiel (chapters 25 through 33), and these messages by Jeremiah.

Taken together, these three sets of prophetic messages to the Gentile nations comprise an important section of Scripture, totaling 603 verses. I find that Christians today have very little acquaintance with these passages of Scripture.

Is it important to know what God said to these nations? I believe it's not just important, it is *essential*! The message Jeremiah delivered to these great nations in his day is still God's urgent warning to the nations of our own day—to North America, South America, the United Kingdom, the European nations, Russia, China, India, the Arab world, the African nations, and every other nation, great and small.

Imagine all the powers and superpowers of this world, with all their armies and navies, their air forces and nuclear arsenals, their wealth and national pride, their belligerence and arrogance. Picture them gathered in one arena to listen to the voice of God as spoken through an obscure man from an obscure village from an ancient time in a distant corner of the world. He is a nobody, without any degrees after his name, without an impressive résumé, without any diplomatic portfolio, without even a nation to call home, now that his land has been absorbed by the Babylonians. But this is the man God has appointed over nations and kingdoms.

In chapter 46, Jeremiah rises to speak. He begins by addressing Egypt, where he was living at the time. He will end his discourse with the empire of Babylon, far to the east, in the land across the Euphrates River. As we listen to Jeremiah speak, we will see once again that the truth of God's Word comes to us in rich, multi-layered levels of meaning and application.

The surface level of Jeremiah's message to the nations is historical and political in nature. These prophecies have to do with actual kingdoms that existed at a specific time in history. God, speaking through Jeremiah, made specific pronouncements about these nations. Four nations would endure throughout the centuries to come, and God would bless them. It's important to note that all four of these nations exist now and have, in fact, awakened from the dust of centuries past to become major political powers today.

Two other nations are mentioned, but without any message of blessing from the Lord; these two nations also exist today. Finally, God names three nations that, He predicts, will disappear from the face of the earth; these three nations have long since been lost to history.

Digging beneath the surface of Jeremiah's message, we find a second level of meaning that we can apply to our lives today. This second level of meaning can be understood as symbolizing the spiritual forces at work within us. One of the clues to understanding the Word of God is to see ourselves whenever we read about these nations. We can better understand our own deceptive flesh and how it tempts us into sin and error as we examine the national character of these kingdoms.

The nine kingdoms God addresses in this series of messages can be divided into three groups. Each group of nations has a significant symbolic application to our lives today.

A MESSAGE FOR EGYPT

We will begin with chapter 46, in which God, through Jeremiah, addresses the nation of Egypt. In fact, chapter 46 comprises two messages that Jeremiah delivered on two separate occasions. The first was apparently delivered before Jeremiah was taken into Egypt, and it deals with the Battle of Carchemish. Jeremiah writes:

> This is the word of the LORD that came to Jeremiah the prophet concerning the nations:
> Concerning Egypt:
> This is the message against the army of Pharaoh Necho king of Egypt, which was defeated at Carchemish on the Euphrates River by Nebuchadnezzar king of Babylon in the fourth year of Jehoiakim son of Josiah king of Judah. (46:1–2)

This introduction to Jeremiah's first message to Egypt takes us back to 605 BC, when Nebuchadnezzar first came up against Judah. Before Nebuchadnezzar reached Judah, he encountered the armies of Egypt at the city of Carchemish on the west bank of the Euphrates River, in what is now northern Syria (which is directly north and east of Israel). The Babylonians and Egyptians met here in one of the most important battles in ancient history. Prior to the Battle of Carchemish, Egypt was the most powerful nation in the known world. In this battle, Babylon broke the power of Egypt, and the Babylonian Empire became the superpower of the region.

God uses poetic yet historically accurate language to describe Egypt in terms of its national character and behavior on the world stage. Looking beneath the surface description, we see that Egypt is a symbolic picture of the world and its influence upon us. God's description of Egypt is that of a nation filled with worldly pride, worldly arrogance, and worldly ambition:

> "Who is this that rises like the Nile,
> like rivers of surging waters?

Egypt rises like the Nile,
    like rivers of surging waters.
She says, 'I will rise and cover the earth;
    I will destroy cities and their people.'" (46:7–8)

Throughout Scripture, Egypt serves as a symbol of the world and the spirit of worldliness. Egypt was a place of tyranny and bondage for the Hebrew people. The Israelites suffered under the yoke of a wicked and cruel Pharaoh who enslaved and oppressed them without mercy. Incredibly, after the Israelites escaped, they often thought nostalgically of the land that had enslaved them.

For example, in Exodus, the people complained to Moses, "If only we had died by the LORD's hand in Egypt! There we sat around pots of meat and ate all the food we wanted, but you have brought us out into this desert to starve this entire assembly to death" (see Exodus 16:3). Somehow, it slipped their minds that they had to spend their days doing backbreaking work, trying to meet an impossible quota while being lashed by their Egyptian slave masters.

Egypt is a fitting symbol of how the world lures believers into its grasp. Egypt kept the Israelites in perpetual bondage, afflicting them with fear and forced labor. Similarly, when we yield ourselves to the world and its pleasures, we invariably end up in bondage, unable to liberate ourselves from the habits, fears, and addictions that keep us enslaved to the world.

Worldliness is an attitude toward life in which you think of living only for your own pleasures and enjoyment. If you are a worldly person, you rarely think about what God wants for your life. You only think about what you want to get out of life.

There's nothing wrong with enjoying life and its pleasures, as long as you enjoy life's pleasures in a context of seeking God, His kingdom, and His righteousness first and foremost. God wants us to experience the incredible joy of knowing Him. As the psalmist said, "You make known to me the path of life; you will fill me with joy in your presence, with eternal pleasures at your right hand" (Psalm 16:11). But if we pursue pleasure or wealth or fame or success more than we pursue God, then we are worldly people, symbolically living under the spell of Egypt.

What does God mean when He says, "Egypt rises like the Nile, like rivers of surging waters"? For centuries, every spring the Nile River would rise and overflow its banks. While this has changed because of the construction of the Aswan Dam, these annual cycles of overflow deposited silt from the river on the surrounding lands, making the farmlands consistently fertile, year after year. But those surging waters sometimes caused flooding and death as well.

The prophet uses the Nile River and its cyclical overflows as a picture of the way the world tempts us and assaults us. The world comes at us in surges and waves. Temptation floods over us, and we feel overwhelmed, lost. Then the temptation subsides, and we think we have conquered those sinful urges. No matter how many times we have gone through these cycles, we forget that the temptation will come at us again and again throughout our lifetime as believers. In our spiritual pilgrimage, the world rises again and again to afflict us, lure us, betray us, and draw us back into bondage.

The chief symbolic characteristic of Egypt is worldliness.

LOUD NOISE AND MISSED OPPORTUNITIES

Jeremiah 46:13–24 contains a second message about Egypt. God gave Jeremiah this message after the prophet was exiled in Egypt. Here he describes the forthcoming invasion of Egypt by Nebuchadnezzar, which took place after Jeremiah's death. In accordance with this prophecy, Nebuchadnezzar and his army swept into Egypt and conquered the land. This prophecy reveals another characteristic of the nation of Egypt:

This is the message the LORD spoke to Jeremiah the prophet about the coming of Nebuchadnezzar king of Babylon to attack Egypt:

"Announce this in Egypt, and proclaim it in Migdol;
proclaim it also in Memphis and Tahpanhes:

'Take your positions and get ready,
  for the sword devours those around you.'
Why will your warriors be laid low?
  They cannot stand, for the LORD will push them down.
They will stumble repeatedly;
  they will fall over each other.
They will say, 'Get up, let us go back
  to our own people and our native lands,
  away from the sword of the oppressor.'
There they will exclaim,
  'Pharaoh king of Egypt is only a loud noise;
  he has missed his opportunity.'" (46:13–17)

God makes a strange statement about Egypt near the end of this chapter:

The LORD Almighty, the God of Israel, says: "I am about to bring punishment on Amon god of Thebes, on Pharaoh, on Egypt and her gods and her kings, and on those who rely on Pharaoh. I will give them into the hands of those who want to kill them—Nebuchadnezzar king of Babylon and his officers. Later, however, Egypt will be inhabited as in times past," declares the LORD. (46:25–26)

This prophecy was fulfilled in 567 BC, when Nebuchadnezzar invaded Egypt, conquering much of the Nile Valley while humiliating Pharaoh. The Persians would carry out a more complete conquest of Egypt in 525 BC under Cambysses, the son of Cyrus the Great.

God not only predicts that Egypt will be conquered but He also says that Egypt will one day be restored and inhabited. I believe the restoration of Egypt took place during my lifetime. For centuries, from the Middle Ages through the subjugation under the Ottoman Empire, from the seventh century AD through most of the nineteenth century, Egypt was a nation asleep. After the Ottoman Empire fell, from about 1867 until the start of World War I in 1914, Europe trampled Egypt underfoot, ransacking Egyptian pyramids and other antiquities to display their findings in European museums. Great Britain held Egypt as a protectorate from 1882 to 1952.

In 1952, the nation of Egypt achieved full statehood through a military coup led by Gamal Abdel Nasser, who eventually became the dictator of Egypt. Under Nasser's strong but oppressive leadership, Egypt awakened and became a sovereign nation once more. In Jeremiah's message to Egypt, God promises to spare Egypt and cause the land to be inhabited once more. We find a similar promise to Egypt in Isaiah 19, where God says that Egypt will be healed, and God will bless the Egyptians and call them His people.

A MESSAGE FOR THE PHILISTINES

In chapter 47, Jeremiah delivers a message from God to a nation closely associated with Egypt: Philistia. Until the rise of the Assyrians, the Philistines were the principal enemy of the Israelites. Philistia and Israel had been in a perpetual state of war for centuries. The Philistines lived along the southern coastline of the land of Palestine. The name *Palestine* comes from the word *Philistine*.

God told the Israelites to avoid the fierce and warlike Philistines during their exodus from Egypt (see Exodus 13:17). Samson single-handedly killed more than a thousand Philistines in a single battle (Judges 15). The Philistines defeated the Israelites at the Battle of Aphek and captured the Ark of the Covenant (see 1 Samuel 4:1–10). Israel defeated the Philistines in battles at Eben-Ezer (1 Samuel 7:3–14) and Michmash (1 Samuel 14). The great Philistine warrior Goliath intimidated even Israel's King Saul, but the shepherd boy David slew him with a single stone from his sling (1 Samuel 17). The Philistines defeated the Israelites at Mount Gilboa, leading to the deaths of King Saul and his three sons (1 Samuel 31). The history of Israelite-Philistine relations was one of perpetual warfare.

The Philistines were in the land that God had promised to the Israelites, but these hostile people were the enemies of God. They are a symbol of the worldling who claims to have a place in the land of promise but who is actually an enemy of faith. We might equate them to so-called "nominal Christians," people who claim to be Christians but who actually subvert and oppose the true faith. They want to enjoy the benefits of living in a place God has blessed, but they refuse to commit themselves to the godly way of life that produces those blessings.

God spoke this message to the Philistines through the prophet Jeremiah:

> This is the word of the LORD that came to Jeremiah the prophet concerning the Philistines before Pharaoh attacked Gaza:
>
>> This is what the LORD says:
>> "See how the waters are rising in the north;
>>   they will become an overflowing torrent.
>> They will overflow the land and everything in it,
>>   the towns and those who live in them.
>> The people will cry out;
>>   all who dwell in the land will wail
>> at the sound of the hooves of galloping steeds,
>>   at the noise of enemy chariots
>>   and the rumble of their wheels.
>> Parents will not turn to help their children;
>>   their hands will hang limp.
>> For the day has come
>>   to destroy all the Philistines
>> and to remove all survivors
>>   who could help Tyre and Sidon.
>> The LORD is about to destroy the Philistines,
>>   the remnant from the coasts of Caphtor." (47:1–4)

This prophecy speaks of a coming invasion by an unnamed army—an invasion that will mean the end of the nation of the Philistines. The Philistines were subjugated by the Assyrians and were later absorbed by the Babylonians and Persians. By about 600 BC, there was no remnant of the Philistine ethnic group in the region, though some modern Palestinians claim to be descended from the Philistines. The Palestinians carry on the ancient grudge wars, using terrorism and rocket attacks against the modern state of Israel.

GOD'S MESSAGE TO MOAB AND AMMON

Jeremiah 48 and 49 contain God's message to a group of five nations—Moab, Ammon, Edom, Damascus, and Kedar (Arabia). These five nations have little in common except that they are all enemies of the nation of Israel. They picture for us what the Bible calls "the flesh," the part of our nature that is inherent in us because of the fall. The flesh is the enemy of faith, and because it is our *inner* enemy and part of our fallen nature, it is a foe from which we cannot escape. It is always with us.

God's message to Moab and Ammon takes up all of Jeremiah 48 and the first six verses of 49. There God describes the downfall of these nations, which are descended from their namesakes, Moab and Ammon, the sons of Lot. After the destruction of Sodom and Gomorrah, Lot fled into the mountains with his two daughters, and they hid in a cave. The daughters feared they would never be able to raise children, since there were no men to marry. They got their father drunk with wine and had sexual relations with him without his being aware of what he was doing. Lot's two daughters each conceived a son by this incestuous relationship, and those two sons were Moab and Ammon. These brothers settled in the land we know as Jordan: Moab to the east of the Dead Sea, and Ammon north of Moab.

Chapter 48 vividly describes the destruction of the cities of Moab by merciless foes and the humiliation of the Moabite demon-god Chemosh, a vengeful deity who demanded human sacrifices:

> "Flee! Run for your lives;
> become like a bush in the desert.
> Since you trust in your deeds and riches,
> you too will be taken captive,

and Chemosh will go into exile,
together with his priests and officials.
The destroyer will come against every town,
and not a town will escape.
The valley will be ruined
and the plateau destroyed,
because the LORD has spoken.
Put salt on Moab,
for she will be laid waste;
her towns will become desolate,
with no one to live in them." (48:6–9)

Moab was off the beaten track, away from the main invasion routes of the various empires. Conquerors came and went in the region, century after century, and usually left Moab alone. God described the Moabites as complacent and self-satisfied:

"Moab has been at rest from youth,
like wine left on its dregs,
not poured from one jar to another—
she has not gone into exile.
So she tastes as she did,
and her aroma is unchanged.
But days are coming,"
declares the LORD,
"when I will send men who pour from pitchers,
and they will pour her out;
they will empty her pitchers
and smash her jars.
Then Moab will be ashamed of Chemosh,
as Israel was ashamed
when they trusted in Bethel. (48:11–13)

God compares Moab to wine in a jar. When wine ferments and ages, particles of yeast, crushed grapes, and other impurities settle to the bottom of the jar in the form of "lees" or settled residue. The clarified wine rests on the lees, and this is a picture of the Moabites, resting complacently on the years and years of peace they have enjoyed.

But a time is coming, the Lord says, when Moab will be stirred and shaken by war, "poured from one jar to another" by the violence of invasion. Just as shaking and pouring wine from a jar will stir up the lees and impurities at the bottom of the wine, making it cloudy, the people of Moab will be shaken and their comfortable, peaceful lives will be disturbed by war. The wine jars of national peace and prosperity will be shattered, and the god of Moab, the demon-god Chemosh, will be shamed for being weak and powerless.

After Jeremiah delivered this message of doom to the Moabites, the land of Moab experienced wave after wave of invasions by tribes from Kedar (northern Arabia) and other nations. During that time, the nation of Moab disappears from the historical records that archaeologists have unearthed in that region.

In verse 13, God says, "Then Moab will be ashamed of Chemosh, as Israel was ashamed when they trusted in Bethel." Why was Israel ashamed for trusting in Bethel? This is a reference to an event that took place after Israel was split into two kingdoms after the death of Solomon. Jeroboam, the first king of the Northern Kingdom of Israel and a wicked leader, made two calves of gold, which he set up in Bethel and Dan (see 1 Kings 12). God refers to the idolatry at Bethel, which brought shame upon the nation. The Lord goes on to say:

> "We have heard of Moab's pride—
>   how great is her arrogance!—
> of her insolence, her pride, her conceit
>   and the haughtiness of her heart.
> I know her insolence but it is futile,"
>   declares the LORD,
> "and her boasts accomplish nothing." (48:29–30)

Whenever you are tempted to feel proud, arrogant, self-sufficient, and boastful, you are being tempted by the spirit of Moab. You are being attacked by Moab, just as the Moabites repeatedly attacked Israel. You are contending with the perpetual enemy of God—the arrogance of the flesh.

The people of Moab became complacent and conceited, thinking they were beyond the reach of God's judgment. When judgment finally fell upon Moab, the people were too stunned to respond, and their destruction was swift. Why was Moab judged? Because the people of that nation defied God and worshiped Chemosh. Chapter 48 ends with these words:

> Woe to you, Moab!
> The people of Chemosh are destroyed;
> your sons are taken into exile
> and your daughters into captivity.
> "Yet I will restore the fortunes of Moab
> in days to come,"
> declares the LORD.
> Here ends the judgment on Moab. (48:46–47)

This is an amazing promise. After predicting Moab's doom because of idolatry, God promises to "restore the fortunes of Moab in days to come" (v. 47). This promise has been fulfilled in our time. You may ask, "Where is the nation of Moab today? If Moab has been restored, why can't I find it on the map?"

Answer: One nation now occupies the territory once known as the kingdoms of Moab and Ammon. That nation is Jordan. The capital of Jordan is Amman, which is derived from the ancient name Ammon. So the descendants of these two sons of Lot live today in the nation of Jordan, which has become a major power broker and stabilizing factor in the Middle East.

In Jeremiah 49:1–6, the Lord pronounces a similar doom on the nation of Ammon. Though Moab and Ammon were both descended from sons of Lot by an incestuous union, Ammon followed a different demon-God than Moab. The Ammonites worshiped Molek (also known as Moloch), a cruel and blasphemous Canaanite deity associated with child sacrifices.

274

So God judged the Ammonites just as he had judged the Moabites. Jeremiah writes:

> "Put on sackcloth and mourn;
>   rush here and there inside the walls,
> for Molek will go into exile,
>   together with his priests and officials.
> Why do you boast of your valleys,
>   boast of your valleys so fruitful?
> Unfaithful Daughter Ammon,
>   you trust in your riches and say,
>   'Who will attack me?'
> I will bring terror on you
>   from all those around you,"
> declares the Lord, the Lord Almighty.
> "Every one of you will be driven away,
>   and no one will gather the fugitives." (49:3–5)

But just as God promised to show grace to the Moabites, so he also promised to restore the Ammonites:

> "Yet afterward, I will restore the fortunes of the Ammonites,"
>   declares the Lord (49:6).

The nation of Jordan exists today because God always keeps His word. He has restored the fortunes of Moab and Ammon, just as He promised, and the descendants of Moab and Ammon still live in that land today.

God's message to Edom, Damascus, and Kedar

Next, God levels His sights on Edom, located south of the Dead Sea. For many centuries, the capital of Edom was Petra, a beautiful city carved out of natural red rock. The people of Edom were descendants of Esau, the twin brother of Jacob. In Scripture, Esau is always a symbolic picture of the man of the flesh, especially as the flesh opposes the Spirit of God.

As the prophet Malachi wrote, "'Wasn't Esau Jacob's brother?' declares the Lord. 'I loved Jacob, but Esau I hated'" (see Malachi 1:2–3). Why did God say that about Esau? It's because Esau was continually in conflict with the Spirit of God. The apostle Paul contrasts the flesh and the Spirit in his letter to the Galatians: "For the flesh desires what is contrary to the Spirit, and the Spirit what is contrary to the flesh. They are in conflict with each other, so that you are not to do whatever you want" (Galatians 5:17).

In Jeremiah 49, God promises to eliminate the nation of Edom, founded by Esau, from the face of the earth. Jeremiah records the message of God to Edom:

> "Turn and flee, hide in deep caves,
>   you who live in Dedan,
> for I will bring disaster on Esau
>   at the time when I punish him.
> If grape pickers came to you,
>   would they not leave a few grapes?
> If thieves came during the night,
>   would they not steal only as much as they wanted?
> But I will strip Esau bare;
>   I will uncover his hiding places,
>   so that he cannot conceal himself . . .
> Edom will become an object of horror;
>   all who pass by will be appalled and will scoff
>   because of all its wounds.
> As Sodom and Gomorrah were overthrown,
>   along with their neighboring towns,"
> says the LORD,
> "so no one will live there;
>   no people will dwell in it." (49:8–10,17–18)

And God was true to His word. The nation and people of Edom passed into history hundreds of years before Christ was born.

Next, the Lord addresses a message to the city-state of Damascus. That city, now the capital of Syria, is one of the oldest continuously inhabited cities in the world. In ancient times, Syria was known as Aram, and the region around Damascus, to the north of Israel, is the source of the Aramean language and culture that had a major influence on life in Israel during the time of Christ.

The people of Damascus were warlike. Tensions between Damascus and Israel go back hundreds of years, and they continue to this day. Concerning Damascus, Jeremiah relates this message from the Lord:

> "Damascus has become feeble,
>   she has turned to flee
>   and panic has gripped her;
> anguish and pain have seized her,
>   pain like that of a woman in labor.
> Why has the city of renown not been abandoned,
>   the town in which I delight?
> Surely, her young men will fall in the streets;
>   all her soldiers will be silenced in that day,"
> declares the LORD Almighty.
> "I will set fire to the walls of Damascus;
>   it will consume the fortresses of Ben-Hadad." (49:24–27)

The ancient name for Syria, *Aram*, means "exalted." Symbolically, Aram was a type or picture of the kind of arrogant pride that goes before a fall. Damascus, as the capital of Aram/Syria, is the epitome of the pride of Aram, which stands against the authority of God. Down through the centuries, many wars have been fought for control of Damascus, but the city has never been completely and finally destroyed. The description of the destruction of Damascus that Jeremiah relates here suggests that a full and final destruction awaits Damascus. In fact, Isaiah 17 contains a prediction of the final destruction of Damascus, and it may be a parallel of Jeremiah's prophecy here. The destruction of Damascus in Isaiah 17 appears to take place in the end times, during the Great Tribulation.

Damascus symbolizes human pride that exalts itself against God. Whenever you see Damascus spoken of in Scripture, it is a symbol of human self-exaltation. The next time you are tempted to brag about your achievements, try to get people to notice you or be impressed with you, or exalt yourself in any way, remember God's judgment against Damascus. Like all human pride, Damascus will one day be leveled. Only the humble will be exalted in that day.

Next, God delivers a message for Kedar, which is the ancient name for Arabia. Kedar was home to the nomadic, desert-dwelling tribes of the region we now call Saudi Arabia. The Arabs of Kedar were descended from Ishmael, the half-brother of Isaac and son of Abraham. So the tribes of Kedar are related to Israel. God's word to Kedar is a message of judgment and affliction:

> Concerning Kedar and the kingdoms of Hazor, which Nebuchadnezzar king of Babylon attacked:
> This is what the LORD says:
>
> "Arise, and attack Kedar
> and destroy the people of the East.
> Their tents and their flocks will be taken;
> their shelters will be carried off
> with all their goods and camels.
> People will shout to them,
> 'Terror on every side!'" (49:28–29)

The Lord's prophecy that Kedar would be attacked, plundered, slaughtered, and terrorized by Babylon is confirmed by the Babylonian Chronicles in the British Museum—tablets that record the actions of the Babylonian Empire. According to the Chronicles, Nebuchadnezzar's army raided many encampments of Kedar in 599 BC. The description of those raids fits the judgment that God speaks of here.

The nomadic, tent-living people of Kedar can be seen as a symbol of the restlessness of our nature. We are constantly searching here and there for the peace that eludes us. The desert-roaming people of Kedar hold a mirror up to our lives, reflecting back our own restlessness as we live out our lives in a desert of dissatisfaction and despair, apart from God.

God's message to Elam and Babylon

The last two nations, Elam and Babylon, are associated with each other. At the time God gave this message to Jeremiah, at the beginning of the reign of King Zedekiah, Elam was one of the provinces of Babylon. Yet God singles Elam out as meriting a significant word from God. The reason God focuses on Elam is stated at the beginning of this section:

> This is the word of the LORD that came to Jeremiah the prophet concerning Elam, early in the reign of Zedekiah king of Judah:
> This is what the LORD Almighty says:
>
> "See, I will break the bow of Elam,
> the mainstay of their might." (49:34–35)

God pictures Elam as an archery bow, which He calls the "mainstay" of Elam's might. A bow symbolizes the ability of an army to strike and wound at a distance. The apostle Paul uses this same symbol when he speaks of spiritual warfare, our struggle against the attacks of Satan. In Ephesians 6:16, Paul urges us to "take up the shield of faith, with which you can extinguish all the flaming arrows of the evil one."

Satan hurls flaming arrows of evil thoughts and sinful imagination at us. These satanic attacks often come when we least expect them, and when we feel invulnerable. You may kneel to pray and suddenly find an evil thought pressing its way into your mind, seemingly out of nowhere. You wonder, "Where did *that* come from?" That was one of the fiery arrows of Satan, symbolized by the bow of Elam.

The fiery arrows of Satan may come as a temptation to sin or doubt God or question our salvation. You are being targeted by the bow and flaming arrows of Satan. You are being attacked at a distance. Satan doesn't dare to attack you face-to-face, at close quarters, because he knows you would recognize him and never fall for such an attack. But the unseen arrow that flies in the darkness, the arrow from the hidden assassin, the arrow that attacks without warning—these are the satanic sneak attacks. The arrow attack was the mainstay of Elam, and it's the trademark of Satan.

God pronounces judgment upon the province of Elam. Nevertheless, on a national level, God promises to restore Elam:

> "Yet I will restore the fortunes of Elam
>   in days to come,"
> declares the LORD. (49:39)

The ancient Babylonian province of Elam still exists today, and it is known as the Ilam province of Iran. So once again, the prophecy of the Lord has been proven true.

Nehemiah 50 and 51 are two of the longest chapters in the book, and they are devoted to the judgment against Babylon. The symbolic significance of Babylon is well known. Everywhere in Scripture, Babylon is a symbol of the great enemy of God. In the book of Revelation, Babylon represents Satan's deceptive, seductive influence through false religion, which is the essence of a way of thinking referred to as Babylonianism.

Some suggest that Babylon was the fountainhead of false religion. Babylon began with the Tower of Babel, after the flood of Noah. Genesis 10:8–10 tells us that Babel (or Babylon) was one of a number of cities founded and ruled by the mighty hunter Nimrod, the son of Cush and great-grandson of Noah, in the region of Shinar (Mesopotamia). As the city of Babel grew, the people said, "Come, let us build ourselves a city, with a tower that reaches to the heavens, so that we may make a name for ourselves" (see Genesis 11:4).

Even though God thwarted the Babylonians' attempt to build a sky-scraping tower for their religion by confusing their language, the spirit of Babylon grew in that place. The city became the mother of religious harlotry and abominations, a fountainhead of idolatry, spreading its blasphemous ideas and demonic gods throughout the world. Most of the false religions that still seduce people in our culture today can be traced to ancient Babylon.

This is why there is a philosophy in the world today sometimes referred to as Babylonianism, which can be defined as an attempt to gain prestige or status in the eyes of the world by wielding religious power and authority. The spirit of Babylon, as it is sometimes called, can permeate any religious group, denomination, or church. It can be seen in any religion in the world that seeks worldly power by wielding religious authority. Babylonianism often seeks to mingle idolatry with watered-down Christianity to produce a pleasant-sounding distortion of the truth to deceive the masses and expand the following (and bank accounts) of false teachers.

This kind of thinking comes through when we use the church or our Christian faith or our knowledge of the Scriptures to bring attention and prestige to ourselves. It is also the basis of those who have ever tried to blend Christianity with ideas from astrology, occultism, Buddhism, or other religious traditions. Also, it's the kind of thinking that causes us to take pride in attending "the prestigious church" in town, or feeling pride at being one of the pastors, elders, or lay leaders at our church.

This began with the Tower of Babel, and it has come under the judgment of God. Here in Jeremiah 50, God predicts the overthrow of Babylon by the Medes and Persians—a prediction fulfilled in 539 BC with the victory of Cyrus the Great, King of Persia, over Babylon in the Battle of Opis. Here is God's prophecy of the fall of Babylon:

> This is the word the LORD spoke through Jeremiah the prophet concerning Babylon and the land of the Babylonians:
>
> "Announce and proclaim among the nations,
>> lift up a banner and proclaim it;
>> keep nothing back, but say,
> 'Babylon will be captured;
>> Bel will be put to shame,
>> Marduk filled with terror.
> Her images will be put to shame
>> and her idols filled with terror.'
> A nation from the north will attack her

and lay waste her land.
No one will live in it;
    both people and animals will flee away." (50:1–3)

Bel (or Baal) is an ancient title meaning "lord," and it was used for centuries to refer to an assortment of Babylonian gods. By the latter years of the Babylonian Empire, when Jeremiah recorded this prophecy, the title Bel was associated almost exclusively with the chief Babylonian god, the god of fertility and weather, also known as Hadad. Marduk was the patron deity of the city of Babylon and was astrologically associated with the king of the planets, Jupiter. God pronounced judgment not only against the Babylonians but also against their false gods.

At the height of its power, the Babylonian Empire had conquered Judah, laid waste to Jerusalem, and leveled the great temple of Solomon. But Babylon's turn for judgment was coming. God, through Jeremiah, prophesied that an enemy would invade out of the north. At that time, the empire of the Medes and Persians extended from modern-day Turkey, to the northwest of Babylon, across modern Armenia, down through Iran, and east as far as modern Afghanistan and Pakistan. The city of Babylon sat on the plains between the Tigris River to the east and the Euphrates River to the west. Thus the best way to attack the city was to sweep down from the north, moving swiftly to the plain between the two rivers. The Medo-Persian Empire arched around the northern and eastern frontiers of Babylon, giving the Medes and Persians an ideal invasion route from the north, as this prophecy foretold.

In 539 BC, Cyrus the Great sent his armies southward into Babylonia to the city of Opis, on the eastern (or near) side of the Tigris River, and directly north of the city of Babylon. After quickly conquering Opis, the Medo-Persians crossed the Tigris and rolled southward to the Babylonian city of Sippar on the eastern (or near) side of the Euphrates. With control of the crossing at Sippar, the Medo-Persians swept southward to Babylon.

Because the walls of Babylon were considered impenetrable, the Medo-Persians devised a plan to exploit a weakness in the Babylonian defenses.

The Babylonians had built a series of metal grates underwater, so that the river could flow beneath the city walls and into Babylon, providing fresh water. During the evening of a Babylonian feast day, the feast described in Daniel 5, Medo-Persian troops worked swiftly and efficiently to dam the Euphrates River upstream from the city. Troops diverted the river waters enough that their fellow soldiers could walk in the riverbed with their heads above water. Upon reaching the metal grate, which was no longer submerged, it was easy to cut the bars and enter the city unopposed.

While the unsuspecting Babylonians were celebrating their feast, Medo-Persian forces swiftly conquered the outlying parts of the city. In spite of Babylon's wealth and might, its supposedly "impenetrable" walls, and its many wonders such as the fabled Hanging Gardens, Babylon was conquered at the height of its power. God describes the ultimate desolation of Babylon:

> "Flee out of Babylon;
>> leave the land of the Babylonians,
>> and be like the goats that lead the flock.
> For I will stir up and bring against Babylon
>> an alliance of great nations from the land of the north.
> They will take up their positions against her,
>> and from the north she will be captured.
> Their arrows will be like skilled warriors
>> who do not return empty-handed.
> So Babylonia will be plundered;
>> all who plunder her will have their fill,"
> declares the LORD. . . .
> "She will be the least of the nations—
>> a wilderness, a dry land, a desert.
> Because of the LORD's anger she will not be inhabited
>> but will be completely desolate.
> All who pass Babylon will be appalled;
>> they will scoff because of all her wounds. . . ."
> "A sword against the Babylonians!"
>> declares the LORD—

"against those who live in Babylon
  and against her officials and wise men!
A sword against her false prophets!
  They will become fools.
A sword against her warriors!
  They will be filled with terror.
A sword against her horses and chariots
  and all the foreigners in her ranks!
  They will become weaklings.
A sword against her treasures!
  They will be plundered.
A drought on her waters!
  They will dry up.
For it is a land of idols,
  idols that will go mad with terror.
So desert creatures and hyenas will live there,
  and there the owl will dwell.
It will never again be inhabited
  or lived in from generation to generation.
As I overthrew Sodom and Gomorrah
  along with their neighboring towns,"
declares the LORD,
"so no one will live there;
  no people will dwell in it." (50:8–10,12–13; 35–40)

God foretold the overthrow of Babylon exactly as it came to pass. Daniel 5 tells us that the night Babylon fell, King Belshazzar was reveling at a great feast with all the lords and ladies of the kingdom. They were engaged in drunken debauchery, defiling the sacred utensils of worship that Nebuchadnezzar had stolen from the temple of Solomon.

During this blasphemous feast, the revelers were shaken by the specter of a disembodied hand writing words of doom upon the wall. Frightened out of his wits, Belshazzar summoned Daniel to interpret the handwriting on the wall. Daniel told him that the message foretold Belshazzar's doom. Both Daniel 5 and Jeremiah's prophecy paint a picture of Belshazzar being stricken with paralysis, unable to respond to the looming threat. Jeremiah records God's prophecy about Belshazzar—a prophecy delivered before Belshazzar was even born:

> "The king of Babylon has heard reports about them,
>   and his hands hang limp.
> Anguish has gripped him,
>   pain like that of a woman in labor." (50:43)

That night, the kingdom was taken from Belshazzar. Even as Daniel was interpreting that handwriting on the wall, the forces of the Medes and Persians were rising up out of the river and swarming into the city. Within hours, the empire of Babylon was overthrown and Belshazzar was dead. The once-mighty empire of Babylon became a province of Persia under Cyrus the Great—the same Cyrus who later permitted the Jews to return to their homeland (see 2 Chronicles 36).

For centuries, the site of the city of Babylon was lost. Humanity didn't even know where the once-great city had been. In the early nineteenth century, explorers of Great Britain's East India Company began excavating the site we now know to be the remains of Babylon. More extensive excavations were conducted years later by the British Museum. Today, we know Babylon as a field of ruins half-buried in the sands of Iraq. In 1978, the Baathist government of Iraq, led by dictator Saddam Hussein, launched a project to rebuild and restore Babylon in our time, but the project was never completed.

As I write these words, the city that once ruled most of the known world in the time of Jeremiah is still a place of desolation in the desert.

GOD'S MESSAGE TO THE JEWS

God not only predicted the destruction of Babylon with devastating accuracy but He also promised the return of the Jews to the land of Judah, as Jeremiah records:

"In those days, at that time,"
  declares the LORD,
"the people of Israel and the people of Judah together
  will go in tears to seek the LORD their God.
They will ask the way to Zion
  and turn their faces toward it.
They will come and bind themselves to the LORD
  in an everlasting covenant
  that will not be forgotten." (50:4–5)

Some Bible expositors believe that ancient Babylon must be rebuilt in order for the end times prophecies to be fulfilled. It's true that the book of Revelation contains references to an entity called "Babylon." For example, in Revelation 18, we read:

Terrified at her torment, they will stand far off and cry: "'Woe! Woe to you, great city, you mighty city of Babylon! In one hour your doom has come!'" (Revelation 18:10)
    Then a mighty angel picked up a boulder the size of a large millstone and threw it into the sea, and said: "With such violence the great city of Babylon will be thrown down, never to be found again." (Revelation 18:21)

Throughout the book of Revelation, Babylon is used as a symbol of the idolatrous practices and arrogance of false religious authorities. The destruction and desolation of the literal Babylon by the Medes and Persians is a foreshadowing of the destruction and desolation of the figurative Babylon—the false religious system of the world—in the last days. When the events foretold in the book of Revelation finally come to pass, all the false religious systems of the world will be swept away, and the One True Faith will take their place, with Jesus the Lord as its King and High Priest. When John describes his vision of the last days, he echoes the message of God through Jeremiah regarding the utter destruction and desolation of the literal, historical city of Babylon on the plains of Mesopotamia.

Jeremiah continues the record of God's pronouncement of judgment against Babylon in chapter 51, and he closes his book of prophecy with these words:

This is what the LORD Almighty says:

> "Babylon's thick wall will be leveled
>   and her high gates set on fire;
> the peoples exhaust themselves for nothing,
>   the nations' labor is only fuel for the flames."

This is the message Jeremiah the prophet gave to the staff officer Seraiah son of Neriah, the son of Mahseiah, when he went to Babylon with Zedekiah king of Judah in the fourth year of his reign. Jeremiah had written on a scroll about all the disasters that would come upon Babylon—all that had been recorded concerning Babylon. He said to Seraiah, "When you get to Babylon, see that you read all these words aloud. Then say, 'LORD, you have said you will destroy this place, so that neither people nor animals will live in it; it will be desolate forever.' When you finish reading this scroll, tie a stone to it and throw it into the Euphrates. Then say, 'So will Babylon sink to rise no more because of the disaster I will bring on her. And her people will fall.'"

The words of Jeremiah end here. (51:58–64)

There is one more chapter in the book, appended by a different writer, recounting the fall of Jerusalem and the eventual release from prison of Judah's deposed king, Jehoiachin. There is no record of the death of Jeremiah, though tradition says that he died in Egypt, martyred by his own countrymen who were enraged by his condemnation of their idolatry.

What is the core message of the book of Jeremiah for you and me today? As we have journeyed through this prophecy, we have watched the prophet Jeremiah as he struggled with the workings and the judgments of God, as he struggled with his own weaknesses and doubts, and as he endured persecution from kings, religious leaders, and others who rejected his message of repentance. We have heard him deliver a series of messages from God to the nations, and we've seen that these nations symbolize the spiritual enemies you and I face every day.

These nations and their hostility toward God's chosen people represent the attacks you and I face from the world, the flesh, and Satan. And the recurring theme of the book of Jeremiah is that God's power and wisdom are adequate for any challenge. Our faith in the True and Living God overcomes the world and demolishes the deceitfulness of the flesh. Our God is more than a match for Satan, no matter how he tries to intimidate us.

You and I can stand—God's man, God's woman—even amid the threats and terrors of this world. Babylon—the false religious system of this world—will sink and never rise again, just as the ancient city of Babylon has fallen, leaving nothing but broken ruins in the sand.

Near the end of his letter to the Romans, the apostle Paul makes an amazing statement: "The God of peace will soon crush Satan under your feet" (see Romans 16:20). Notice, Paul does not say God will crush Satan under His feet—he says "under your feet." God, carrying out His eternal plan through us, shall soon crush Satan under our feet! Do not be intimidated by Satan or any other enemy you face. God, living out His life through us, wielding His limitless power through us, will soon make Satan our doormat.

We're surrounded by enemies who seek to destroy us, just as the kingdom of Judah was ringed by enemies. But by faith in God, we can walk through their midst without fear, because God is with us. That is the comfort and blessing of God's message to the nations.

And that is God's message to you and me from the book of Jeremiah.

NOTES

1. Charles Colson, *Loving God* (Grand Rapids, MI: Zondervan, 1996), 92.

2. Dietrich Bonhoeffer, *The Cost of Discipleship* (New York: Simon & Shuster, 1995), 44–45.

3. C. S. Lewis, *The Problem of Pain* (New York: Macmillan, 1963), 81.

4. T. S. Eliot, *The Rock: A Pageant Play* (New York: Harcourt, Brace and Co., 1934), 7.

5. From "How Firm a Foundation," a hymn first published in 1787 by John Rippon in *A Selection of Hymns from the Best Authors*, attributed to "K," which is generally believed to refer to Robert Keene; public domain.

6. Jeremiah F. O'Sullivan, translator, *The Fathers of the Church: The Writings of Salvian, the Presbyter* (Washington, DC: The Catholic University Press, 1947), 193–194; 222.

7. Zosimus, *New History*, Book 5 (London: Green and Chaplin, 1814), http://www.tertullian.org/fathers/zosimus05_book5.htm.

8. George Washington, "Farewell Address" (1796), Yale Law School (Lillian Goldman Law Library) website, http://avalon.law.yale.edu/18th_century/washing.asp.

9. Larry P. Arnn, *Churchill's Trial: Winston Churchill and the Salvation of Free Government* (Nashville, TN: Thomas Nelson, 2015), 272–273.

10. Rudyard Kipling, "Tomlinson," *Collected Verse of Rudyard Kipling* (Garden City, NY: Doubleday, 1916), 241.

11. William Bell Riley, *The Perennial Revival: A Plea for Evangelism* (Philadelphia: American Baptist Publication Society, 1916), 37–38.

12. William Matthew Flinders Petrie with A. S. Murray and F. L. Griffith, *Tanis: Part II, Nebesheh (Am) and Defenneh (Tahpanhes)* (London: Trubner & Co., 1888), 52.

13. Jacques Monod, *Chance and Necessity: An Essay on the Natural Philosophy of Modern Biology* (New York: Alfred A. Knopf, 1971), 180.

Help us get the word out!

Our Daily Bread Publishing exists to feed the soul with the Word of God.

If you appreciated this book, please let others know.

- Pick up another copy to give as a gift.
- Share a link to the book or mention it on social media.
- Write a review on your blog, on a book-seller's website, or at our own site (odb.org/store).
- Recommend this book for your church, book club, or small group.

Connect with us:

 @ourdailybread

 @ourdailybread

 @ourdailybread

Our Daily Bread Publishing
PO Box 3566
Grand Rapids, Michigan 49501 USA

 books@odb.org